T0334390

"I have worked with Timmy Mac for 20 years, teaching together at NYU and consulting together on things business, life and family. He is one of those rare strategic and marketing communicators who has 'done it' and 'taught it' at high levels. Everywhere, he sees leadership as organic to success. Whether you're sitting with Tim over coffee in Manhattan or Omaha, in a classroom or business meeting, you are never bored. Meet McMahon, one heck of a storyteller."

John Doorley, *Associate Professor of Strategic Communications at Elon University, USA, and Co-author of* Reputation Management *and* Rethinking Reputation

"McMahon sat in the chair at a high level and knows first-hand what happens when leaders communicate effectively. With scholarly support he draws out the critical keys to unlock the power of buy-in. Recognize the cues and opportunities; then energize your team!"

Bruce C. Rohde, *Chairman & CEO Emeritus, ConAgra Foods*

"Tim brings the application of provocative theories to life by incorporating them into the everyday struggles of an enlightened leader who effectively fosters true buy-in. A delightful read."

Helio Fred Garcia, *President, Logos Consulting Group, and Adjunct Associate Professor of Leadership, Ethics and Communication, New York University and Columbia University, USA*

"Leadership communication is at the heart of many social business challenges and opportunities. Tim McMahon has described the importance of principled servant leadership built through communities of practice that focus upon customer and stakeholder value."

Jeremy Harris Lipschultz, *Peter Kiewit Distinguished Professor, University of Nebraska at Omaha, USA*

" 'The problem today is that everything communicates…,' and this book does just that - communicates the author's passion for customer-privileged leadership by communicating his experience and scholarship through the generously peppered anecdotes from real-life successes. The book is meant for students, scholars and laypersons alike. I loved every bit of it."

Dr. Richard Rego, S.J., *Associate Professor and Director of the Global Engagement Center, St. Joseph's College Autonomous, Bangalore, India*

"This book is deceptively simple. Amid extensive use of tales, analogies and metaphors outflows the essence of the author's lifelong study of leadership and communication. Key components leading to effective leadership communication are expounded and bolstered—in an intimate tone—with findings in philosophy, literature and cognitive science, just to name a few. The book gains life from the characters who vividly embody the author's wisdom, keen observations and hands-on experiences in the field. The book itself is a masterpiece of communication. Besides scholars and practitioners of management, students of language and cross-cultural studies may also benefit from the communication techniques employed in the book."

Fang Song, *Lecturer of linguistics and business English, Shandong Jiaotong University, Jinan, Shandong, China*

FOSTERING EMPLOYEE BUY-IN THROUGH EFFECTIVE LEADERSHIP COMMUNICATION

Based on a case study of leadership communication in a time of organizational change, this book gives new leaders insights into the tools and skills needed to become effective, motivating communicators in their leadership careers.

Taking a holistic approach to communication and leadership, the book argues that employees buy in to change when they collectively feel engaged in meaningful work that will enrich the lives of customers, employees, and investors. Based on ethnographic research, it approaches the topic through an absorbing fictional retelling of an organization's successful navigation of change against the backdrop of the 2007 mortgage crisis. In doing so, it establishes a framework for leaders to understand the principles behind how and why buy-in is generated in organizations. This unique approach allows readers to visualize leadership communication principles in practice.

Fostering Employee Buy-in Through Effective Leadership Communication is ideal as a supplementary text in introductory leadership communication, management, and business courses or as a text for new leaders interested in inspiring organizational change.

Tim P. McMahon is Associate Professor of Practice in the Heider College of Business at Creighton University, USA. He has founded and led radio stations, restaurants and marketing agencies and was senior marketing communications officer at a Fortune 100 company. He holds an earned Ph.D. from Gonzaga University.

FOSTERING EMPLOYEE BUY-IN THROUGH EFFECTIVE LEADERSHIP COMMUNICATION

Tim P. McMahon

Routledge
Taylor & Francis Group

NEW YORK AND LONDON

First published 2022
by Routledge
605 Third Avenue, New York, NY 10158

and by Routledge
2 Park Square, Milton Park, Abingdon, Oxon, OX14 4RN

Routledge is an imprint of the Taylor & Francis Group, an informa business

Library of Congress Cataloging-in-Publication Data
Names: McMahon, Tim P. (Timothy Patrick), 1954- author.
Title: Fostering employee buy-in through effective leadership
communication / Tim P. McMahon.
Description: New York, NY : Routledge, 2022. |
Includes bibliographical references and index.
Subjects: LCSH: Leadership. | Communication in management. |
Organizational change.
Classification: LCC HD57.7 .M3988 2022 (print) |
LCC HD57.7 (ebook) | DDC 658.4/092--dc23
LC record available at https://lccn.loc.gov/2021006440
LC ebook record available at https://lccn.loc.gov/2021006441

ISBN: 978-0-367-63045-4 (hbk)
ISBN: 978-0-367-62636-5 (pbk)
ISBN: 978-1-003-19512-2 (ebk)

Typeset in Bembo
by MPS Limited, Dehradun

To my wife and partner, Debbie, who has supported my dreams and balanced my inadequacies throughout our life together.

CONTENTS

ABOUT THE AUTHOR

Tim P. McMahon is an accomplished business leader. He has founded, owned, and operated businesses, including radio stations, marketing agencies, and restaurants. He has led sustainable growth in large-scale multinationals and small businesses alike using effective strategy, cutting-edge technology, and authentic human engagement. He has published on leadership, new media, and distance learning and has presented and taught internationally.

He is a lifelong learner and for more than a decade has focused on the challenges of higher education, learning, marketing, and productivity. After a successful career in business including founding and managing an award-winning marketing services agency and serving as the chief marketing and communication officer at a Fortune 100 company, he returned to higher education and earned a MA from Seton Hall University and a PhD from Gonzaga University. He has also served in key positions leading learning initiatives, advancing experiential learning, and as serving as a senior officer in administration in business and higher education. In recent years he has been an invited lecturer at universities in China and India.

Tim and his wife Debbie have three adult children, and two granddaughters (AJ & Luna).

PREFACE

This book grew out of a career in business with experiences at every level and viewed from every angle. It is written as a survey of the many leaders and their encounters in moving people to act in a favorable manner. I established the basis of this work in my doctoral dissertation, a case study of a firm with a highly successful charismatic leader. He is the inspiration for Chris, the principal character of the story. It is through his eyes that the reader sees and hears the problem unfold and through whom the multi-faceted approach to fostering buy-in is revealed.

Throughout my career, I've had the distinct pleasure to work side-by-side with extraordinarily successful leaders—both charismatic and not—who got true buy-in resulting in financial success. Common to each was a commitment to customer. That is why the customer is the hero of this story. However, the customer is not king. People aren't supposed to question an aristocrat.

Chris is not a sycophant. If anything, he is a true friend who expects and delivers honesty. Whether friend or customer or boss, he sees people will value you as a partner principally because you provide value to them—it's an exchange.

Value is the Holy Grail. It is the secret sauce that draws people to give you something in exchange for what you have to offer: a product or service that helps them make progress against their situation, whatever that may be. In speeches and classroom discussions I will ask, what is the purpose of a business? Unquestionably, the universal answer: to make money. It is a trick question, of course.

The purpose of a business is to get and keep customers. By the way, making money is a requisite. Fail to do that for too long and you'll need to find something else to do! Customers pay the way with what they have to exchange for what you have to offer, and broadly speaking, that's value. Narrowly is what must be defined.

Accepting this perspective will help keep the firm on task with helping the customer make progress against their situation. Lose sight of that and you will soon be chasing bright, shiny objects that appear valuable but may not live up to the task. The test is, will your target customer hire you—your product, whether it is a good or service or both—to help them make the progress they were struggling to achieve?

This idea of hiring a product to do a job comes from Clayton Christensen's "Theory of Jobs to be Done," which focuses on deeply understanding your customer's *struggle for progress* and then creating the right solutions and attendant set of experiences to ensure you solve your customers' jobs well, every time."[1] This is the stuff from which value is created. The task before the firm is to create, capture and sustain value over time.

You create value by studying and analyzing your best prospect for business. Success rides on understanding your customer and the situation they face. For this reason alone, you must have every member of the organization bought in to your challenge so as to benefit from their unique perspectives. In the words of veteran business consultant Ron Rhody, "Buy-in is that happy state when the people who are important to the success of your initiatives understand what you want to do. They approve of it." They support it."[2] This happens through sincere engagement. When all hands are involved in value creation, an executable strategy emerges that will likely survive the first assault—the true test of its worth in the marketplace.

Firms capture value through execution of the strategy. It is measured in the price your customer will pay, both in what they are willing to exchange (e.g., money, loyalty) combined with how well your firm is able to deliver the value it promises. You sustain value through vigilance, being mindful of external threats that may change or alter the value proposition or your firm's ability to deliver. So, *creating* something they value is how you get and keep customers. You *capture* it through the exchange and *sustain* it by being mindful and proactive to external threats. Buy-in drives that process.

Leadership has changed over time. At some point, it might have been possible to compel people to follow out of fear or blind allegiance. That might still apply someplace, but to attract the best people, it is wise to engage their commitment through both their hearts and minds. For that reason, this book is based on leadership that recognizes leaders and followers in an influence relationship.

The second section explains the three elements that fuel this concept of interdependence: vigorously confront reality, expand individual and organizational knowledge, and create safety for members to take bold action. These elements underpin the remaining part of our definition of leadership: it intends real changes that reflect their mutual purposes. Real changes are necessary to raise the firm to a higher level of performance in both actions that create value and those that uphold the highest ethical standards. By the way, ethics are not a social duty, they are a benefit. Be ethical and people will trust you. It all begins there.

Explaining the dimensions of the definition of leadership upon which this book is premised is the role of the third section of this book, the essentials of leadership: setting direction, effective use of persuasion and influence, developing adaptive capacity, and cultivating a learning climate. The reader will gain a greater appreciation for how true leaders *foster* buy-in, by promoting growth and development.

In the fourth section, the reader will experience various thought-provoking concepts to inspire fresh perspectives that may lead to greater possibilities. In this sense, this book is not a "how-to" as it does not prescribe a specific step-by-step manual to obtain commitment from employees. Rather, it takes the reader on a journey through thoughts, ideas, and theories that are intended to broaden and reveal ways to expand leadership.

So, why do so many people on the job feel uninformed, confused, and unsure? We'll address these issues in this book from a positive perspective: how do you inform, clarify and make certain. The fact is, in successful organizations, buy-in and communication are inextricably connected. Too often, communication is simply not taken seriously. Oh, there's plenty of lip service. But, if you asked a CEO what's more important—profits or communication—well, you know the answer. The task here is to help people see the connection.

This book is multi-disciplinary in that is not restricted to a single source of knowledge. It will serve as a valuable resource in studying leadership, communication, and business. One fundamental reality is the importance of communication. Our main character didn't delegate communication, didn't think of it as one-way messaging. He recognized effective communication had better make sense to the head while firing up the heart, or the loop would remain open and the desired action stubbed or misguided.

This is a fictionalized tale. That is, the scholarly information is presented alongside a running fictional narrative of a leader facing a significant challenge brought on by the real-world event, the subprime mortgage crisis erupting in 2007. In classic storytelling form, the main character (Chris) has a problem (a decision that will lead to a major loss of business). He meets a guide (well, it's his mother and he has known her for some time) who helps him think through a plan that calls him to action so the firm will thrive, not merely survive. In the end, he avoids failure, and his company emerges to deliver value better than ever.[3]

There are many books that you may read to address the challenge of moving people to desired outcomes. This one is not intended to be a cookbook for whipping up the main course of an important dinner. Moreover, it is intended to provide the reader with a source of nourishment to stoke the fires of believing in one another and in doing so recognizing the startling power of teamwork.

Notes

1 Christensen, C. M., Hall, T., Dillon, K., and Duncan, D. S. (2016). *Competing against luck: The story of innovation and customer choice.* New York, NY: HarperCollins, (p. xiv).

2 Rhody, R. (1999). *The CEO's playback: Managing the outside forces that shape success.* Sacramento, CA: Academy Publishing, (p. 102).

3 Miller, D. (2017). Building a story brand. New York, NY: HarperCollins Leadership. This book served as inspiration for framing the information in a fictionalized story.

ACKNOWLEDGMENTS

This book is the result of years of contemplation. From the first experience I had working in an organization, individuals have contributed to this work in some fashion, whether as an example, a voice of experience, wisdom, or example of how and why people buy-in. Too numerous to name all. Above all, I acknowledge Bill Mackintosh, the inspiration for the main character of this book. Rest his soul, Bill and I were a two-man learning team over a 30-year friendship. I miss him greatly, but can still hear his hearty laugh, see his broad smile and feel his warm presence. He speaks to me still and most certainly in the writing of this book.

There are many others who have taught me business and provided insights I could never have gotten from university. Bruce Rohde and I have a lifelong relationship dating back to the old neighborhood where we once counted 100 kids living in homes on a block long street. He is wicked smart and I have struggled mightily to challenge his extraordinary intellect with my wits and street smarts. It has been my fortune that he engages me and in so doing shapes my thoughts.

My gratitude to my many academic colleagues at Seton Hall, Gonzaga, University of Nebraska-Omaha, Elon University, St, Joseph's, Northwest Missouri State, New York University, and my longest and strongest relationship at Creighton University Heider College of Business. The number in the hundreds and I am eternally grateful for the lessons they have taught me about teaching, learning, and remaining open to new possibilities.

My enduring gratitude to my support team: Professor Karen Weber from the University of Nebraska-Omaha for her expert editing, World class cartoonist Jeffrey Koterba for his illustration of Milgram's experiment, and nationally recognized designer Dave Webster for his art direction and creation of all the figures in this book. I have known their talents all my life and am so grateful I could bring them to bear on the quality of this work. Mike Mackintosh and Ashley Mackintosh contributed to the authenticity and accuracy of this story as well.

I am very thankful for the team at Routledge, most importantly Felisa Salvago-Keyes for inviting me to submit a concept that resulted in this manuscript, to Grant Schatzman for his guidance and patience through my first experience with a book publisher, and to Sumit Kumar for copyediting expertise.

To my wife, Debbie, two sons, Tim, Jr. and Ryan, my daughter Maureen and son-in-law Jay, and my two beautiful and inspiring granddaughters, AJ and Luna. Thank you all for your patience and ever-present interest and encouragement.

Finally, to Darlene, who started it all.

PART I
Setting the Scene

Buy-in is a magic word—the Holy Grail for many leaders. They invoke its presence even when it's not present. Buy-in is frequently touted as an agenda item when a leader takes the reins of an organization. Consultants promise they can help leaders achieve it. And employees will often tell their bosses, "they're in" (meaning *bought*-in) even when they're not. Too often, leaders ask for it before they've even earned it.

Communication is what all leaders claim is the single-most-important ingredient in leading an organization. They hang banners, send e-mails, hold town hall meetings, and allocate dollars to keep the channels open and broadcasting. They don't hold back when it comes to getting the message to the people.

Chapter 1 sets the scene for the story of Chris and his company Apex. Chris is a seasoned executive having founded and led organizations that generated significant revenue because he kept all workers focused on providing products and services the customer valued. Chris believed a firm must make a profit. It is a requisite for the business to continue. But the goal of a business is to get and keep customers. Producing value is the road to that outcome.

This book posits that members of an organization will buy-in to actions they see as creating and delivering a beneficial future for them and their organization. Buy-in is driven by leaders and followers in an influence relationship. Leaders provide assurance and clarity in the face of an adaptive challenge. The leader is the emotional guide; the follower is the loyal skeptic. Together they forge the authority that impels a firm to address the real changes that reflect their mutual purposes.

So, we begin our tale with an introduction of Chris, the subject at the center of our story. We see first-hand how leadership is created through contemporary sensemaking and effective communication. On with the story.

1

SUCCESS RUNS THROUGH THE CUSTOMER

The main character of this story is Chris, an accomplished businessman who faces a crisis that threatens the existence of his firm and the livelihood of more than 300 employees. While inspired by real events experienced by real people, it's a tale, a fictional narrative imaginatively recounted. It establishes a simple truth: the path to success runs through the customer.[1] If a firm holds fast to advancing the progress of its customers, it advances its own fortunes as well.

Chris is not the hero. He is a leader who believes in the power of relationships to weather the most challenging problems. Chris will need his people to help identify a looming external threat and construct a response that will empower the company to not just survive but thrive. As the story unfolds, you'll witness the challenge in human terms through the lens of sound business practices built on instructive theories that, when effectively executed, deliver success.

However, there's often a big gap between strategic intent and effective execution. This story provides the reader a front-row seat to the well-worn challenge of change management, and the critical task of generating employee buy-in to close the gap.

The Main Character and His Development

Chris had experienced success. Out of college, he landed a job selling a popular product to businesses in need—a perfect job because Chris had been selling all his life. As a young boy in a small Nebraska town, Chris hit the streets selling door-to-door to neighbors and strangers. His mother had prepared him well. She had a knack for understanding people and for teaching life lessons. She had a Dale Carnegie understanding of people.

Mom may have even read the book. She was a voracious reader. Simply put, she just plain "got it" when it involved the nature of human beings and she unwittingly passed this gift onto young Chris. She was quite the opposite of her husband, a dedicated large animal veterinarian. "Doc" was book smart and a tremendous asset to the farm community where people depended on the health of their animals. "Doc" met life head-on, a valuable talent since he often confronted the business end of a 900-pound heifer at birth. He passed his brutally honest approach to life on to Chris.

Chris is a study in contrasts. A blend of mom and dad. He had dad's smarts, "but not too smart" as he might say. Once you met his mother it became clear he favored her practical wisdom and harmless devilishness. Chris enjoyed his shenanigans with the guys. During his monthly poker games he'd demonstrate his keen card sense, yet regularly punctuated his play with a clear recognition of the value of humility when it came to competition.

"Win one and then pop off," he'd say to the young feller at the table who bragged about his cards. Turning to his own hand, he'd take a big puff off his fat old stogie and announce, "I gotta a hand like a foot." Then he'd plug the well-worn joke with a hearty laugh. Fond of horseracing and other forms of gambling, you might confuse Chris for the stereotypical used-car salesman at first blush. But behind his gregarious façade, Chris brought meaningful values to life in ways that will surprise and delight.

"Values," you say? "How could a man with such seemingly crude personal habits simultaneously embody Stephen Covey's *principle-centered* concept of leadership?" Covey's principled leaders are not saints; they embrace behaviors like lifelong learning, service-orientation, belief in other people, with a commitment to living balanced lives. They see life as an adventure. They are change catalysts.[2] Further, they practice self-renewal, which helps them remain energized and serves as a means to shirk off the fatigue of the cycle of sacrifice[3] inherent in leading.

A principled leader is trustworthy and dependable and sacrifices much in pursuit of his dreams. Moreover, he understands that when leaders resonate with followers they "will confer authority or volunteer to follow you because they are looking to you to provide a service, or to be a champion, a representative, an expert, a doer who can provide solutions *within the terms that they understand the situation.*"[4] In other words, followers entrust leaders with power in exchange for services—the definitive concept of buy-in—specifically for "serving a set of goals ... [they] ... hold dear."[5] Too often, the strain of leading takes a toll and the leader falls into dissonance with those he leads.

A leading cause of stress in all human beings is the sense they're not in control. For leaders, the inherent stressor lies in the fact followers have expectations the leader will lead them in the way they expect to be led and will reward leaders who comply (and tacitly dismiss those who don't).

However, leading in changing conditions requires challenging some of those expectations. Inevitably, you must move people out of their comfort zone. Further, this must be accomplished in a manner that inevitably creates conflict. Therein lies the stress. Most people don't like and aren't equipped to deal with conflict, especially when it challenges their inherent assumptions. Chris frames it as constructive engagement, as a means to examine held beliefs juxtaposed against greater possibilities.

For decades, scholars have endeavored to describe leaders by listing their traits, often in heroic terms rooted in battlefield imagery. However, the distinguishing qualities of a leader can be paradoxical, and there's no definitive description or combination of traits or characteristics that embody a leader. Heroism is relative. Leaders aren't born as leaders; they emerge through their life experiences.

For centuries, a leader was characterized as a great man, and it was always a man, riding in on a white horse to singlehandedly save the day—a stereotype retained by far too many romantics for far too long. Heroism involves "motivating oneself to above-and-beyond performance by focusing on the richest potential of every moment."[6] That means expanding beyond the terms in which followers conceive of the solution. This requires challenging assumptions, redefining expectations, and inevitably disappointing people in your charge.

The conventional response to this dilemma is that a leader will be best served by developing a compelling vision of the future—a destination followers will see as beneficial and achievable. Yet, often lost in the vision is the driving force of the enterprise, namely the customer or client. We're much better advised to remember if there're any heroes in the picture, it's the people who buy the products and services because they literally deposit their money at the door in exchange for what they need to make progress in their lives. They fund the enterprise. It is natural to serve them.

If a leader can create an environment where the people of the firm coalesce around the customer, everyone wins because the customer delivers what the firm needs to thrive: money. But someone in the enterprise must articulate the self-serving benefits of this relationship. The leader must lead the charge to identify exactly what value members of the firm deliver that the customer covets. The litmus test of a leader—which Chris fits to a T—is answered by the question "will people follow him?" The answer as you will see, is that people follow Chris.

Leading isn't about being perfect or never making a mistake. While we like to lionize leaders, great leaders are flawed. Donald Phillips wrote of Abraham Lincoln, "All human beings have their weaknesses, but not all of us realize them, come to grips with them, or offset their negative impact."[7] When leaders embrace their weaknesses, they sweeten their influence and expand their authority because they're unafraid of confronting reality even about their own shortcomings.

Make the Customer the Hero

When Chris launched his first business, he found success in IT, performing maintenance and repair on computers dedicated to the financial industry. Who would have thought that repair and maintenance was the issue customers needed to make progress against? Chris made this discovery after setting out to peddle new, improved software—the better mousetrap—that he thought customers would snap up in a heartbeat. There were no takers. The mousetrap they had was working fine.

Disappointed, Chris replayed the tapes in his mind. What did they say at the end of the call? "Nice presentation, Chris, we'll get back to you." Words of doom to a salesperson who was left with hope but no order. Then he remembered, "You guys don't fix these things, do you?" Eureka! Upon reflection, Chris identified the customer's pain: when the stuff broke, downtime was costly and held them back from making progress against their production.

Chris returned home, recruited a talented crew of problem-solvers, and devised a proactive, yet nimble service solution that kept customers up and running to the max. His innovative new service included preventive maintenance to stave off downtime and provide an on-the-spot substitute board to quickly restore operations hampered by the outage. The service immediately caught fire with customers. The business grew rapidly because Chris made the customer the hero. Customer demand made Chris's business profitable and kept his people focused and busy. Chris made sure everyone in the firm knew exactly what job their customers hired them to perform and saw to it people consistently delivered on the promise.

This is in line with guidance from business guru Clayton Christensen, who advised firms would succeed when their products and services were "conceived, developed, and launched into the market with a clear understanding of how these products would help consumers make the progress they were struggling to achieve."[8] In creating his first business, Chris learned a valuable lesson: we are best served and more committed when our people take their orders from the situation, and not arbitrary, autocratic decision makers who often could not articulate their real needs.[9] The lesson here is when you make the customer the hero everyone succeeds. Employees buy-in because are appreciated by their customers.

After a decade of growing the firm into a national business, Chris sold it to a large publicly held service organization that needed the results Chris' firm delivered to bolster their revenue and earnings. However, he retained the secrets of his success.

A Little Coffee Break with Mom

Chris often took a mid-morning break and headed to his Mom's place nearby to clear his mind and re-connect with the old-fashioned values and beliefs that gave him perspective as a leader. In running his first company he learned that being "the guy" at the top, you often find yourself in a fog that can accumulate in the day-to-day activities of an organization with hundreds of employees. So, what better way to clear the air, than a coffee chat with your mother?

Here's an example of the nature of his visit, this one shortly after he sold his first business. His mother, Agnes, lived through nearly eight full decades of good and bad times and had a perspective on life, and in particular, Chris' experiences—the greatest teacher of all. Chris read somewhere it's good to remove yourself from the dance floor and take a look from the balcony to regain perspective.[10] A visit with mom served that purpose for him.

A VISIT WITH MOM TO CLEAR THE FOG

AGNES: *Idle hands ...*
Chris knew the finish of that old saw ...
CHRIS: *Are the devil's workshop!*
AGNES: *You must be really proud of what you've done. Now, I bet, you're asking yourself, "Can I do it again?"*
CHRIS: *You got that right. Business looks simple enough and that's where a lot of people get confused.*
AGNES: *Well, my money is on you, son.*
CHRIS: *But I need to get busy. I am a little antsy. I am pretty confident I have learned important lessons as a CEO, but I'm itching to get at it again and prove it out.*
AGNES: *That's good. The message is the devil tempts all, but the idle man tempts the devil.*
CHRIS: *Message received!*

The conversation moved on to pithy topics like the weather and grocery prices, but Chris carried a wise message with him out the door as he had many times before. It's time to buy a new business!

Second Verse, Same as the First

Chris' son had graduated college and taken a job in sales with a mortgage services firm. Apex Enterprises had a pretty good list of customers. Chris had heard Danny talk about his new job and the crazy practices of his new boss. From what he heard from Danny's war stories on the job, Chris saw great opportunity.

In his business life, Chris developed a deeper appreciation for how and why people thrived in organizations. For people to be productive and motivated, they needed clear direction each day they walked into work. Clarity is a powerful job motivator. When you know what is expected of you each day, you can set about the challenge with your attention on that which truly mattered to customers.

In listening to Danny's tales, Chris learned Apex and its boss didn't focus on performance on behalf of the customer; rather they focused on apologizing and explaining away service shortcomings. Apex was not good at operations but excelled at mollifying the customer through concessions, discounts, golf outings, gifts, or delightful dinners. This placation practice created a false sense of customer satisfaction. Below the surface, Apex managers knew operations were sub-par and ill-equipped to address the customer's issues, so they took to blaming employees for not working hard enough. This led to poor morale and more mistakes.

When a mistake created ill will with a client, there would be hell to pay. Managers rode employees hard and berated anyone they saw complicit in creating embarrassment, often venting in full view of customers. Leaders painted a picture that Apex ran a tight ship when in fact the vessel was slowly sinking. At Apex, appearance was more important than performance, Danny would say. This was a drastic departure from the way Chris ran his business, and Danny could see Apex was running on empty. Yet, Apex made a pretty good buck. It helped that competition operated in a similar manner, so customer expectations were low. No one in the competitive set offered the client relief from their real need: swift, error-free reports.

A Tale of Two Firms

Chris bought Apex. And the before and after pictures were like night and day. Chris' management style focused on catching his people doing something right! He would frequently ask, "What are you doing for the customer today?" If one couldn't answer the question quickly and simply, it was time to discuss, assess, and coach both the employee and their supervisor. There were no raised voices. Chris established a "praise in public, coach in private" policy. "Model the behavior you want to see," he regularly reminded.

This was unlike the Apex he inherited that operated as an autocracy where direction was top-down, ill-informed, and hostile. Such operations are in a death spiral and the army of ants could not see a way out of the toxic environment.[11] But, the founder could; he jumped at the offer Chris made to take over Apex.

Chris' first act at Apex was to interview each of its 15 supervisors. He discovered more than half of them loathed coming to work every day. They felt burdened by the disturbances of overseeing workers. They liked the status but felt beleaguered and ill-prepared for the accountability that accompanied the title. This stood in stark contrast with Chris' principal task of management: *get the right people in the right places doing the right things*. The *enfeebled supervisor* situation needed to be remedied quickly. Chris got busy.

In his one-on-one chats with the group, Chris learned that these people had great institutional and functional knowledge. Being new to the business himself, he saw this as a valuable asset as it was granular intelligence of an industry he had yet to apprehend. Yet, he doubted most of them would ever take to the role of managing. So, he devised a plan to remedy the problem.

For those who had no desire to manage, Chris relieved them of their duties and turned these failing supervisors on to a new position as subject matter expert (SME), an area where he figured they would thrive. They could serve the organization in ways they felt valued, and in a manner that delivered value to the firm's heroes, its customers; and its second most important constituents: the employees.

He discovered the remaining supervisors had the desire and a knack for managing but hadn't the foggiest idea how to do it, so he created a management training program. Such decisive and immediate moves sent a message to all members of the firm there're new assumptions about the way the business would be operated: people shall be empowered to act on behalf of the customer. The empowerment would be bolstered by training and accompanied by accountability. This first move signaled a shift in governance, from autocracy to meritocracy.

One more point. Remember the supervisors turned SMEs? When he adjusted their duties, he restructured their compensation from salaried to hourly. They were no longer exempt from overtime as they had been as supervisors. In actual practice, SMEs annual compensation netted out about the same as their previous supervisor roles, so no jolt to their income. And, in the way Chris presented it to the entirety of the firm, they didn't experience any loss in their feeling of, or others' perception of their self-worth. He celebrated the change at a town hall meeting.

Over time, SMEs defined critical aspects of industry knowledge and refined the work processes within Apex. This, when combined with development of management and emotional intelligence of the newly recruited and trained managers, helped the former supervisors with management potential grow into their new role by sharpening their business acumen and developing their management chops. Chris took the words of Edward Hess to heart: "We build confidence in our efficacy by being put into challenging situations that we have the potential to handle well—those in which we have the requisite capabilities and tools."[12]

Chris repeatedly turned to teaching and learning as a means to inform and prepare people in the organization to become more enlightened and capable servants of the mission. From the moment one walked into the building, a visitor would see the lending library with multiple copies of books that Chris had read and encouraged others to read. As witnessed in his approach to the enfeebled supervisor issue, Chris' approach to problem solving began with gathering an understanding of the problem; facing it directly; then, devising a solution that met the needs of all involved. Elegant. Simple. Effective.

Orders didn't come from the boss, they flowed from an understanding of the situation at hand. And the process was punctuated with an outsized quantity of communication. Town hall meetings, exit interviews, detailed onboarding, executive welcomes, and weekly, monthly, and quarterly one-on-ones filled the calendar. Of special note, the one-on-ones included everyone in the building and were conducted by members of the senior management team who regularly took the pulse of the people and met to share the vibe with their colleagues. About communication, Chris joked, "If your employees are not mocking you for your overabundance of communication, you are not communicating enough!"[13]

Communities of Practice Tied to Learning

Chris recalled learning about the concept of the *community of practice* and knew he wanted to give it a try. It works like this. Where a group of people share a passion for something in which they commonly participate,[14] people were encouraged to form a community that would meet regularly. Their aim was to provide members help with everyday challenges, identify best practices worthy of spread, and where needed, form strike teams to address bottlenecks in productivity and innovation. This is an effective way to bring new members up to speed on the practices of the firm and while giving seasoned members a chance to re-examine current behaviors and practices.

With a deep commitment to learning and communication, Chris placed big demands on members to stretch and move out of their comfort zone by embracing new challenges and personal learning, distinct earmarks of the *learning* culture Chris aimed to cultivate and implement at Apex.

Peter Senge says learning cultures offer three distinct advantages: (a) a better way to manage and lead change; (b) an overall organizational capacity for continual adaptation to change; and (c) a way to improve performance because it "creates the types of workplaces in which most of us would truly like to work."[15] When an organization knows how to learn, it can accomplish these outcomes. Not prone to naïveté, Chris recognized learning is fraught with roadblocks.

Hess warned: "Learning requires deliberate, higher level thinking that challenges and changes an individual's existing views of the world and of self. Although we all strive to be rational and logical and think we are, we all too often, don't respond like rational beings. Emotions influence almost every step in the cognitive and communication processes necessary for learning."[16] Further, it often defies logic.

Daniel Kahneman warns that rational thinking[17] is often influenced by a measure of our brain's activity called *cognitive ease*. "Easy is a sign all is well—no threats, no major news, no need to redirect attention to activate a response. Strained indicates that a problem exists"[18] which will require mobilization of a deeper more strenuous level of thinking. "When you feel strained, you're more likely to be vigilant and suspicious, invest in more effort in what you are doing, feel less comfortable, and make fewer errors, but you also are less intuitive and less creative than usual."[19] This is clearly not the comfort zone for most people. Learning may be necessary to reveal new possibilities, but learning is hard to do.

The Learning Mindsets

The learning challenge is illuminated by a deeper understanding of how people approach goal setting and achievement. Generally, people are motivated in one of two ways. Some people actually love to learn for learning sake (intrinsic); while for others learning is simply a path to rewards (extrinsic) like receiving a degree or certificate. Extrinsic learners are easily motivated by success, and can be quite competitive, but are more likely to be self-oriented rather than team oriented. They worry about scorekeeping and rewards; are more likely to fudge the results to show their accomplishment. The intrinsic approach favors closing the gap between mastering and performing.

Daniel Pink wrote these *intrinsic* learners "have higher self-esteem, better interpersonal relationships, and greater general well-being."[20] Carol Dweck added to this when she distinguished two types of learners: fixed and growth. Those with a fixed mindset are likely to avoid challenges because failure would signal their lack of intelligence.[21]

These learners default to a perception of performance as a definitive assessment of innate ability, that is, they fail to see a person can acquire skills not directly related to performance. On the other hand, those who have a mastery, or growth mindset, are internally driven and believe that intelligence is not fixed but can grow with effort. They see putting forth an effort as a path to "mastery—the desire to get better and better at something that matters."[22]

Dweck distinguishes the difference between leaders with a growth mindset as people who "don't highlight the pecking order with themselves at the top, don't claim credit for other people's contributions, and they don't undermine others to feel powerful. ... [rather] they surround themselves with the most able people they can find, they look squarely at their own mistakes and deficiencies, and they ask frankly what skills they and the company will need in the future."[23]

As it turns out, a good learning environment is one where there are "good role models (teachers) for learning and creativity, and where the style of teaching meets the diverse needs of learners ... [in that it] resembles a journey of discovery in which the learner plays the main character and is encouraged to be creative and socially and authentically connected to the learning community."[24]

What is Leadership?

At this point, let's make a key distinction about the term leadership often intermixed with the term leader. They are not one in the same. We've described an effective leader in our description of Chris. But what is *leadership*? Joseph Rost introduced a definition of leadership that sets the tone for this book: "Leadership is an influence relationship among leaders and followers who intend real changes that reflect their mutual purposes."[25] We will take that definition apart piece-by-piece in Part III, as we proceed through this book, but one fact must leap out at you: if the preceding definition of leadership serves our purpose, how do we create leadership? How do we know when it is happening?

Leadership occurs when leaders and followers act in concert to address their mutual concerns by setting direction, obtaining commitment, and facing adaptive challenge. Leaders set the pace but are best served when they create an environment of open, honest communication that acts to inform members of the organization so they can act accordingly. Additionally, it opens the door for employees to challenge the assumptions put forth by leaders. Ironically, when a firm has established this kind of a culture, change management is not a program, it's a way of life. People are not intimidated by conflict; they openly accept it and feed on it.

In other words, one reason traditional change efforts fail is because leaders and followers don't recognize the potency in cultivating their interdependence. Maybe members of the firm have failed to articulate their mutual purposes or unable to create common ground; each of which, if held jointly, might unleash collective power. Without it, invisible opposition forms and is often displayed in a passive-aggressive manner, which gives the appearance of buy-in when no such possibility exist. "The transformational leadership style affects the organizational change process. In this type of leadership, the leader coordinates with employees, shares their knowledge, gives opportunity in making decisions in organizational level."[26]

When a firm like Apex faces a long, slow slide into extinction, ironically change is not perceived as a solution. To the contrary, change is a clear and present threat to the integrity and autonomy of the group. Changing when the wolf is at the door presents risk of the unknown. As the old phrase suggests, "better the devil I know."[27]

Nearly 75 years ago, pioneering organizational psychologist Kurt Lewin discovered the more forceful an attempt to persuade the group that a problem exists, the more resistance the group will muster in opposition to the idea. When people sense change is in the offing, they become bracketed by anxiety, knowing "the way we do things around here"[28] is under attack.[29]

Many factors thwart a firm's ability to manage change. People need to see the threat, recognize a need to adapt, and be given a framework to throw out the old while holding on to that which they value dearly. That may be "some deeply held belief about right or wrong about the way the world works or should work. Or it may be nothing deeper than a desire to maintain what is stable, predictable, and familiar in their lives."[30] Ignoring this need may shut off buy-in before a case can be made. Failing to see this may mean buy-in is dead-on-arrival.

A Framework of Trust Built on Efficacy

When Chris acquired Apex in 2004, sweeping changes were put into place to transform the business from a collegial autocracy, where employees earn reward for their tenure with the company, to a meritocracy, which places value on achievement of business goals related to customer needs. For legacy employees, this was a dramatic shift that affected performance expectations. For legacy leaders, this was a threat to their power. Under the founder, long work and loyalty were valued, equating time with achievement.

With Chris, productivity through engagement became the gold standard. He'd often say, "don't confuse activity with accomplishment." Communication was ever-present, honesty and truth were expected, and simplicity was valued. Doing the right thing was sacrosanct. It was all reflected in Apex' newly published values:

THE MOTHER STANDARD

The Meaning of Our Values

We will treat all stakeholders respectfully, fairly, and ethically. We will use the "Mother Standard." If you would feel comfortable explaining to your mother what you are doing, it is almost certainly the right thing to do from a values standpoint. If you would not feel comfortable explaining to your mother what you are doing, then it is almost certainly wrong, and you should reconsider your actions.

This is quite a departure from the status quo under previous ownership. In the early days of the transition, plenty of unrest existed and in a very public way, those who chose to hold on to their ideas about the ways and means of the old Apex were summarily dismissed. This was entirely necessary. "Every new group or organization must develop a shared concept of the ultimate survival problem, from which usually is derived its most basic sense of core mission, primary task, or even 'reason to be.'"[31] Peter Northouse wrote of power, "as a relational concern for both leaders and followers." The concept of power and authority differs greatly.

The Role of Power and Authority

In the words of leadership scholar Northouse: Members of the organization "pay attention to how leaders work with followers to reach common goals."[32] At Apex, legacy employees saw two distinct views that were on opposite sides of the power spectrum from dominance on one side to authority on the other. Under the founder, power was closer to *habitual deference*[33] while under Chris' management concept the employee had the freedom to authorize, a sort of buy-in by the employee.

As such, they were expected to take part in decisions. In this shift, leadership is not necessarily the outcome of leader influence as much as it's the product of the leader and follower conspiring to understand the reality of their situation—where influence flowed in both directions. Chris was quick to point out Apex is not a democracy! It's better understood that leadership flows from meaning and not meaning from leadership. However, the final decision was in the hands of the appointed leader. This establishes the basis for accountability that is informed collectively but held individually by a single individual.

Why does this matter? Leaders are often disappointed in their belief that a logical argument will carry the day in the workplace because on its face, it won't. Jack Welch, the hard-edged leader of General Electric, wrote: "there is a core of people who absolutely will not accept change, no matter how good your case."[34] We have all heard executives refer to these dissenters as rogues, the antithesis of the team player. But are they?

Welch considered resistance to be recalcitrance, "Either their personalities just can't take it, or they are so entrenched—emotionally, intellectually, or politically—in the way things are, they cannot see a way to make them better."[35] This is a tough stance, in such situations leaders must deliberate wisely. Welch offered three reasons for a legitimate employee dismissal: (a) for integrity violations, (b) layoffs due to the economy, and (c) firings for non-performance.[36]

Chris considered this sound guidance. However, he embellished it a bit by adding a couple of distinctions. Chris recognized employees operating under an assumption that "they had a job for life" were going to rightfully struggle with a change in culture that rejected that thought. Chris said, "These folks were feeling tremendous loss of security. Suddenly, they realized they could lose their job in an instant. Telling them, 'As long as you perform, you're fine' offers little relief. They have no history that tells them they should trust those words. They legitimately feel the rules changed and they are leery of just how that will play out, and they should be!" In Chris' mind, these workers were not being obstinate, they were being reactionary. This posed a transitional challenge: how would he signal adoption of a new set of rules that would guide behavior?

First, Chris relied on the guidance of having *the right people in the right places doing the right things* as the framework for organizational effectiveness. So, if someone was deemed to be underperforming in a given area (like the supervisors in the early stages at Apex mentioned earlier) it may be because they were serving in the wrong place or doing the wrong things. It is up to management to reassign based on fit and not dismiss people arbitrarily.

Secondly, it's better to coach frequently than to critique annually. Coaching is centered on performance against agreed-upon goals, often called key performance indicators (KPI)[37]. Further, coaching is two-way and aims to get everyone on the same page premised on identifying a gap that may exist between employee performance and their personal skills and competencies. Chris was first and foremost a coach and thereby considered his firm a team in every sense of the word.

What Could Go Wrong?

Have you ever felt that creeping feeling that something isn't right? As a matter of fact, it was terribly wrong? We all had that feeling when we watched the first jetliner crash into the north tower of the World Trade Center on September 11, 2001. And then a second one piled into the south tower all in a period of 16 minutes. During such times we struggle to make sense of such events. These unexplainable acts had the effect of what Daniel Goleman called *hijacking the amygdala*.[38] Figure 1.1 locates the amygdala in the brain and provides a rough depiction of what happens.

The amygdala is part of the brain's limbic system which is responsible for processing strong emotions. In such moments as the initial events of 9/11, "when an impulsive feeling overrides the rational … the newly discovered role of the amygdala is … something like a psychological sentinel, challenging every situation, every perception, with but one kind of question in mind, the most primitive: Is this something I hate? Something that hurts me? Something I fear?"[39] If so, the amygdala sends urgent messages to every part of the brain summoning hormones to mobilize action, activating the circulatory system, muscles, and gut to enable a response. So, it is no wonder why we sometimes fail to act rationally in such circumstances.

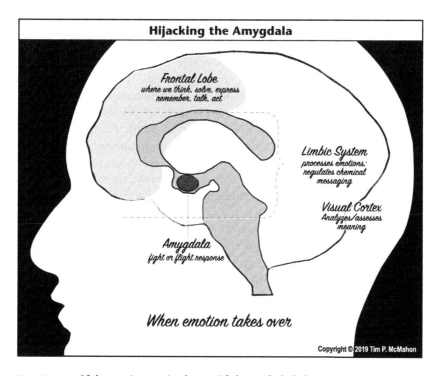

FIGURE 1.1 If danger is perceived, our "fight or flight" decision is triggered overriding our rational response

This is sort of condition can occur in both shocking and subtle ways, but both can be gravely disturbing. Chris faced this when his vp-sales came to him with a strong message from their largest account. They wanted a bare-bones underwriting report. One that could be used when a customer showed up over their lunch hour seeking a quick answer to a mortgage application. It had to be lightning quick because if the client didn't have such a report, the hot prospect would walk out the door and down the street to a competitor who had such a product. If Apex couldn't deliver it, the customer would go elsewhere. Fact is, it was a competitor who developed this report. Such a report might facilitate issuance of a mortgage, but it would not identify high-risk borrowers.

Early Warning Signal

Chris was hit with the rush of confusing signals that essentially had the power to hijack his amygdala and put him on an emotional path to a possibly tragic response in either of two ways he might act. His immediate instinct was to lash out at the vp-sales for not seeing the ridiculousness of the request. At the heart of his concern—though unforeseen by many at the time—was a looming crisis in mortgage lending that eventually dealt a catastrophic blow to the industry and in the end to the entire global economy.

Chris had recognized for some time that clients requested quicker turns on underwriting reports to qualify mortgage applicants. He saw it as a massive departure from assumptions that the purpose of his firm's reports was to ward off default-prone applicants. At the moment of that request, he determined the mortgage companies had done an about face on sound business practices. They were willing to sacrifice quality for speed, a move certain to accommodate low quality applicants and significantly increase the risk of mortgage default. Chris saw his customer—the hero—on the cusp of a freefall. However, this wasn't the time to rattle the troops with an outburst. It was a time to ramp up dialogue to muster the will to make tough decisions.

The experts suggest that when we're confronted with a situation that hijacks our amygdala, we must summons a rational response: Count to 6. Re-engage with your reasoned mind by sorting out the dynamics clouded by the emotion driven by the fear. Chris responded, "Looks like an opportunity. We need to get the whole team to weigh in on this one!" Chris had regained his balance. He avoided an outburst that surely would have unsettled everyone within earshot; he resolved to identify and address the threat directly.

Chris called upon his people to gain a clear view of the market in which Apex was now operating. It had changed. What did that mean for Apex? How would it respond?

Almost No One Saw it Coming

Looking back, in 2007 the subprime mortgage crisis surprised all the experts. Years later, financial journalist and best-selling author Michael Lewis wrote *The Doomsday Machine* that explained how the U.S. housing bubble triggered the financial crisis of 2007–2008. His account was made into *The Big Short*, a movie about an obscure group of investors who tried to warn the industry of impending doom in the mortgage lending market but were ignored. So, they bet against the market (a short) and made a fortune. How did they know? Common sense. It just didn't square that a stripper could have five mortgages (true account from the movie).

Mortgage bankers—the customers of Chris' firm—over-sold mortgages to feed the demand for mortgage-backed securities sold through the secondary market.[40] As preposterous as it may sound, mortgage lenders shirked off their concern for risk and were demanding quick approval products from vendors like Chris. These quickie products were designed to gloss over the risk factors of many borrowers so as to justify granting them a loan.[41] The mortgage market was under the spell of irrational exuberance.[42] Complicating things further, these risky mortgages were then lumped in with the traditionally solid mortgage loans that had undergone much more rigid underwriting standards. This unusual phenomenon was blindly ignored by almost everyone, except the hedge fund group Lewis wrote about, and Chris, a new entrant into the world of mortgage underwriting who, as he says, could see it because he was not blinded by the boom.

The Right Response Depends on Preparation

Armed with a passion for life, Chris felt deeply about the potential in human beings. He understood the distinction between Theory X and Theory Y workers.[43] Theory X believers assume workers do not enjoy work and are ex-trinsically motivated, that is, they respond to financial rewards. Leaders who adopt a Theory Y version of people embrace the idea that workers enjoy their work and are motivated by a challenge, particularly one that makes a difference.

Daniel Pink argues that whichever you choose to embrace, you are better served to believe in the human potential: "If you believe in the 'mediocrity of the masses,' then mediocrity became the ceiling on what you could achieve. But if your starting point was Theory Y, the possibilities were vast—not simply for the individual's potential, but for the company's bottom line as well."[44] He concluded Theory Y people are fed by *autonomy, mastery*, and *purpose*.

Chris believes in people. He held the distinct view that people flourish when they address their self-interests. In ethics, it's called enlightened self-interest. In plain terms, it is the Golden Rule: treat others as you would like to be treated. In psychology, it's explicated in Self-Determination Theory (SDT), and "examines how biological, social, and cultural conditions either enhance or undermine the inherent human capacities for psychological growth, engagement, and wellness, both in general and in specific domains and endeavors."[45]

A practical application of the theory points to the importance of context, specifically, how well certain environments (e.g., families, teams, classrooms) either support or impair human thriving. By identifying that which regulates motivation and by understanding the conditions that foster such behavior, we can effectively apply SDT to challenges in the workplace. "Simply stated, individual organisms are endowed with, and energized by, propensities to expand and elaborate themselves in the direction of organized complexity and integrated functioning."[46] From infancy to adulthood, we strive to assimilate, we crave relatedness, we seek connection to others in creating something greater than we can create by our self. We relate through events and experiences normally in a healthy, self-affirming manner.

Making Sense of the Situation

The context in this book strives to create a coherent picture of organizing principles that come together to create a place where people are not only empowered, but expected to respond to the situation at hand, whatever that may be at the time. If leaders and followers recognize the power of freely influencing one another of their intention for real change that reflects their mutual purposes, the organization need not *manage* change, but *activate* "a system of communication and a language that permits interpretation of what is going on."[47] It is called sensemaking.

Karl Weick advised: "A crucial property of sensemaking is that human situations are progressively clarified,"[48] through an ongoing engagement. Nelson Goodman pointed out that in such evolving arrangements, the value is not in proving truth; rather, it is "for its efficacy in worldmaking and understanding."[49] In other words, it is not about following the leader as much as it is about the group recognizing what it can do when it collectively makes sense of a situation. In a compound word, culture-building.

When a leader fashions a culture that functions effectively to deal with external challenges, the firm is capable of integrating an internal response based on broad consensus of its members because the response serves their mutual purposes. This isn't about instituting a change initiative; it's about unleashing an organizational response well-suited to adapt to troubling external threats. That said, it helps if a firm can fall in love with tough decisions.[50]

Think of it this way, human beings have a keen sense of what serves their interests. When their interests are engaged, they are motivated to perform, so to act is a natural response. Change is not a preferred response. Change suggests we are wrong. So, we should not manage change, we should lead people to act on their interests, much in the manner Chris has established with his people. Deliver the truth. Human beings have an inherent need to satisfy psychological needs for competence, relatedness, and autonomy.[51] Leaders who recognize these fundamental human needs may leverage them to address organizational challenges.

Nurturing the Culture

From the time he purchased the firm in 2004, Chris began to instill in its people a culture that valued a meritocracy. During one of his early town hall meetings Chris held with his people, he focused on the organizing principle that set his firm apart from the predecessor firm. The slide was simple. Three basic forms of workplace power structures are: (a) autocracy, (b) democracy, and (c) meritocracy. The slide identified each style and the source of power, as well as the role of the boss. See Figure 1.2 for a simple visual to understand the operating structure at Apex, a meritocracy. What followed were discussions across the organization, both formal and informal, so that members of the organization could make sense of the governing system and how the firm would integrate internal responses to external challenges.

A culture evolves through sociology and group dynamics. The slide is one aspect of culture formation, which, in a sense is "identical to the process of group formation in that the very essence of groupness or group identity—the shared patterns of thought, belief, feelings, and the values that result from shared experience and common learning—results in the pattern of shared assumptions that … [Edgar Schein] calls the *culture* of the group."[52]

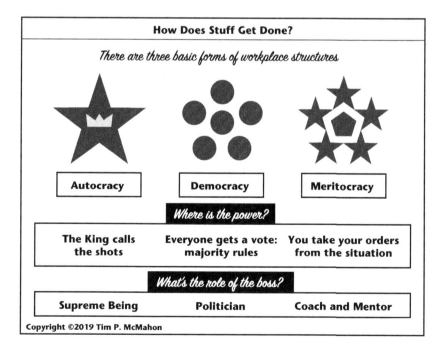

FIGURE 1.2 This depiction was used in an Apex Town Hall meeting to show ways things get done

Change for Change Sake?

Chris fully embraced challenging his people. Furthermore, he understood that people needed safety to act boldly because it is bold action that succeeds boldly. Chris had a framed quote on his office desk that read, "No guts, no blue chips." This is not the reflection of a river boat gambler, rather, it is the conviction that conventional, safe, and low-risk actions produce low value rewards. Yet, bold action is borne of insight and rigor and produces outsized returns. Insight bubbles up from the front lines and rigor is exerted by management. Insight plus rigor is an effective prescription for delivering value to the customer.

Yet, many leaders are fixed on change. That's because they perform a gap analysis and discover there's something between the organization's desired behaviors and its actual performance. Make no mistake, the gap analysis is a valid and useful tool as you will see. In reality, members of the firm, particularly those customer-facing people, must be brought into the discussion because they are closer to the front line. When leaders solicit their perspective, they bring perspective into focus resulting in a clear picture of necessary action.

When change strategy "is top-down it's considered *revolutionary*, ... the organization waits until it believes that the costs of not changing exceed the costs of overcoming organizational inertia and then introduces its master plan for change."[53] This is good. It's short-sighted to think a logical argument will sway the masses for as we have explained, a need to change is equated with failure, and people fundamentally resist such efforts.

Chris and his management team met regularly to update their understanding of internal capabilities and external challenges. Preliminary to the assessment was a review of the business with the frontline workers. Then, and only then, could management proceed. At the center of the review was a well-practiced SWOT, a process for assessing the internal Strengths and Weaknesses and the external Opportunities and Threats. See Figure 1.3 that depicts the outcomes of a session just months prior to the crisis. The team grappled with a particularly disturbing and growing reality found in the first bullet point under Threats: *The loss of a major account would be devastating.* As the team pondered the challenge, little did they know that it would not be the loss of their largest account, which was unduly oversized, rather, it would be the loss of the entire mortgage industry as they knew it!

As described, under its founder, Apex operated as an autocracy where the owner directed activities and workers operated from within their area of specialty. The functions of the firm lacked interchange between functions, the proverbial silo problem. Chris knew this situation had to change if the new Apex were to improve its profitability and competitive stance. Once he gained control and understanding of the situation, he started a revolution.

INTERNAL CONTEXT	**Apex Enterprises SWOT Analysis**

Apex Enterprises SWOT Analysis

STRENGTHS

1. Vendor database (access to hinterlands)

2. People: approach and engagement, trust, sense of urgency, ability to dead with complexity, passion, manage expections

3. Customer focus: product ease-of-use

4. Nimble size (rare: not too big, not too small - in an elite group)

5. Own proprietary operating technology (differentiator)

6. State-of-the-art buildings and facilities

OPPORTUNITIES

1. Available revenue in marketplace (existing pipeline, new customers, new categories

2. Off-shoring opportunities to move non-core competencies out of shop (speed, savings, scale-up)

3. Project VC product

4. Legislative / political changes are driving change in environment and may cause new business opportunities

WEAKNESSES

1. NUCLEON process is not serving basic customer needs

2. Disadvantaged in large market data access

3. Execution (variance, productivity, process

4. Shrinking form dominant position

5. Not known as employer of choice

6. Communication is lacking in content and frequency

7. Line management is youthful, inexperience

THREATS

1. Loss of major account would be devastating

2. Market conditions softening consumer demand

3. Rise in raw costs squeezing all margins; could stoke price pressure

4. Technological advances reducing demand/ need for parts of our bundle of benefits

5. Legislative oversight uncertainty

Copyright ©2019 Tim P. McMahon

FIGURE 1.3   A snapshot in time

Being Aware is More Important Than Being Smart[54]

When it represents certain threat, overcoming the status quo is the first challenge of any leader charged with accomplishing growth and profits for the firm. This is more difficult than it appears. Growth shows viability and profits permit the organization to continue its mission. It's so important, we become slaves to that which is its cause. This is true for both profit and not-for-profit companies.

However, organizations must thrive, not simply survive. We are often deceived, believing they are one and the same. Surviving describes the long slow march to the end. Survival is triggered by a firm's inability to respond to change in the environment. The taxi industry failed to respond to the emergence of ride-sharing services. Uber and Lyft thrived. In the nonprofit arena, school districts with stagnant population growth succumb to cost creep and administrators seldom make cuts in non-essential resources. So, administrators choose survival because they are risk averse. They retain resources that bear a high cost, but little fruit. Their response is not to re-birth the system, but to go to the taxpayers with a bond issue. Ugh!

That's why when the skies get cloudy, management must spring into action. If their business model is under stress, leaders must engage their people to respond. If your school district falls prey to stagnant growth, boards must insist administrators find ways to re-focus the limited resources on the mission. Reaching out to the front lines, the teachers, is a powerful move. Yet, in many organizations, workers have endured an onslaught of interventions that become synonymous with failure. Teachers are just such an example. In other words, the organization remains mired in survival. Survival is not a viable strategy. Leaders must create an effective response to change if a firm is to thrive, rather than dreadfully survive.

We know that most efforts of this sort fail. But why? This book suggests it lies in false assumptions fueled by a failure to confront reality, expand individual and organizational knowledge in purposeful ways, and in creating safety for members taking legitimate bold action. This book offers a root-cause explanation of this failure to thrive: Leaders fail to act when they lose sight that the real hero is the customer.

TAKEAWAYS

- Now you have met Chris and see he is a successful businessman who sticks to tried-and-true rules while demonstrating a true respect for the people with whom he works. You also see his common sense comes from his mother, who in regular kitchen visits, Chris regains his perspective to do the right thing. He fosters interdependence.
- You probably recognized he is the product of a solid upbringing provided by a father with strong cognitive skills and a mother with exceptional emotional skills. And, while his mental skills are ample, his ability to understand himself and others—practical wisdom—serves him in leading people.
- You see he approaches leadership not from the perspective of a boss, but as more of a leader creating leadership where the group works smarter and more effective together than its individual members acting alone.
- He seeks to have a clear picture of a situation from which he takes his orders. And, he lays a foundation of trust with whom he works which serves to tap into followers' needs to contribute to something bigger than themselves. This is all grounded in the customer, lest we forget, who pays the bills.
- You may have learned, Chris's success flows from having the *right people* in the *right places* doing the *right things*. He believes that this is best accomplished in a meritocracy, where members of the firm are rewarded for creating value that retains customers and engages employees.
- While remarkably simple, it requires a relentless pursuit of learning, practice, understanding, and communication. Communication in all

ways, always. The problem today is that everything communicates; and, we have never had more knowledge or more ways to observe it, express it, and put it into practice than exists in the world we live in today.

- Underlying all of this, we have unprecedented levels of change in our world. External change demands effective internal adaptation so the organization can not merely survive but thrive.
- Chris marches to a definition of leadership that comprises four essential elements: based on an influence relationship, of leaders and followers, who intend real changes, that serve their mutual purposes. In this sense, effective buy-in flows from a movement, not an initiative or campaign.
- Finally, failure to confront reality, expand individual and organizational knowledge in purposeful ways, and in creating safety for members taking legitimate bold action.

Notes

1 I hope to demonstrate that every business exists to serve someone, somehow, with some special ability to advance the progress that someone is attempting to make against a situation they face. This fundamental premise stems from the brilliant work of Clayton Christensen, a truly gifted researcher, teacher, and human being whose life was cut short far too soon.
2 Covey, S. R. (1990/1991). *Principle-centered leadership.* New York, NY: Fireside.
3 Boyatzis, R. & McKee, A. (2005). *Resonant leadership: Renewing yourself and connecting others through mindfulness, hope, and compassion.* Boston, MA: Harvard Business School Press., (p. 7). The authors warn "the constant sacrifices and stress inherent in effective leadership can cause us to lose ourselves and sink into dissonance" (p. 58), a condition they term the Sacrifice Syndrome.
4 Heifetz, R., Grashow, A., & Linsky, M. (2009). *The practice of adaptive leadership: Tools and tactics for changing your organization and the world.* Boston, MA: Harvard Business Press, (p. 24).
5 Ibid, p. 24.
6 Lowney, C. (2003). *Heroic leadership: Best practices from a 450-year-old company that changed the world.* Chicago, IL: Loyola Press, (p. 209).
7 Phillips, D. T. (1992). *Lincoln on leadership: Executive strategies for tough times.* Illinois, USA: DTP/Companion Books, (p. 80).
8 Christensen, C. M., Hall, T., Dillon, K., & Duncan, D. S. (2016). *Competing against luck: The story of innovation and customer choice.* New York, NY: HarperCollins, (pp. xiii–xiv). The authors illustrate that "to elevate innovation from hit-or-miss to predictable, you have to understand the underlying causal mechanism—the progress a consumer is trying to make in particular circumstances" (p. 21).
9 Tonn, J. C. (2003). *Mary P. Follett: Creating democracy, transforming management.* New Haven, CT: Yale University Press. Scientific management pioneer Mary P. Follett wrote "one creates a joint, interpenetrating responsibility [by recognizing there is] … no necessary opposition between obedience to orders and freedom—as long as orders are 'the composite conclusion of those who give and those who receive them' and express 'the integration of the people concerned and the situation'" (p. 400).
10 Heifetz, Grashow, & Linsky (2009). *The practice of adaptive leadership.* Cambridge, MA: Harvard Business Review Press, (pp. 7–8).

11 In an article about the pandemic published in *The Atlantic,* author Ed Yong wrote: "Army ants will sometimes walk in circles until they die. The workers navigate by smelling the pheromone trails of workers in front of them, while laying down pheromones for others to follow. If these trails accidentally loop back on themselves, the ants are trapped. They become a thick, swirling vortex of bodies that resembles a hurricane as viewed from space. They march endlessly until they're felled by exhaustion or dehydration. The ants can sense no picture bigger than what's immediately ahead. They have no coordinating force to guide them to safety. They are imprisoned by a wall of their own instincts. This phenomenon is called the death spiral." Retrieved September 12, 2020, from https://www.theatlantic.com/health/archive/2020/09/pandemic-intuition-nightmare-spiral-winter/616204/.

12 Hess, E. D. (2014). *Learn or die: Using science to build a leading-edge learning organization.* New York, NY: Columbia University Press, (p. 35).

13 Chris was a fan of Verne Harnish's *Rockefeller Habits,* a book along with its successor, *Scaling Up,* served as the likely source for such comments.

14 The community of practice concept was introduced in a book titled *Situated Learning,* written by Jean Lave, an anthropologist, and Etienne Wegner, an educational theorist.

15 Senge, P. M. (2006). *The fifth discipline: The art and practice of the learning organization* (Rev. ed.). New York: Currency Doubleday, (p. 273). Senge is recognized as a leader in building learning organizations. He wrote, "There seem to be three overlapping but distinct motivations that compel people to take on the difficult work of building learning organizations. Some seek a better model for how to manage and lead change. Some are trying to build an organization's overall capacity for continual adaptation to change. All seem to believe that there is way of managing and organizing work that is superior in both pragmatic and human terms, that significantly improves performance and creates types of workplaces in which most of us would truly like to work" (p. 273).

16 Hess, E. D. (2014). *Learn or die: Using science to build a leading-edge learning organization.* New York, NY: Columbia University Press, (p. 108).

17 Rational thinking defined as the use of reason, the capacity to make sense of things, and the use of logic to verify facts. Retrieved November 22, 2020 from https://www.sciencedirect.com/science/article/abs/pii/S1546144012003791.

18 Kahneman, D. (2011). *Thinking, fast and slow.* New York, NY: Farrar, Straus and Giroux, (p. 59).

19 Ibid, p. 60.

20 Pink, D. H. (2009). *Drive: The surprising truth about what motivates us.* New York, NY: Riverhead Books, (p. 111).

21 Writing in the *New Yorker,* Malcolm Gladwell speculated that the Enron disaster sprouted from a culture that demanded top talent, distinguished by degrees from top colleges, and considered to be the smartest people in the room. It created a culture that honored talented people. So, if you worked at Enron, you had better make sure everyone know you were smart, smarter than anyone, and incapable of failure. These folks have stopped learning. They are entrenched in a fixed mindset. They have all the answers. Therefore, there is no learning. The problem, as we later understood, was that all these talented people were incapable of recognizing a big problem that eventually toppled the firm.

22 Pink, (p. 98). Pink emphasizes the benefit of moving people from compliance to engagement. This theme recurs in this book as we investigate ways leaders and followers can move to effective coaching, or mentoring of one another, arrive at engagement. While compliance worked for the better part of the 20th century, but the complex problems of the 21st century require engagement of inquiring minds willing to explore new possibilities.

23 Dweck, C. S. (2006/2016). *Mindset: The new psychology of success.* New York, NY: Random House, (p. 110). Dweck reflected on Jim Collins *Good to Great* study that identified leaders who inspired a firm to thrive were self-effacing, inquisitive, confronted reality, and refused to accept failure, but, rather, maintained the faith that they would succeed in the end.

24 Hess, F. D. (2014). *Learn or die: Using science to build a leading-edge learning organization.* New York, NY: Columbia University Press, (p. 46).

25 Rost, J. C. (1993). *Leadership for the 21st century.* Westport, CT: Praeger, (p. 102).

26 Hussain, S. T., Lei, S., Akram, T., Haider, M. J., Hussain, S.H., & Ali, M. (June 22, 2016). Kurt Lewin's change model: A critical review of the role of leadership and employee involvement in organizational change. *Journal of Innovation & Knowledge.* Retrieved November 23, 2020, from https://reader.elsevier.com/reader/sd/pii/S2444569X16300087?token=5 ED1B6F3DCF3D1E0A42122B380C58A8F6D5C1003B4AB5524E64B3C1A251440F5 640478514328CC924277B00AB843BC78.

27 "Better the devil you know than the devil you don't know - It is better to deal with something bad you know than with something new you don't; the new thing might be even worse. The proverb is of Irish origin and has been traced back to the 1539 Collection of proverbs by R. Taverner. First attested in the United States in 'Dodd Cases' by K. Livingston…" *Random House Dictionary of Popular Proverbs and Sayings* by Gregory Y. Titelman (Random House, New York, 1996).

28 Schein, E. H. (2017). *Organizational culture and leadership* (5th ed.). Hoboken, NJ: Wiley & Sons, Inc., (p. 205).

29 Lewin, K. (1947). Group decision and social change. In T. N. Newcomb & E. L. Hartley (Eds.), *Readings in social psychology* (pp. 340–344). New York: Holt, Rinehart and Winston.

30 Heifetz, et al. (p. 96).

31 Schein, E. H. (2017). *Organizational culture and leadership* (5th ed.). Hoboken, NJ: Wiley & Sons, Inc., (p. 89).

32 Northouse, P. G. (2007). *Leadership: Theory and practice* (4th ed.). Thousand Oaks, CA: Sage, (p. 8).

33 Heifetz, R. A. (1994). *Leadership without easy answers.* Cambridge, MA: Belknap., (pp. 58–61). Ronald Heifetz wrote about the difference between dominance and authorization. Dominance relationships are based on coercion. Heifetz cites the work of Stanley Milgram on obedience to explain *habitual deference* and cites the example that while authority relationships involve the employee to authorize the power, in dominant relationships, the employee is deferential, like a victim would defer to a mugger with a gun. Sure, there is an exchange—freedom for money—but the victim has no real choice in the matter.

34 Welch, J., & Welch, S. (2005). *Winning.* New York: HarperBusiness, (pp. 141–142).

35 Ibid, p. 141.

36 Ibid, p. 120.

37 Key performance indicators (KPIs) refer to a set of quantifiable measurements used to gauge a company's overall long-term performance. KPIs specifically help determine a company's strategic, financial, and operational achievements, especially compared to those of other businesses within the same sector. See https://www.investopedia.com/terms/k/kpi.asp

38 Goleman, D. (2006). *Emotional intelligence.* New York: Bantam Books. When we experience shocking events the amygdala, operating in nanoseconds, proclaims an emergency before the neocortex (the thinking brain) even has a chance to react. The "hallmark of such a hijack is that once the moment passes, those so possessed have the sense of not knowing what came over them" (p. 13).

39 Ibid, p. 16.

40 In fairness, many mortgage lenders bought mortgages from third-party marketers. They may or may not have had a true appreciation for the precarious nature of the

recipients of these loans due to a lack of transparency or some degree of opacity accompanying the conveyance of these loans.

41 Friedman, T. L. (2009). *Hot, flat, and crowded* (Release 2.0). New York: Picador/ Farrar/Straus and Giroux. Friedman wrote, "The meltdown that occurred in the market was triggered by subprime mortgages which allowed people with low incomes and tarnished or no credit histories to buy homes" (p. 193). Friedman characterized the fervor as a binge of loaning treating the risk as if it were a U.S. Savings bond when in fact it was a massively risky note.

42 Irrational exuberance refers to a situation where economic agents develop confidence in the economy and financial markets that is misplaced. The term was originally coined by the then Federal Reserve Board chairman, Alan Greenspan, in a speech given at the American Enterprise Institute during the dot-com bubble of the 1990s. The phrase was interpreted as a warning that the stock market might be overvalued.

43 McGregor, D. (1960). *The human side of enterprise*. New York, NY: McGraw-Hill.

44 Pink, D. H. (2009). *Drive: The surprising truth about what motivates us*. New York, NY: Riverhead Books, (p. 71).

45 Ryan, R. M. & Deci, E. L. (2017). *Self-determination theory: Basic psychological needs in motivation, development, and wellness*. New York, NY: The Guilford Press, (p. 4).

46 Ibid, p. 3. The authors state that Self-Determination Theory "(SDT) specifically assumes humans have evolved to be inherently curious, physically active, and deeply social beings. Individual human development is characterized by proactive engagement, assimilating information and behavioral regulations, and finding integration within social groups" (p. 3). People express a need to master both their internal and external worlds, specifically in the areas of intrinsic motivation, internalization, and social integration. "SDT posits that inherent in such pursuits are satisfactions in feeling competencies, autonomy, and relatedness. These proximal satisfactions reflect, in the deepest sense, the essence of human thriving, and they predict any number of indicators of wellness and vitality (pp. 3–4).

47 Schein, E. H. (2017). *Organizational culture and leadership* (5th ed.). Hoboken, NJ: Wiley & Sons, Inc., (p. 111).

48 Weick, K. E. (1995). *Sensemaking in organizations*. Thousand Oaks, CA: Sage, (p. 11).

49 Goodman, N. (1978). *Ways of worldmaking*. Indianapolis, IN: Hackett, (p. 129).

50 Heifetz, Grashow, & Linsky (2009). *The practice of adaptive leadership: Tools and tactics for changing your organization and the world*. Boston, MA: Harvard Business Press. How do you strengthen your capacity to make tough decisions? "On the other side of any tough decision facing you, there inevitably will be another one. You can choose to be annoyed or anxious about these choices, or you can embrace them" (p. 256).

51 Pink, D. H. (2009). *Drive: The surprising truth about what motivates us*. New York, NY: Penguin. Pink advises that we inherently respond to positive and negative reinforcements, as he writes, "zippy calculators of our self-interest, or lumpy duffel bags of psychosexual conflict" (p. 72).

52 Schein, E. H. (2017). *Organizational culture and leadership* (5th ed.). Hoboken, NJ: Wiley & Sons, Inc., (p. 87, pp. 87–88).

53 Jones, G. R. (2001). *Organizational theory: Text and cases*. Upper Saddle River, NJ: Prentice-Hall, p. 401.

54 Jackson, P., & Delehanty, H. (1995). *Sacred hoops: Spiritual lessons of a hardwood warrior*. New York, NY: Hyperion, (p. 113). Phil Jackson quoted Chinese philosopher Wu Men in describing the value of presence of mind: "If your mind isn't clouded by unnecessary things, this is the best season of your life." The message is that whatever you do, "pay precise attention, moment by moment" (p. 116).

PART II

One Road; Three Milestones

You will recall from the introduction chapter we defined leadership as *an influence relationship among leaders and followers who intend real changes that reflect their mutual purposes*[1]. This definition provides a roadmap for plotting the role of leadership in creating buy-in. Based on empirical findings,[2] this suggests leadership flows from meaning. Leaders and followers gain an understanding of the circumstance they occupy and are guided by understanding their mutual purposes.

An important distinction to note is leaders don't micromanage followers, indicating a subservient role for members of an organization. Rather, leaders *and* followers act in relational dialogue[3]. Influence is present but it flows both ways. But, make no mistake, a leader must be accountable to setting direction, driving commitment, and adapting to external challenges—the recipe for thriving in the 21st century.

This approach is rooted in James MacGregor Burns' concept of *"transforming leadership,* while more complex, is a more engaging form of leading people than the transactional kind, which focuses more on leaders forcing compliance upon followers. The transforming leader recognizes and exploits an existing need or demand of a potential follower."[4]

This idea is fundamental to how the leader forms and shapes engagement with followers. The leader looks for "potential motives, seeks to satisfy higher needs, and engages the full person of the follower."[5] Thus, we prefer an alternative view: leadership flows from meaning. In other words, through two-way, symmetrical communication,[6] people buy-in more fully to the challenge at hand because they're dealt the truth, provided the tools and training, and offered the psychological safety to take bold action.

In observing the contributing factors of effective leadership from a theoretical perspective, three principles emerge as the foundation for exemplary practice that cultivate employee buy-in. These are the milestones[7] of the journey, by definition *a significant point in development*. Effective communication is fundamental because when these practices are understood and functioning, the CEO can more effectively inspire decision making to generate committed buy-in from members.

The three developmental factors (milestones) represent significant points in the journey: (a) vigorously confronting reality, (b) expanding individual and organizational knowledge in purposeful ways, and (c) creating safety to members taking legitimate bold action, demonstrated in Figure 2.1. In the next three chapters, we'll begin to understand how these principles work in concert to generate active employee support and participation.

You will see a closer look at these three practices that serve vital roles in recognizing when effective leadership is happening in the organization. We begin by accepting the notion that leaders must not arbitrarily set the marching orders for the troops. A more direct way to say it: the organization takes its direction from the circumstances. For that to work, members of the firm must see reality, know how to respond, and do so with confidence and support from the top; the leader must assure that is happening—she is accountable.

In Chapter 1, the introduction, you met Chris, a proven success story in business. You got a glimpse of his formation and values. Though he would never describe it in these terms, Chris lives the perspective that leadership flows from meaning that's socially constructed through unfettered communication—both speaking and listening—as a means to create understanding, agreement, and commitment.

Don't be confused. Apex' governing structure is a meritocracy where an individual's worth is reflected in the value he or she contributes to the firm. Chapter 2 addresses an inherent obstacle to success: failing to confront reality; Chapter 3 focuses on the merits and means to expand individual and

FIGURE 2.1 If you want their hearts and minds, give them yours

organizational knowledge; and Chapter 4 explains in detail the value of creating safety for members taking bold, legitimate action. We must never lose sight that the end game is for the organization to thrive; the measure of success is ultimately in its ability to get and keep customers for the long haul.

2

FRICTION CREATES THE PEARL

Metaphors help us understand difficult-to-explain concepts or ideas. Forty years ago, George Lakoff and Mark Johnson asserted: "most concepts are partially understood in terms of other concepts."[8] The pair established that abstract thought is largely metaphorical. Love, for example, "is not love without metaphors of magic, attraction, madness, union, nurturance, and so on."[9] In his manner of speaking, Chris uses conceptual metaphors to provide clarity and understanding for customers and employees. For example, on his desk is a plaque that reads: "No guts. No blue chips." So, when we use a metaphor to describe the process of confronting reality, it fits, and the idea resonates.

Friction creates the pearl. This metaphor explains how the beauty of the pearl is created from the oyster when a tiny irritant, such as a parasite, enters the shell and secretions from the mollusk form around the object. Over time, layers build up and after several years of this repetitive activity, the jewel grows in size and value. While researching this, it was discovered that friction is the concept most often used to describe the creation of a pearl.

This phrase does the work of a conceptual metaphor when used to suggest conflict is not inherently bad, as a matter of fact, among human beings it often yields breakthrough outcomes. Just as an oyster creates a pearl from the proverbial grain of sand, so too, is pushback when an organization must adapt to a threat. If the organization can embrace the process, the treasure awaits. If not, no pearl exists, just an irritating foreign object lodged in the mechanics of the organization.

In this chapter, you are introduced to the first of three concepts that support the principle that leadership flows from meaning: *vigorously confront reality*. You'll recall from the last chapter the working definition of leadership is *an influence relationship among leaders and followers who intend real changes that reflect their mutual purposes.*[10] As noted at the outset of this section, the distinction is not leaders *over* followers, indicating a subservient role for members of an organization, rather it's leaders *and* followers.

Leadership then, is an interdependent relationship where leaders and followers accept the roles of accountability (of leaders) and responsibility (of followers). Together, they establish a strong bond with customers who are hungry for a vendor partner who will help them make progress against the situation they face at any given time. This relies on each holding an objective view of reality built on truth.

Truth Is Mysterious, Elusive, Always to Be Conquered[11]

French poet/philosopher Paul Valéry mused: "the best way to make your dreams come true is to wake up." As Chris might say, "Stop dreaming and make it happen." Valéry's words make it clear that presence of mind is a tremendous gift. The trouble is, we resist becoming fully aware because it often threatens our life as we know it, so truth becomes a casualty. Sometimes facing up to the truth presents too much of a threat. When the facts are distressing, it's easier to reframe or ignore them than to deal with them directly. Years of research have informed us that unless there's sufficient interest to push past the initial set of disconfirming facts, the information is disregarded, or deemed irrelevant.

British polymath Bertrand Russell wrote: "Every great idea starts out as blasphemy." That explains why new ideas are rejected out of hand. Anthony De Mello reminds us this is why it is so difficult to get buy-in on new ideas. In this manner, truth is not just ugly, it is not to be believed. To cope with a changing world, one must wake up to new ideas. That "doesn't mean swallowing whatever the speaker is saying. Oh no. You've got to challenge everything. ... But challenge it from an attitude of openness, not from an attitude of stubbornness. And challenge it all."[12]

That requires significant energy; energy we don't always possess. Too many decisions fly at us at any moment that, as Daniel Kahneman put it, get relegated to the fast-thinking system in the brain.[13] Called System 1, it responds to and considers familiar situations to be accurate, or true. "The human mind specializes in analogy and metaphor, on a sweeping together of chaotic sensory experience into workable categories labeled by words and stacked into hierarchies for quick recovery."[14]

When we experience a problem and muster an effective response, our brain logs that incident in our memory. So, what sticks? Put in digital media terms: the question is: What clicks and what sticks.

The Brain and the New Stimulus

MIT physicist-turned-author Joseph Romm points to storytelling. Citing neurological studies, he found that "telling a compelling story actually lights up the same parts of the brains of both speaker and the audience,"[15] so, he concluded neural connection is rudimentary in the task of persuasion. Romm reported figures of speech, such as irony (Taylor Swift's lyric, "he's so bad, but he does it so well") and metaphor (Lady Gaga's Poker Face) are highly effective mind grabbers. By the way, philosopher Frederich Nietzsche recognized the persuasive power of music when he wrote: "At times the experience of music is so over-powering that one fears for one's poor ego, which threatens to be submerged in the pure rapture of music ...."[16]

Perhaps the strongest influence combo is *repetition* teamed up with *hyperbole* as masterfully demonstrated by President Trump on many occasions, including his repeated claim that he would construct a wall the entire length of the southern border and Mexico would pay for it. The Trump faithful fully believed it would happen. Yet, by October 6, 2020, about 350 miles of barrier had been con-structed during the Trump presidency, and only 15 miles were new, that is, not replacement or secondary wall, and none of it paid for by Mexico.[17] That not-withstanding, the president stands hard and fast by the rule that if you repeat a statement frequently, people will eventually believe it to be true, regardless of its veracity; he does so with good reason. Think: the election was stolen.

Repetition of a statement is hard to ignore; when it resonates with an audience it proves both memorable and considered true, even if false, famously dubbed the alternative truth. Consider this, in a study measuring the memorability of myths regarding the flu vaccine, respondents were provided CDC information cor-recting myths, such as, *the side effects of the vaccine were worse than the flu*—a patently false statement. Yet, when researchers measured memorability a mere 30 minutes later, 28% of respondents misremembered the false statement to be true; three days later they remembered 40% of the myths to be factual. What are the im-plications of this phenomena?

Informed by this reliable peer-reviewed research, journalist Shankar Vendantam wrote: "Someone trying to manipulate public opinion can take ad-vantage of this aspect of brain functioning. In politics and elsewhere, this means that whoever makes the first assertion about something has a large advantage over everyone who denies it later." When a speaker repeats a recognizable solution to a problem previously encountered, the receiver matches the solution with the pattern in their mind—established by what they first perceived about the matter. This mental shortcut is considered reliable. If a communicator can burn an image or thought into a receiver's brain, it's not only embedded, it's perceived to be true. In many minds, Mexico paid for the wall that was built coast-to-coast. Yet, that statement is false.

How does one deliver the truth so it's received and understood by the re-ceiver? As we have discovered, fact has little to do with it. The challenge is to master the tools of rhetoric. Reverting to the wisdom of the ancients, we discover in Plato's dialogue, *Gorgias*, that a skilled rhetorician would more ef-fectively persuade an audience that he was more a doctor than a real doctor.

Rhetoric is a language device that works and has for more than a couple of thousand years.

To Confront Truth, Speak Truthfully

While we see truth can be subjective, it is useful when it is, in fact, true. Chris would tell his people one of the benefits of buying a business he wasn't entirely familiar with, was the advantage of *not* knowing everything. In other words, he had no pre-conditioned response to certain facts that others might find discomforting, or even meaningless.

He needed to learn to use System 2 of his brain—the slower, more deliberative, and logical part—to work through the unfamiliar. Then, he needed to quantify the pro's and con's and settle on a course of action. In this way, he confronted the reality of the situation, countering any bias he may have, so he could embrace the uncomfortable truth if it reared its ugly head.

To explain this, Chris would say, "If I became aware that one of our key performance indicators (KPI)[18] was trending in the wrong direction, then I'd be curious to discover the cause. However, if it was me that should have known better, it was *me* that was to be blamed, so I'd be defensive. I'd feel like I'd missed something. So, I wouldn't be seeking the root-cause as I should, I'd be questioning if it were true that it was me who created the problem, or that there was a problem at all." Chris laid it on the line, people are human and tend to preserve self above all things. So, when truth presents a threat, they seek an alternate explanation for reality.

Chris reminded himself of that prophetic quote from the film "The Big Short:" "It ain't what you don't know that gets you into trouble. It's what you know for sure that just ain't so."[19] In that film about the 2007 subprime mortgage crisis, four outsiders saw what the experts failed to see: a disastrous housing bubble built on poorly vetted mortgage loans.

Having great business instincts provided Chris reliable judgment of right from wrong and good from bad even without intimate knowledge of the details. Perhaps, it's because he is well-disciplined, intellectually honest, or simply selflessly curious that Chris invites inquiry into the unknown. More importantly, as an authority figure, he pushes past the fear of the known. As the boss, he could see the benefit in pursuing the unvarnished truth. "You cannot fear something you do not know. ... What you really fear is the loss of the known."[20]

Put differently, when one is confronted with something that's not going as planned, the need is to determine if one must unlearn something that is no longer true. Too often, truth is not expressed in words, it's seen and felt. That's why truth is not subject to advocacy or debate, it's true because you feel it's true or not true because you don't. Even crazier, you have your truth and I have mine and they aren't the same. Due to this, we don't struggle with truth as much as we fight the obstacles standing in the way of the truth. So yes, sometimes it's simply a matter of waking up. Chris sees it much as his mother taught him growing up: "Wake up, son, or the world will pass you by."

Early Warning Systems Yield an Advantage

Organizations today face external challenges at an increasingly fast pace. Whether it's an innovation brought on by a competitor who introduces a compelling new value proposition for your customer—think Uber if you were in the taxi business—or some external change, like a natural disaster, adaptability is essential. If it's not a competitor, maybe it's a black swan event, like the global pandemic that changed all the rules overnight. The questions are: Is your organization able to adapt? Can it *vigorously confront reality*? And most importantly, will it merely survive, or will it thrive.

Perhaps it's unfair to cite examples from the Coronavirus pandemic in illustrating the way people and organizations confront reality. After all, who could have predicted such an epic phenomenon, right? Well, actually, both near- and long-term advanced notice existed. On New Year's Eve, 2019, a small Canadian company called BlueDot tapped into a potentially disturbing piece of news. Its computers, driven by a news-thirsty algorithm, collected an account from a Chinese business newspaper that reported "27 cases of a mysterious, flu-like disease in Wuhan, a city of 11-million people."[21]

This is believed to be the first identification outside of China of the novel Coronavirus. The service that produced this startling finding is a product dubbed Outbreak Science, described by the company as an early warning system of pandemics. Who knew there was such a thing?

BlueDot's founder, Dr. Kamran Khan, an infectious disease physician, started the firm on the heels of the 2003 SARS epidemic that had spread from Hong Kong to Toronto, causing an outbreak that resulted in 44 deaths, including three of Dr. Khan's colleagues, and caused $2-billion in financial losses. In creating BlueDot, Dr. Khan assembled an eclectic set of curious, knowledgeable experts to devise a means to rapidly identify potential virile threats. BlueDot's early adopter clients—who all valued the concept of vigorously confronting reality—signed up for the service.

While the Chinese government was mum on the details of the virus it need not be the sole source of understanding. BlueDot's algorithm was "processing data including medical bulletins, even livestock reports, to predict where the virus would go next."[22] In retrospect, it is quite possible that the preponderance of the Coronavirus cases that landed on US shores were from Europe. The company scanned the airline ticket data from 4,000 airports tracking flights and calculating cities at the greatest risk. So, once the 27 cases were discovered in Wuhan, BlueDot tracked the volume of travelers to destinations across the globe. New York City was one of the highest

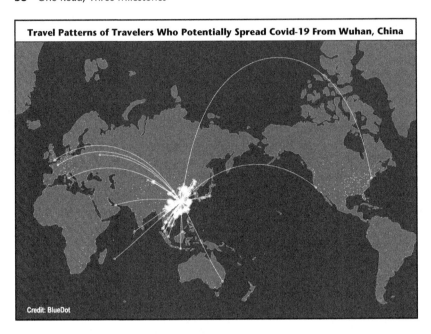

Travel Patterns of Travelers Who Potentially Spread Covid-19 From Wuhan, China

Credit: BlueDot

FIGURE 2.2 Map by BlueDot's Outbreak Science product. It depicts patterns of spread of the virus from Wuhan, China

volume destinations. In Dr. Khan's words, "If you think of an outbreak like a fire with embers flying off into different locations"[23] the map (Figure 2.2) shows where the embers are landing and where the virus is most likely to expand.

CBS 60 Minutes interviewer Bill Whitaker suggested to Dr. Khan, "those embers landed in New York and started a wildfire" to which he emphatically agreed. He added with more than 4-billion world airline travelers yearly, tracking their movement is critical in telling us where and how diseases spread. Khan determined if an airline company can track a traveler down to the specific seat in which he or she sits, BlueDot people could certainly tap into that data to depict the spread of a virus.

Besides tracking global passenger movement, BlueDot has licensed access to anonymized cell phone data that enables it to track devices. Using this data, the firm could track travel during specific time periods from Wuhan to other cities in Asia and across the globe. The combination of these databases working through an effective algorithm to track global movement gave BlueDot's clients, like Humber River Hospital in Toronto, a canary in the coal mine perspective.

By using the early warning information, Humber River got a jump on sourcing and ordering essential personal protective equipment (PPE) that once word of the outbreak was out the supply quickly tightened. This is a prime example that by vigorously confronting reality, it's possible to reduce risk and, as

BlueDot envisions, reduce the uncontrolled spread of pathogens. The takeaway here is that we are far better served by developing the technology to permit ourselves to identify patterns emerging from data. Far better than playing the blame game.

No hospitals in the United States had contracted with BlueDot to receive the Outbreak Science product. Neither did the U.S. federal government. The federal response earned criticism for acting too late and further failing to mitigate the costly effects of states outbidding one another for PPE once the outbreak hit in full force. By the way, in March, California became the first state in the country to lockdown its cities. California is a BlueDot client. Moreover, it marshals its own similarly constructed algorithm to identify patterns of virus spread and social distancing in public spaces.

Even with this window into spread, it was the masses who thwarted California's ability to flatten the curve. This is a lesson in itself, that even when leaders confront reality, if followers don't buy-in by taking basic actions like wearing masks and social distancing, the benefit is lost. For any number of reasons, and with a few notable exceptions, global leaders disastrously failed to win the hearts and minds of nations of followers. New Zealand Prime Minister Jacinda Ardern was one such favorable example. By late Fall 2020, life in New Zealand had returned to normal with a total of 25 deaths in a country with about 5 million people. By April, 2021, there were 26 deaths from COVID.

To Confront Reality, Mobilize Response

To confront reality, one must be prepared to see it, feel it, and know its implications. In the previous account, we saw a tale of two responses; one that vigorously confronted reality by employing forward-thinking tools that identified a significant risk, and the rest of the world that ignored the possibilities of a pathogen catastrophe. This despite clear warnings well in advance. What's more, the delay in recognizing the spread of the novel Coronavirus stalled what should have been a robust effort by the government to communicate individual citizen's role in controlling spread.

As we now know, three simple practices go a long way here, namely: wear a mask, wash your hands, and watch your distance. Further, accurate and rapidly deployed testing in adequate quantities and widely distributed, is an invaluable tool to identify spread and plan for an effective response from the nation's health care providers. Finally, if you want to nip the virus in the bud, so to speak, you must have robust contact tracing *before* the spread gets out of hand. Once the virus is unleashed this is a near-impossible task.

Ironically, these simple measures were spelled out in a White House document titled, "Playbook for Early Response to High-Consequence Emerging infectious Disease Threats," otherwise called "The Pandemic Playbook" (Figure 2.3) which was originally created in 2016 by the Obama Administration and subsequently

They Had a Plan ...

FIGURE 2.3 The Pandemic Playbook issued by both Obama and Trump administrations

updated by the Trump administration.[24] Moreover, Trump administrators conducted a tabletop exercise just months before the outbreak.

So, years before, despite issuing warning signs and putting planning place, when the pandemic struck, the response proved too little too late. This is a grim reminder that to truly confront reality, leaders must gather the will of the people to act. All the preparedness matters not if leaders cannot connect the dots for all to see. As David Maister wrote, "the necessary outcome of strategic planning is not analytical insight but resolve."[25]

When Truth Is Mistaken for a Trojan Horse

In March 2015, Bill Gates presented a Ted Talk where he warned that "the greatest risk of global catastrophe doesn't look like this [pointing to a mushroom cloud], it looks like this [pointing to the now famous virus microbe with its red-topped plumes jutting out from a ball-like center]. The worldwide disaster is most likely to be an infectious virus rather than a war."[26] This startling prediction from such a credible source as Bill Gates failed to shake the world into action. Rather, it sat dormant for five years. Then, after the Coronavirus landed on American soil, the talk generated 25-million views, roughly five times the views in the previous five years.

Interestingly, the *New York Times* reported that Gates has since "become the star of an explosion of conspiracy theories ... [now] being falsely portrayed as a profiteer from a virus vaccine, and as part of a dastardly plot to use the illness to cull or surveil the global population."[27] Ironically, as we stated before, reality, or truth, is in the eye of the beholder. Novelist Anaïs Nin popularized a perspective that may explain this communication phenomena: *We don't see things as they are, we see things as we are.*[28]

While the arrival of the novel Coronavirus was published in high-level reports early in the month, by January 29, 2020, the White House became aware of the Coronavirus when Peter Navarro, a high-ranking West Wing official and President Trump's trade chief, advised: "The lack of immune protection or an existing cure or vaccine would leave Americans defenseless in the case of a full-blown coronavirus outbreak on U.S. soil."

Mr. Navarro's memo reported, "This lack of protection elevates the risk of the coronavirus evolving into a full-blown pandemic, imperiling the lives of millions of Americans."[29] On February 23, 2020, Navarro resurfaced the threat when he warned of an "increasing probability of a full-blown COVID-19 pandemic that could infect as many as 100 million Americans, with a loss of life of as many as 1–2 million souls."[30]

In retrospect, these events presented a clear lesson that underscores the theme of this chapter: vigorously confront reality. But, as we discovered, knowing is not confronting, especially when the gift of advance notice is dismissed as a threat to the status quo. If reality is not vividly presented, it cannot be used to create buy-in.

Shadow Group Dynamics: The Formation of Teleopathy and Groupthink

Human beings are dutiful to their commitments, particularly when going along means getting along. Consequently, if our livelihoods come first, it's not likely we'll go against the flow. Adopting this stance, we're vulnerable to prejudice—judging before hearing full and sufficient examination.[31] Further, as we've learned, people become adept at choosing the truth they want to hear if it threatens to disturb their collective zeitgeist.

In the terminology of the day, this is known as the echo chamber, a metaphor used to describe an individual's ability to tailor digital/social media. When individuals shape their internet feed through personal selection of platforms and sites; when their search behavior is captured by search engine algorithms, they are filtering their content in a manner that unwittingly shuts off competing ideas and opposing thoughts.

Journalist Eli Pariser called it the filter bubble. In a 2005 Ted Talk, he extolled the virtue of the Internet as a means of giving people who had previously been unable to express their ideas, the unlimited power in what became known as citizen journalism. Moreover, search engines like Google, are adept at organizing the massive data in the World Wide Web in a manner that makes it easy to access actionable data to inform ideas and innovation by creating networks of individuals with diverse thoughts.

Yet, Pariser, the author of the *Wisdom of Crowds* states, "the more tightly we become linked to each other, the harder it is for each of us to remain independent."[32] One of the fundamental outcomes of a network is that it begins to shape the views of its members by constraining its views and interactions. When members lose their independence, the group becomes myopic.

With the ability to tailor information to feed our needs and sooth ourselves, we can readily minimize the effects of cognitive dissonance[33] a source of fret and worry. Even before we could create our own self-affirming news feed, we devised ways to reduce the dissonance in our life. To understand this, it helps to apprehend the idea of teleology, the explanation of phenomena in terms of the purpose they serve rather than of the cause by which they arise.[34] Simply said, teleology says everything has a purpose. However, holding that worldview stands in opposition to experiencing life as a way of being, a means to explore possibilities as they emerge.

It can be problematic to say everything happens for a reason and, at the same time, remain open to the idea that phenomena may change the course of one's life. After all, sometimes events arise for unexplainable reasons and new prospects are presented. Yet, our personal teleology can effectively move us to be blind to biases causing us to act, ignoring the possibilities in life driven by experience. When this leads to an imbalance, we may obsess on a destination. This suppresses the diverse voices that serve to protect the organization. By succumbing to fatalism, we dismiss the messages that we can control our own destiny and buy-in is thwarted. Suppressing opposition can be dangerous, even disastrous.

Teleopathic Dangers

Derived from teleology, Kenneth E. Goodpaster coined the word *teleopathy*,[35] and defined it as unbalanced pursuit of purpose. Goodpaster attributes this to a mindset overly fixated on goals. He describes mindsets as "a person's or group's practical orientation, including not only general values like competence, achievement, and satisfaction, but also more work-related attitudes."

"*Mindsets carry thoughts and values into action*, and this fact makes them particularly important in the guidance of persons and organizations."[36] In other words, mindsets not only drive thought, they drive action. Goodpaster points to three symptoms of an organization that has devolved into teleopathy:

- *Fixation* or singleness of purpose under stress;
- *Rationalization* of behavior through selective perception about context and consequence; and
- *Detachment*, a kind of self-imposed cultural fence that impairs open communication between leaders and followers.[37]

In this kind of environment, organizational leaders place outsized attention on achieving the goal at all costs. Top-down leader messaging—both verbal and behavioral—encourages strict compliance, unquestioning loyalty, and short-term thinking. Supported through policy and compensation, members of the organization are held to narrow measures of success and are encouraged to reject conflicting data that may deter, or challenge established goals.

This condition is similar to groupthink,[38] a "pattern of thought characterized by self-deception, forced manufacture of consent, and conformity to group values and ethics."[39] When we deny honest feedback and discourage candid observations among members of the workplace, we make ourselves vulnerable to groupthink, when the desire for consensus quashes common sense and peer review, essential to high quality decision-making and problem-solving.[40] A notable example of groupthink in action was the Challenger Space Shuttle disaster in 1986, when a diverse team of experts—many aware of faulty parts and questionable launch conditions—proceeded as planned leading to a disastrous explosion 73 seconds after launch killing all seven aboard.

Groupthink and teleopathy may have beneficial outcomes in the appearance of group cohesion and low internal conflict that stimulate swift and timely completion of tasks. However, effective decision-making requires loyal opposition as when an opposing view surfaces from the role of the *devil's advocate*. Like any leader with an agenda, Chris appreciated consensus. However, he recognized the importance of accommodating diverse, or opposing views.

Vigorously confronting truth is essential for a firm to understand and effectively create an open and honest workplace. In meetings, Chris would intentionally hold back on voicing his position on an issue until others had exhausted their ideas and options. Also, he would ask for an individual to adopt the "devil's advocate" role by asking, "Okay, who wants to throw water on this idea?" On major decisions, he would take the time to casually sample the opinions of others privately. This often led to a "second look" session where members have the opportunity to second-guess without fear of retribution. This is the essence of deliberation, decision-making guided by careful and thoughtful consideration.

Work Out Differences Before Asking for Buy-In

In his guide to life,[41] Dale Carnegie offered this bit of advice about getting people on board with your idea or plan. He titled the first chapter, "If You Want to Gather Honey, Don' Kick Over the Beehive." To Carnegie, kicking over the beehive was akin to diminishing others, robbing them of their dignity. In life, giving praise is more effective than dispatching criticism. One of the most genuine ways to praise others is to recognize the value of their thoughts, but never in a patronizing way.

Chris cultivated many aspects of General Electric's Work-Out program as a practice to reduce hierarchy as a barrier to ideas. Frustration over leaders who failed to "walk the talk" to embed change resulted in the creation of Work-Out, a forum for dialogue aimed at eliminating bureaucracy and tapping into front-line workers' observations thereby enlisting them in the solution.

This form of vigorously confronting reality meant, "getting people to face facts and take responsibility—an astoundingly difficult thing to achieve, especially in large organizations."[42] But, if a leader can demonstrate genuine trustworthiness,[43] trust will likely take root. At GE, the Work-Out ethic eventually went virile within the organization, a testament to the power of seeking genuine consensus.

From the initial employee engagement of Work-Out, GE extended its reach to "suppliers and customers into the intimacy of GE's candid discussions."[44] This inspired a revolution inside the company and it "spawned the explicit value of 'boundaryless' behavior."[45] Boundarylessness meant the firm refused to limit free exchange of information and ideas. How committed was management to this concept? GE fired people for bullying or suppressing information or ideas.

Chris admired this tough commitment to facing reality because he could see how it could empower and motivate people up and down the organization, including suppliers who were accomplices in value creation and customers who were the ultimate funders of the business. His commitment took shape in outreach sessions, during which Chris hired a trusted third-party representative to travel to customers' offices to interview them on a variety of issues to get the true view.

By using a third-party, Chris felt customers would feel more unencumbered and would speak frankly on their perspective of the firm's dealing with the customer. When the third-party returned to report on customer findings, the management team received a briefing and a lively no-holds-barred discussion ensued. Finally, Chris would personally report back to the customer on what he and his team learned thereby closing the loop on matters of importance to the customer.

LISTENING FOR WHAT HE DIDN'T HEAR

During this visit to Mom's, Chris was struggling with truth. Was truth always necessary? Or, did it have a place and time?

CHRIS: *Do you remember when I made a house call with Doc?* (From the time he was a young boy, Chris called his dad what everyone else called him, "Doc").

AGNES: *That was an eye-opener for you ... the night you lost your boyhood innocence.*

CHRIS: *Also, that was the night I decided I didn't want to be a vet! Well, we went to Gunderson's place. And it was obvious to Doc that the calf being raised by Janey was not going to make it. But Doc did something I'd never seen him do, he got soft and held back. I was surprised.*

AGNES: *You mean he didn't lay it out in his usual manner ... straight and to the point.*

CHRIS: *Yes, he knew that calf was soon to go, but he told Janey and Mr. Gunderson to nurse the calf. He probably should have put it down right then and there ...*

AGNES: *But he didn't say anything even though he knew. He was bound to tell the truth, but even old Doc had a soft spot.*

CHRIS: *Yea, but it surprised me. He always shot straight from the hip.*

AGNES: *Even for your dad, looking into that little girl's eyes he couldn't tell her straight out. And good thing, she had a chance to spend a little time with the calf and prepare herself for loss. Big lesson for all.*

CHRIS: *I think I am in Janie's position. I didn't like what I didn't hear when I visited the Big Client this week. We've had some internal discussions about the "quickie report" that people are calling it. It's a joke. It's barely a report at all. But the client wants it because competition is brutal and ready to approve anybody that can fog a mirror! I left the meeting not hearing what I had hoped to hear ...*

AGNES: *What's that?*

CHRIS: *They didn't level with us. They knew the product was dicey but told us to go back and re-think it. There was nothing to re-think.*

AGNES: *Sounds to me like you feel a little like Janey ... you're about to lose something and there is nothing you can do about it.*

Chris drove back to the office with a big thought. He questioned ... if there was an elephant in the room at the client, namely the catastrophic outcome of the quickie report, would his people confront it? Would they buy-in to the agonizing decision of losing all the business that would befall Apex when they refused to offer the slipshod product?

Buy-In Runs Through the Customer

If there's ever a time in history when vigorously confronting reality on behalf of the customer is productive, the time is now. Three words characterize our current marketing communication environment: authenticity, transparency, and relevance. Authenticity is when you let the real brand DNA shine through warts and all. No polish. No spin. Just the unvarnished truth. No brand is expected to be perfect. The brand is expected to be authentic, the best version of its real self. So, if your firm has a culture that rewards honesty and open dialogue, your brand is likely transparent—no hidden agendas or sacred cows. That's good because with authenticity and transparency embraced, your brand can be relevant, that is, you can engage with your customer because you know the value you deliver and provide a culture that lives and supports the essence of your brand.

QUICK MARKETING LESSON

Firms, whether for-profit or not-for-profit, must get and keep customers. The money that patrons and customers contribute permits the organization to continue to operate. What they buy is *value*—defined as what you get for what you pay. The customer's specific needs determine what specific category of purchase may be considered. Knowing flows from peers' experiences and recommendations. The moment of purchase triggers the reality test. Does this purchase do the job I hired it to do?[46] Your choice is dependent on the what you specify in the job you are trying to get done and whether that brand/product is up to the task. Fail to perform and your brand will not be asked back again.

The firm must assess what it does best; which customer is its best prospect for what it can do. This requires the participation of all brains in the game, not just employees, but also customers, suppliers, distributors, and retailers. Most importantly, determining what your customer wants—the job to be performed—is dependent on open, honest dialogue. This is true in any exchange, whether it's retail, wholesale, product, service, idea, or any combination of these.

Before Chris acquired Apex, a distinctly different style of leader managed the firm. The former owner had a mechanistic, controlling style and preferred a command-and-control approach to leading people. This stood in stark contrast to Chris, who considered influence to be more collaborative—a give and take—that's accomplished through a free flow of information and observations.

Dennis, a supervisor who had worked under the previous regime said, "it is quite different now. We are all about better relationships between our people and our clients because if our people build relationships, they build trust and an environment of honesty. The customer will let us know if we are getting the job done for them. This is a way of doing business now. Chris reminds us all the time, if we want to be trusted we must be trustworthy. So, each of us must assume the responsibility in speaking our minds in an open and honest relationship."

In keeping with the theme of leadership in this text, consider this observation from Ronald A. Heifetz: "Rather than define leadership as a position of authority in a social structure or as a personal set of characteristics, we may find it a great deal more useful to define leadership as an *activity*."[47] In this manner, anyone in the firm can be a leader or follower at any given time. The dependent factors are not status, rather they hinge on the needs of the organization at the time. All members of the firm must have working knowledge of the skills and traits of their co-workers and, of course, themselves. Managers must see to it this happens.

"Personal abilities are resources for leadership applied differently in different contexts"[48] In this conception of leadership, everyone must rise to the leadership occasion when presented. Failure to do so would be dereliction of duty. Conversely, assuming a leadership role when clearly incapable, is a waste of time and effort.

Chris offered a sailing analogy for knowing when leadership was necessary: "It's needed in setting direction, getting everyone on board, and facing the winds of change. Without knowing where the ship is headed, it's perilous to act. If people aren't engaged, they won't have enough energy to complete the trip. And, if you don't know when a course correction is due, arrival at our destination is a crap shoot."

Can't See the Forest for the Trees?

Sometimes we are simply too engaged to see the big picture or recognize the meaningful pattern in random data. Sometimes, we see what we are looking for, not what is there. We do have selective perception and a free will, so sometimes, we can't see the forest for the trees. Ironically, we are either too close or too far away. Or, our focus is not properly adjusted. Larry Bossidy and Ram Charan wrote: "People often miss the external realities because they're overly focused on internal processes, policies, and politics [but, ironically] ... that doesn't stop them from misjudging the internal realities. They overestimate their capabilities and underestimate the difficulty of achieving their goals."[49]

Why does this happen? This may be why Jim Collins (2001) called for a culture of discipline in people, thought, and action as a means of providing a framework in which people can freely act without the stifling effects of being managed or controlled. In this manner, a firm has an early warning device and a means to identify and ward off looming threats to the organization.[50]

The sustainable success of a business lies in it providing a differential advantage.[51] This is the basis of its market strategy. Having an open, honest relationship with customers at all levels doesn't automatically deliver competitive advantage but the two-way communication that results, helps a firm identify *how* it delivers value and *why* it will uniquely stand out from its competitors.

Additionally, in an environment of open communication, employees know how they contribute to the success in the firm, and therefore, how they might share in its success, a true motivator. Also, with better relationships, communication is forthcoming because with candor there is a greater expectation that what they say will be heard and acted upon.

Dennis said, "the 'my way or the highway' style worked, for the most part. But that was when the market was strong and, you know what they say, 'big sales cover a multitude of sins.'" That's true. Sales growth has a tendency to deceive, and unintentionally promote a lack of accountability. So, when sales drop, underperformers can't help the firm out of its slump, they have no learning that applies.

Just Do It and Don't Ask Questions

For a period of time under the original owners, the firm was successful and produced measurable results. Sales increased, so people figured, the company must be on a good course. With a "don't-rock-the-boat" attitude, previous management stifled ideas that were in conflict with their views. This is a matter of focusing on doing things right as opposed to doing the right things.

This concept is central to an argument advanced by Abraham Zaleznik contrasting management and leadership. In his study, Zaleznik[52] enumerated three distinctions between leadership and management that offer insight into thoughts and perceptions of knowledgeable employees working in contemporary business settings today. He found that managers focus on procedure, communicate in signals, and are preoccupied with presenting every scenario as win-win.

On the other hand, leaders focus on substance, communicate in messages, and deal with the reality that in some situations people lose. Zaleznik concluded that management control is overrated and breeds a sense of being manipulated, while leadership sacrifices the appearance of order for authentic employee engagement.

The principles of organizational effectiveness related in the preceding paragraphs provide a foundation for understanding the situation faced by Apex, specifically, how to create and keep customers. This challenge is fundamentally tied to the way the organization makes decisions, generates commitment, and faces adaptive challenge. The ultimate measure of success in these activities lies in successfully getting and keeping customers. It's necessary to vigorously confront reality and to relentlessly spread that practice. Management and leadership each have a role in the firm. Management is making sure work gets done; leadership is about making sure the right things get done right.

Pushing Through the Barriers of Communication to the Truth of the Matter

When we think of barriers to communication in the workplace, we often think of a variety of challenges. These challenges may be overcoming disinterest, inability to listen, accuracy of information, mismatched communication styles, inherent conflict, channel noise, cultural differences, or emotional challenges. Volumes have been written on process, barriers, and prescriptive advice to overcome these issues. Scholars have diligently pursued this topic and built a vast library of knowledge much of which we have investigated in this chapter. Suffice to say, confronting reality is to remove the illusions and fears. It is true, perception is reality. However, unless we rigorously pursue the truth of the matter, we run the risk of perception being an illusion rather than a reflection.

TAKEAWAYS

- For an organization to succeed it must confront reality, that means all members must be free to call out the truth and leaders must create the safety for the truth to emerge through its members.
- When a firm is unafraid to deal with the facts, it can inspire a healthy, efficacious internal response to external challenges. Leadership is an interdependent relationship where leaders are *accountable* for setting direction and followers *responsible* for executing as directed. This is best accomplished if both parties are facing the truth of the matter.
- Meritocracy is the preferred form of organizing in that it focuses on the merit one brings to the firm and the value they can generate through their ability to create value. For a meritocracy to work, everyone must be engaged and aware of their selves and their surroundings. Healthy skepticism, especially when it's supported by keen observations from the front lines, is highly sought-after asset in firms that recognize the customer is the hero and makes the work of the enterprise possible.
- The environment is ever-changing, the firm must adapt. It's not a matter of surviving (who gets enthused about that), it is about thriving. An early warning system is essential, as is abidance to the warnings it may deliver.
- Confronting reality requires the skills and competencies to deal with the threats it may identify. The sequence is to see, know, and act. While it sounds straightforward enough, group dynamics, such as teleopathy and groupthink, can nullify the benefit of early warning.
- Leaders must recognize the value of loyal opposition. Yes, followers are responsible to carry out orders, but they must also alert their leaders when an unexpected challenge appears. Leaders cannot expect this to happen if they have not established an engaging workplace of trust.
- Customers hold the key to growth and happiness. While customer is king may sound good, it's not a good rule to follow. Customers want

help making progress against their hopes and dreams. That's why the firm must demonstrate authenticity, transparency, and relevance.

- There are two vantage points of the business playing field: the front lines and the press box. Toggling back and forth between these two gives the leader a true perspective of the progress being made against the needs of customers and employees.
- Management and leadership each have a role in the firm. Management is making sure things get done; leadership is about making sure the right things get done right.

Notes

1 Rost, (p. 102).
2 McMahon, T. P. (2009), The data gathered in my dissertation "represented themes, relational issues, and factors that support the thesis that ... leadership is not necessarily the outcome of leader influence as much as it is the product of the leader and follower conspiring to understand the reality of their situation. In other words, leadership flows from meaning and not meaning from leadership," (p. 127).
3 Drath, W. (2001). *The deep blue sea: Rethinking the source of leadership*. San Francisco, CA: Jossey-Bass. Relational dialogue is what Drath called a leadership *knowledge principle*, a set of ideas, or rules about the nature of reality and life that are taken to be true. He considered relational dialogue as "a way of understanding that leadership happens when people who acknowledge shared work use dialogue and collaborative learning to create contexts in which that work can be accomplished across line of differing perspectives, value, beliefs, cultures, and more generally what I will refer to as differing worldviews," (pp. 14–15).
4 Burns, (p. 4.)
5 Ibid, p. 4.
6 Grunig, Grunig & Dozier, (p. 308).
7 Milestone. *Merriam-Webster's Collegiate Dictionary*. ©2020
8 Lakoff & Johnson, (p. 5).
9 Ibid, p. 272.
10 Rost, (p. 102).
11 This is a part of a quote attributed to French Philosopher Albert Camus.
12 De Mello, (p. 18).
13 Kahneman, (p. 25). Daniel Kahneman wrote "System 1 (the fast, low-effort mode) ... models familiar situations ... [that] are accurate. Its short-term predictions are usually accurate as well, and its initial reactions to challenges are swift and generally appropriate. System 1 has biases, however, systematic errors that it is prone to make in specified situations. ... and has little understanding of logic and statistics."
14 Wilson. E. O., (p. 60).
15 Romm, (p. 30).
16 Safranski, R. (2003). *Nietzsche: A philosophical biography* (S. Frisch, Trans.). New York, NY: W.W. Norton & Company. (p. 14).
17 Rodgers, L. & Bailey, D. (October 31, 2020) Trump wall: How much has actually been built? *BBC News*. Retrieved from https://www.bbc.com/news/world-us-canada-46824649.

18 Key performance indicators. Investopedia. Retrieved from https://www.investopedia.com/terms/k/kpi.asp. KPIs refer to a set of quantifiable measurements used to gauge a company's overall long-term performance. KPIs specifically help determine a company's strategic, financial, and operational achievements, especially compared to those of other businesses within the same sector.

19 Pitt, B., Kleiner, J., Gardner, D., & Milchan, A. (Producers), McKay, A. (Director). (2015). *The Big Short* [Motion Picture]. USA: Regency Pictures; Plan B Entertainment. This quote is often attributed to Abraham Lincoln and others. However, in researching it, this is the definitive source that could be ascertained.

20 De Mello, (p. 29).

21 Abbott, H. (Producer). 2020, April 26. Outbreak Science (Season 52, Episode 30) [TV series episode]. In W. Owens (Executive Producer). *60 minutes*. CBS Television.

22 Ibid.

23 Ibid.

24 Balding & Beacham.

25 Maister, (p. 6).

26 TED.

27 Wakabayashi, Alba & Tracy.

28 Though Nin passed away more than 40 years ago, has become widely quoted on the internet social media influencer and style muse, defined as a woman who is the source of inspiration for a creative artist. Retrieved from styleclinic.co.

29 Haberman, M. (April 6, 2020). Trade adviser warned White House in January of risks of a pandemic. *New York Times*.https://www.nytimes.com/2020/04/06/us/politics/navarro-warning-trump-coronavirus.html.

30 Ibid.

31 Prejudice. *Merriam-Webster's Collegiate Dictionary*. ©2018 Merriam-Webster, Inc.

32 TED. (2004, February).

33 Cognitive dissonance occurs when a person holds two or more contradictory beliefs, ideas, or values and acts contrary to at least one of the three. This is psychologically stressful, so people tend to seek channels of information that support their beliefs, ideas, and values.

34 Teleology. *Merriam-Webster's Collegiate Dictionary*. ©2018 Merriam-Webster, Inc.

35 Goodpaster, (p. 15).

36 Ibid, p. 33.

37 Ibid, p. 27.

38 The word groupthink was originally coined by Irving L. Janis in his 1972 book *Groupthink,* published in 1972. It was the outcome of his research into why teams reach obtain an excellent outcome on one occasion and disastrous results on the next.

39 Conformity. *Merriam-Webster's Collegiate Dictionary*. ©2018 Merriam-Webster, Inc.

40 Psychology Today, (n.d.). *Groupthink*. Retrieved June 12, 2020 from https://www.psychologytoday.com/us/basics/groupthink. Groupthink occurs when a group of well-intentioned people make irrational or non-optimal decisions spurred by the urge to conform or the discouragement of dissent. This problematic or premature consensus may be fueled by a particular agenda or simply because group members value harmony and coherence above rational thinking. while it is often invoked at the level of geopolitics, groupthink can also refer to subtle processes of social or ideological conformity.

41 Dale Carnegie wrote the eponymous *How to Win Friends and Influence People* in 1936. Warren Buffett has a copy of the book behind the glass on the entry to his office. Moreover, he credits Carnegie's course that he took when he was 20 years old with bringing him out of the shadows, providing him with the understanding and courage to lead people. Carnegie's book has 30-million copies and 9-million people have taken his course.

42 Tichy & Sherman, (p. 119).

43 Matthews, M. D. (May 3, 2016). The three C's of trust. *Psychology Today,* https://www.psychologytoday.com/us/blog/head-strong/201605/the-3-c-s-trust. Competence, character, and caring. First, to be trusted leaders must be viewed by their soldiers as competent. They had to know their jobs and communicate clearly to their subordinates that they possessed the knowledge and skills needed to get the job done. Second, they must have character, found in these traits: selfless service, honor, integrity, and personal courage. Finally, caring, a clear and heartfelt commitment to doing the right thing under very trying circumstances.

44 Ibid, p. 10.

45 Ibid, p. 10.

46 Christensen, Hall, Dillon, & Duncan. "Customers don't buy products or services; they pull them into their lives to make progress. We call this progress the 'job' they are trying to get done, and in our metaphor, we say that customers 'hire' products or services to solve these jobs. When you understand that concept, the idea of uncovering consumer jobs makes intuitive sense. But as we have suggested, our definition of a Job to Be Done is precise—and we need to take a step back and unpack the elements to develop a complete theory of jobs. We define a 'job' as the *progress that a person is trying to make in a particular circumstance.* This definition of a job is not simply a new way of categorizing customers or their problems. It's key to understanding *why* they make the choices they make," p. 27.

47 Heifetz, (p. 20).

48 Ibid, p. 20.

49 Bossidy, L. & Charan, R. (2004). *Confronting reality: Doing what matters to get things right.* New York, NY: Crown Books, p. 22. The authors identify six flaws that hamper leaders when it comes to confronting reality. They are: (a) filtered information, (b) selective hearing, (c) wishful thinking, (d) fear, (e) emotional overinvestment, and (f) unrealistic expectations of capital markets.

50 Schein, (p. 155).

51 Silk, (p. 93).

52 Zaleznik, (p. 76).

3

KNOWING IS DOING

The academic word for the study of the ways of knowing is epistemology, a branch of philosophy that analyzes the nature of knowledge and how it relates to truth, belief and justification. Practically speaking, knowing is the way knowledge becomes apparent to us, the way we apprehend and put knowledge into practice. While scholars have determined as many as eight different ways we come to know, two modes resonate with most people: what we see and what we hear. Yet, if we limit ourselves to these two, we fail to make use of the full spectrum of learning inherent in human beings. If this occurs in organizations, we'll likely fall short when we need "to solve problems, or to create products valued within one or more cultural settings."[1] Leaders must make every attempt in every way to engage hearts and minds.

So, when we say, knowing is doing, what do we mean? Acquiring knowledge is not enough. If I know something but I fail to act on the knowledge have I missed an opportunity? If I know people have different modes of intelligence, but limit the means by which I engage them, am I failing to engage people who may be important to the cause? The answers in your head right now, as a result of addressing these questions, are the first steps to knowing is doing, a path to creating employee buy-in.

One of the first movies I remember as a child was a motion picture called "The Miracle Worker."[2] The film was based on the life of Helen Keller, a young girl, blind and deaf, after suffering a fever as a baby. Her parents grew frustrated when they couldn't communicate with her, leaving Helen equally frustrated and occasionally violent. Enter Annie Sullivan, herself visually impaired, who discovers a way to teach Helen how to communicate. "During one lesson, Annie finger-spelled the word 'water' on one of Helen's hands as she ran water over her student's other hand."

Helen made her first major breakthrough, "connecting the concept of sign language with the objects around her."[3] By appealing to Helen's sensory-perception skills of touch and motion in a side-by-side manner, Annie helped Helen connect the strokes of the word water with concept of water. This is *knowing* through use of perception by alternate senses of touch and motion, bypassing the eyes and ears. We learn it is possible to know in ways other than sight and sound, and this opens a wide range of possibilities for teaching and learning.

Recognizing Multiple Intelligences

Howard Gardner developed the theory of Multiple Intelligences (MI) in an effort to challenge two assumptions about intelligence: (a) that there was a "single, general capacity that every human being possessed"; and (b) that it "could be measured by standardized verbal instruments, such as short-answer, paper-and-pencil tests."[4] Gardner found both assumptions inadequate in describing intelligence. So, he set out to identify modalities of intelligence, rather than viewing intelligence as a single general ability.

In his book "Frames of Mind," he identified seven intelligences. He conceptualized them in the following way. The object-related—visual-spatial, logic-mathematical, bodily-kinesthetic; the object-free—language and music; and the personal—intrapersonal-self, intrapersonal-other. Gardner explicated these "personal forms of intelligence reflect a set of powerful and competing constraints: the existence of one's own person; [and] the existence of other persons; the culture's presentations and interpretations of selves. Universal features of any sense of person or self, but also considerably cultural nuances, reflect a host of historical and individuating factors"[5]

A decade later, he added an eighth modality he labeled naturalistic, described as an intelligence related to hunting, gathering, and farming, all activities attributed to the knowledge of nature. Gardner added a ninth construct he labeled existential, purposefully avoiding the term spiritual. Also, in the later understandings of the theory, Gardner distinguished, "intelligence (the computing power of an individual's musical or spatial or interpersonal capacity) is not at all the same as a style (the way in which one allegedly approaches a range of tasks)."[6]

This cursory grounding in ways of knowing is offered as a means to provide descriptive understanding of the intelligences that are individually and collectively available in the members of an enterprise. This chart summarizes the way Chris and Apex engaged members of the organization in buy-in from the perspective of knowing is doing. You see that by consciously appealing to the range of intelligences inherent in individual members of the organization, the application of knowledge to accomplish an organizational purpose or goal could be maximized.

Multiple Intelligences Mapped to Apex

	Intelligence	What is it?	How does it work?	Methods & Tools	Desired Outcome
OBJECT-RELATED	**Logical Mathematical**	Using logic, reasoning, critical thinking. Most requently associated with general intelligence that measures cognitive abilities	Best engagement is that which engages thinking. Socratic method, that is, cooperative argumentative (not antagonistic) dialogue	Game adaptations like that of Jeopardy, Monopoly, and Jumble puzzles	Greater individual and group understanding and clarity of details and implications of actions
	Visual Spatial	Deals with spatial judgment and the ability to visualize with the mind's eye. Spatial ability is one of the three IQ factors	By engaging employees and visitors to engage in visual depictions, people can see, construct and understand their reality	Show the history of the firm on the walls, allow people to comment, draw, or photograph answers to challenges like Picture our Culture	Show the history of the firm on the walls, allow people to comment, draw, or photograph answers to challenges like Picture our Culture
	Bodily Kinesthetic	Control of one's bodily motions and the capacity to handle objects skillfully. Includes timing, physical action and trained responses	Enhances one's ability of physical expression and controlling of body movement	Build it, act it out, touch it, get a "gut feeling" of it, dance it	Using gestures, dramatic expressions
OBJECT-FREE	**Verbal Linguistic**	Display a facility with words/languages. Good at reading, writing, telling stories and memorization of words and dates. High on verbal IQ measures	Display a facility with words/languages. Good at reading, writing, telling stories and memorization of words and dates. High on verbal IQ measures	Read about it, write about it, talk about it, listen to it	Teaching through storytelling
	Musical Rhythmic	Sensitivity to sounds, rhythms, tones and music. Good pitch, able to sing	Using voice rhythmically	Sing it, rap it, listen to it	Distinct/recognizable voice
	Interpersonal	Sensitive to moods, feelings, motivations, and temperament. Communicate effectively and empathize easily	Interacting with colleagues	Teach it, collaborate on it, interact with respect to it	Dynamically interacting with participants
PERSONAL	**Intrapersonal**	Introspection and and self-reflective capacities. Knows self, strengths/weaknesses and can control actions	Brings feeling into the environment	Connect it to your personal life, make choices with regard to it	Bringing feeling into the environment of working and playing together
	Naturalist* *Added in 1995*	Nurturing and relating to environment in a natural world so as to make distinctions that matter	Ability to classify nature forms provides insight into hunting, gathering, and farming	Hunting, gathering, and farming of past translate into roles of botanists, gardeners and chefs in feeding all	Provides a sensitive, ecological and holistic understanding of our world as it relates to humanity

Copyright ©2019 Tim P. McMahon

FIGURE 3.1 The total is greater than the sum of the parts

Figure 3.1 shows the eight intelligences, briefly describes each and how it works; then shows ways Apex used various methods and tools to accomplish a desired outcome for the business. This is a snapshot in time of an ever-growing box of tools to engage, teach and learn inside Apex.

Broadly, we understand that different ways of perception create different ways of knowing, and different ways of knowing create greater possibilities for creating buy-in. Acquiring a business of which he knew little about its inner workings provided Chris with a genuine way to involve members of the firm. This also provided the opportunity to express his true appreciation for their special knowledge of the inner workings within the firm. As you can see from the chart, it provided a map for understanding, and pursuing, the expansion of knowledge at Apex. Additionally, it would permit him to assess gaps that may exist, creating an opportunity for developing specific areas of learning. Finally, these activities were ways employees could have some fun. Chris would often say, "if we aren't having fun, why are we doing this?"

The Alluring Benefit of Tapping Into Organizational Knowledge

Exercising his own version of management by walking around (MBWA),[7] Chris favored personal interaction with members of the firm to bring clarity to his understanding of the business. This simultaneously exposed his style and clarified purpose to the people who brought the enterprise to life each day at work.

As a residual benefit, Chris became more familiar with the people who did the work. He could readily connect names with faces and their purpose. He developed an appreciation for what each member contributed to the purpose of Apex. This provided the added benefit of the well-worn advice of Dale Carnegie: "You can make more friends in two months by becoming interested in other people than you can in two years by trying to get other people interested in you."[8]

AT THE CORNER OF DUTY AND REWARD

On this particular trip to his mom's place, Chris thought about how he could get his people to make the connection between their personal knowledge and their responsibilities to their family, their community, and their workplace. He boiled it down to a single question: what moves people to commit to their responsibilities? Mom had a ready answer.

CHRIS: *We have good people. Some aren't in the right places. They can't fully use their strengths because we don't recognize what they do best. If we take a little more time to understand their potential and even help them develop their skills, they will become more committed.*

AGNES: *Do you remember why you wanted to join the Boy Scouts?*

CHRIS: *Yes, I wanted to go camping with my buds.*

AGNES: *But, when you came home from your first meeting, you had one thing on your mind, learn that oath. Do you remember it?*

CHRIS: *Oh yes, (Chris proceeded to recite) On my honor I will do my best to do my duty to God and my country and to obey the Scout law. To help other people at all times. To keep myself physically strong, mentally awake, and morally straight. Some stuff you learn you just never forget.*

AGNES: *The word that always stood out to me was oath. That oath is your promise. I'm not one much in favor of loyalty pledges. My spouse, yes. That's fidelity. My boss? I have found that people that ask for loyalty do not always deserve it. Commitment runs both ways. Look at the Boy Scouts. You had a great experience. But we know now that despite that beautiful oath and all that it promises, not all their leaders honored that pledge, so not all scouts had a good experience. Some were tragic. Had they all honored the oath things would be different.*

CHRIS: *I made that oath because it was a requirement for being a Boy Scout; but I kept it because it made my life better. If I ask people at Apex to commit, I must commit. And we do that because it creates a better life for all.*

AGNES: *I'm never surprised how people get confused about that stuff and miss the whole point. You should commit because it is a good thing to do! Your ultimate duty is not to blindly follow rules, but to commit to something you believe because it is its own reward.*

Chris returned to the office that day with a sense of clarity about his mission to create an environment where people could learn and rise to a higher sense of purpose.

Chris eventually gained a deeper understanding of the knowledge and information that contributed to individual empowerment in the workplace and that which did not. In these routine interactions, he became approachable to workers and the informal familiarity eventually encouraged honest and candid feedback. Chris would say, "people don't owe you respect and trust, you have to earn it." He spread this philosophy to his team.

Brutally Honest Up and Down

Chris and his executive management team would often jump in and help out if the workload overwhelmed one particular team. Once on scene, he would take the lowest skill level job, "something I can do without messing up everything!" On one such occasion, after a morning of work, the manager of the department sidled up to Chris and gently suggested it may be more productive for him to move on to his regular duties as he was making too many mistakes. Chris laughed heartily and commended the manager for his candid performance evaluation. Yet, the incident was instructive to the manager and to Chris. If Apex wanted people to personally commit, leaders and followers must develop their personal mastery of their job, honestly assess when it was or wasn't happening and take steps to make sure it did.

In keeping with the idea that people learn in different ways, Chris was always pushing his management team to find ways to draw on diversity of intelligences in the Apex workforce. They got very creative:

- To recognize winners of quarterly goal accomplishments, they set up a dunk tank in the parking lot and gave employees a chance to drop Chris in the cold water;
- As a summer event, Apex held a talent contest under the lights in the parking lot where teams of employees presented skits, singing acts, comedy, and other routines, all loosely themed around company challenges and accomplishments;
- A manager could, at any time, call for a five-minute energizer during the workday, called "Up-and-At 'Em." This was a deskside stretch, isometric and deep-breathing routine designed to get the blood moving through the body as a means to refresh and invigorate;
- When workers replaced one of the bulky pieces of trouble-riddled equipment with new sleek gear to improve performance, Apex held a "Toss the Problem" lunchtime session. Employees cued up in a contest to throw the piece of gear as far as they could with the winner getting a chunk of the equipment mounted on a plaque;
- Chris and a couple of key executives professionally filmed a music video complete with tailor-made company lyrics sung to the tune of "Nine to Five" and played at the annual company Talent Show;
- Each Summer, Apex held a Picnic in the Parking Lot with catered BBQ and a Talent Show with winners honored with a photo of their "act" posted in the company lobby;
- They created a company version of Jeopardy with Chris playing the role of host asking trivia questions about the company, its competitors, and employees;
- Teams of employees used assigned hallway space to design and build wall displays expressing the company's values and purpose with the wall artwork serving as instructional lessons for new hires and customer visitors;
- They placed whiteboard kiosks around the building for employees to draw, write, and/or affix photos and exhibits of great moments in Apex Work Life;
- Chris ordered an Apex onesie for himself that he wore at a one of the quarterly Town Hall meetings when he announced that anyone having a baby would receive a similar onesie for their newborn; and
- For special-occasion lunches, Chris would prepare a special meal called "Come and Get It If You Dare" (he and the management were cooks and servers) and they would serve lunch for all employees and any family members they wanted to invite.

These let-your-hair-down ideas became a way of doing business at Apex and Chris encouraged employees to come up with ideas to tap into the power of their multitude of intelligences and talents. Chris was adamant about all of these activities centering around the life and operations of Apex. So, while it further developed understanding of Apex, it also made learning fun.

A Different Kind of Intelligence Rounds Out the Approach

Along with his understanding of the application of Gardner's multiple intelligences theory, Chris had a keen appreciation for Daniel Goleman's Emotional Intelligence concept, dubbed EQ for emotional quotient. He saw Goleman's work as a perfect complement to Gardner's view, which recognized the importance of cognition—the understanding of self and others in motives and habits of working. This is bolstered by Goleman's theory there's sense in emotion but it's unavailable in the cognitive processing of events. Moreover, there's scalability in Goleman's framework, which occurs on two dimensions: Figure 3.2 illustrates the relationship between managing self and others; in conjunction with knowing (aware) and doing (act).

In viewing the chart, take note that Gardner's Multiple Intelligences theory focuses on the cognitive and Goleman's Emotional Intelligence theory focuses on

Goleman's Emotional Intelligence and Competencies	
Understanding and Developing Our Self and Our Organization	
SELF	**OTHERS**
AWARE How we manage ourselves **Emotional self-awareness:** Reading one's own emotions and recognizing their impact; using gut instincts to guide decisions **Accurate self-assessment:** Knowing one's strengths and weaknesses **Self-confidence:** Having a strong sense of one's self-worth and capabilities.	Available revenue in marketplace (existing pipeline, new customers, new categories Off-shoring opportunities to move non-core competencies out of shop (speed, savings, scale-up) Project VC product Legislative / political changes are driving change in environment and may cause new business opportunities
ACT NUCLEON process is not serving basic customer needs Disadvantaged in large market data access Execution (variance, productivity, process Shrinking form dominant position Not known as employer of choice Communication is lacking in content and frequency	Loss of major account would be devastating Market conditions softening consumer demand Rise in raw costs squeezing all margins; could stoke price pressure Technological advances reducing demand/ need for parts of our bundle of benefits
Copyright ©2019 Tim P. McMahon	

FIGURE 3.2   Relationship of Aware/Act by Self/Others

the emotional. They work in harness to complete our development as competent people. In a discussion with Goleman, Gardner observed: "to broaden our notion of the spectrum of talents. The single most important contribution education can make to a child's development is to help him toward a field where his talents best suit him, where he will be satisfied and competent."[9]

This is not the primary purpose as expressed of our education system. Think about it, No Child Left Behind (NLCB) was the law for K-12 students in the United States between 2002 and 2015. Chris thought it missed the point. He'd say, "that focuses on a collective outcome at the expense of the individual kid. It places the burden on dragging the slow learner into a world in which they are not suited. Teachers shouldn't be burdened with grading students who don't fit the mold, they should be helping them connect with their unique skills and talents."

Sir Kenneth Robinson wrote: "For the most part education systems inhibit creativity and are organized on the false assumptions that life is linear and inorganic. The conventional story is that if you study particular disciplines and stay with the prescribed program, and pass all the tests your life will fall neatly into place. If you don't, it won't."[10] Robinson calls for a better course of child development, one that recognizes personal development is based on three principles: "your life is unique, you create your life, your life is organic."[11]

Chris believes it's up to each of us to seek this knowledge and develop a means to practice it in the safety of people with a mutual appreciation for this idea. Chris often said, "one of our biggest challenges is to learn how to learn. And when we do this together, the potential greatness of the whole place expands." That is why developing cognitive and emotional intelligence go hand-in-hand.

Goleman wrote that he considered competence models for leadership at the highest levels consist of anywhere between 80 to 100% EI-based abilities. "As head of research at a global executive search firm put it, 'CEOs are hired for their intellect and business expertise—and fired for a lack of emotional intelligence.'"[12] Goleman advised that emotional intelligence contributes to our ability to develop potential.

These are learned abilities—having the skill to manage self and others—but doesn't guarantee one has the "ability to handle a customer adeptly or to resolve conflict."[13] In other words, potential must be developed into an emotional competence. "A cognitive analog would be the student who has excellent spatial abilities yet never learns geometry, let alone becomes an architect."[14] One of the motivators for learning difficult concepts is understanding how they can be used in the real world.

Chris considered the role of intelligence in the organization to be a source of productivity and problem solving. Gardner himself, wrote: "To my mind, a human intellectual competence must entail a set of skills of problem solving—enabling the individuals to *resolve genuine problems or difficulties* that he encounters and, when appropriate, to create an effective product—and must also entail the potential for *finding or creating problems*—thereby laying the groundwork for the acquisition of new knowledge."[15] But, how does one unlock the possibilities inherent in organizations?

Wouldn't It Be Nice if a Test Could Pick Your People?

Early in his career, Chris recognized the value of measuring one's intelligence. He became familiar with an IQ assessment called the Wonderlic Contemporary Cognitive Ability Test. He used it in his first company as an assessment to determine the cognitive ability and problem-solving aptitude of candidates for a range of jobs. The test consists of 50 multiple choice questions to be answered in 12 minutes. Developed by Eldon F. Wonderlic, a score of 20 indicates average intelligence.

Today, the test is available on the cloud and is called the WonScore and is considered an effective measure of cognitive ability. Chris found it as a means to raise a red flag, so to speak. In other words, scoring well (20 or above) didn't mean the test-taker was a sure winner; but a score below 20 was a good indicator an applicant may need some additional help learning and performing tasks.

"The Wonderlic" is famously used by the National Football League, which makes it a part of its Scouting Combine. Rumor is that quarterback Tom Brady scored a 33, well above average. Brady was the 199th pick in the 6th round of the 2000 draft. Given this information and eventual accomplishments in his career, perhaps the Wonderlic results identified an underrated prospect, who deserved to be taken more seriously. Its real value it appears lies in identifying shortcomings. As asked in Figure 3.3, is it possible that the NFL is powered by cognitive testing?

FIGURE 3.3   The NFL has long used cognitive testing to assess player cognitive ability

Experience has shown players scoring less than a 20 on the Wonderlic might not be successful learning plays, especially under time constraints. While enlightening, the test was not a foolproof measure.[16] As an interesting sidebar to test your biases, answer this question: Which overall position group in the NFL has the highest average Wonderlic score? The answer is offensive linemen, who rise to the top with an average Wonderlic score of 26. Test scores are only an indicator. Chris thought it was wise to let the results, not our gut instincts, inform our decisions, and tools like the Wonderlic are a valuable assessment, but not the whole picture.

All leaders would like to have an assessment that's a sure-fire predictor of success, but the magic of testing is not the score, rather how the leader uses it to learn the strengths and weaknesses of a candidate. A significant consideration in employee selection is chemistry, that is, how the style of the potential recruit will succeed in the organization. In that case, it's informative to have candidates submit a personality test, like the Myers-Briggs Type Indicator (MBTI), or the CliftonStrengths 34 by Gallup.

The MBTI identifies 16 personality types identified by Carl Jung, who identified the primary modes of psychological functioning of people.[17] The theory is based on the assumption that people have different attitudes and functions of consciousness. These assumptions are derived from perceiving non-rational functions of sensation and intuition, and rational functions of thinking and feeling. The functions are modified by two attitude types: introversion and extraversion. The MBTI is designed to make this theory understandable by providing 16 types of personality and a description of the associated behaviors of each. With some training and understanding, leaders can use the results of this assessment of their people to create more harmonious and productive working relationships. While critics are skeptical, it is widely used in the workplace.

The CliftonStrengths 34 is a means to assess one's talents and "natural patterns of thinking, feeling, and behaving."[18] Developers claim the test will help determine what people naturally do best, help them learn how to develop their greatest talents into strengths, and use the results to maximize potential. These tools require involvement of leader and follower, but those who have taken part generally believe the results are both accurate assessments of self and provide actionable guidance.

First Things First: People Must Be Well Adapted to Their Positions

As referenced in Chapter 1, Apex had 15 supervisors with frontline responsibility. After several weeks of contact with these folks, Chris arrived at a troubling discovery: 13 of them hated their role as supervisor! As Chris said, "This is a startling headline that I bought a company where 86.6% of our frontline overseers ran out of the building at quittin' time with their hair on fire!" It's hard to explain, but the firm that Chris bought was profitable, yet it was operated in a seemingly dysfunctional manner. How could that be?

Heifetz, Grashow, and Linsky wrote it's a myth the organization is dysfunctional or broken. "The reality is that any social system (including an organization or country or a family) is the way it is because the people in that system (at least the individuals and factions with the most leverage) want it that way. In that sense, on the whole, on balance, the system works fine, even though it may appear 'dysfunctional' in some respects to some members and outside observers, and even though it faces danger just over the horizon."[19] Chris was well aware he needed to address this creeping acceptance of mediocrity and could see trouble brewing if he didn't address this issue.

When he took over, the outward signs of inept management were present. Right in front of the building were two parking spots, both reserved for the owner. Not for the customer, not for the employee of the month, but for the owner. Culture guru Edgar Schein wrote an organization displays its culture through shared assumptions that develop over time, heavily influenced by the leader.[20] Those two parking spots spoke loudly about what the culture valued. For many, though they never said it, it was just too much. Not only was the culture maladapted for Chris's meritocratic operating style, it caused managers to function in a suboptimal manner—more tied to their paycheck and status as supervisor than to any good feeling the job delivered. The prevailing advice: "Don't rock the boat. Keep your head down and don't complain."

Though confounding, the idea that such poorly managed firms are unprofitable is simply not true. They often make money in spite of poor practices. Through the motivation of fear, the old Apex promoted and compensated its people irrespective of their contribution to the firm. As a younger man, Chris recalled the companies he worked for that promoted people because they could do the job, not because they could manage or lead people to do the job. Many firms place no value on management training and have ineffective evaluation procedures.

Chris learned that the magic of management is to first make it clear to everyone that getting and keeping business is the purpose of the business. That purpose is served when customers are happy, and that happens when "every brain in the chain was actively engaged in providing value the customer wanted." The only way that happens is having the right people in the right places doing the right things. This must be a conscious, disciplined effort; rigorous, not ruthless.

When faced with an absence of active management, Chris took two steps to remedy the problem. First, he re-designed the job. For example, with supervisors, he elevated it from a supervisory role to a manager role, set specific manager accountabilities, and then he charged his human resource people with designing a training program that would teach managers how to manage and lead the Apex Way. Simultaneously, he developed a new job description called subject matter expert (SME). This job doesn't carry with it any direct reports. Rather, it frees up the time of this person to function as an authority in a specific function critical to some aspect of successful operations.

In line with his straight-forward style of communication, Chris visited each supervisor individually and explained the change. To some, he delivered the hard news: they were not cut out to manage. But if interested, they might be a great SME. To the others, he asked their opinion of the change in job description and asked if they had an interest in becoming a manager. Overall, 13 of the 15 were relieved and excited about the news.

For new SMEs, while they moved from salaried to hourly, their compensation with overtime and bonus for performance, wouldn't suffer greatly. Two of them found the option unacceptable and left the firm. The other two identified as potential managers, were delighted and placed in the management development program.

At a town hall meeting, Chris delivered the news. He gave great credit and appreciation for the newly minted SMEs and described to all how they should be used to assist the firm in improving operational performance. He also announced a transition plan that would take place over the next 90 to 120 days as new managers were hired and trained. Announcing transitions signals change is coming.

Without a Transition Plan, People Have No Context to Explain What is Happening

When organizations attempt change, it stems from a situation that's not acceptable to decision makers. An event occurs, like profits erode, or ownership changes, or a successful leader unexpectedly leaves the firm. To those in the know, the response is clear: change, now. However, too often, change is set in motion without a transition. In other words, to inhabitants of the organization, it's as if winter shows up in the middle of summer.

Such a change, unaccompanied by well-worn rituals that accompany seasonal change, leads to a profound sense of loss, confusion, even grief, and certainly, anxiety. Under normal change of seasons, we experience, even anticipate, the arrival of a new season. When winter comes, just like bears who stock up for hibernation, human beings get set for different needs and necessities. This helps us understand what we can put away and that which we must bring out of storage.

Transitions help us make sense out of change; because while change is situational, transition is psychological. William Bridges identified two essential rules apply: First, "when you're in transition, you find yourself coming back in new ways to old activities"[21]; and "every transition begins with an ending. We have to let go of the old thing before we can pick up the new one."[22] The message is that change—that is to deliver the results sought—means people must stop the old things and begin the new.

In announcing and discussing the management program, Chris passed along sage advice about change: "We are making a fundamental change in the way we conduct business at Apex. If we hope to be successful in our journey, we'll need a transition from what we're currently doing to what we need to be doing to adapt to the change that's happening before our very eyes."

Chris explained the rationale for the need to change, and the transition that would be underway soon. However, he fully anticipated people would need more, much more, to help them through this transition. But, at least calling it out—a transition—was a good start.

Mistakes Can Be a Motivator for Learning

As good as you might think Chris is as leader, he makes an occasional faux pas in developing the new manager development plan he heard about it swiftly. It went down something like this. In his discussions with his management team—all new on the job—they concurred that the organization needed a more highly prepared individual for the role of manager. So, they built the program on the notion of recruiting college graduates from outside the organization. All thought that was a good plan. New company, new blood. However, during his daily MBWA, Chris learned that many loyal and long-term employees voiced great concern about being overlooked for the new opportunity; how demoralizing it was to have an outsider to come in and tell them what to do! Chris realized he had erred and quickly resolved the problem by identifying prospective managers from inside the organization. He also apologized and gave props to the "heroes" who called him out for overlooking internal resources.

People at Apex regularly hear the truth from Chris and his entire management team. It was truly a meritocracy where you advanced in the organization because of the value you delivered. Bosses provided the direction and the resources and then got out of the way. Chris would remind everyone, "we need to be on the same page and headed the same direction." Chris cautioned, "that doesn't mean we don't pay attention. We are constantly talking to people just to keep a dialogue going. We can't build trust if we aren't brutally honest with one another. If I make a mistake, I will own up and I expect it from everyone I work with, that means employees and customers."

Effective Transitions Provide Context for Understanding

In the transition from old management to new, customers needed attention. To develop valued relationships, Apex needed to fundamentally improve the way the company sold services, so customers had no doubt where they stood in the relationship. So too, employees needed attention. Endings are scary.

Under the previous leader, the reflex reaction from the firm was the "customer is wrong" or "customer is a pain-in-the-neck" attitude. It would seem natural to dispense with this attitude. It is not that easy. People may intellectually understand the shift to customer is hero, but old habits die hard. When in transition, while we can intellectually explain why we are doing something, and even see how it might be better, the new behaviors "break our setting in which we know ourselves."[23] Chris asked himself, how could we ever get to *Awesome Customer Service* with a group of people who still held deep resentment, even blame, for customers?

Bridges wrote for all transitions there are three parts: "first, an ending, then a beginning and an important or fallow time in between."[24]

Engage With Customers from Top to Bottom

Upon buying the firm, Chris and key managers visited all of their customers. The objective was to understand how much work was ahead of them in identifying and repairing relationships created by previous management. Chris sent trained listeners to visit customers and hear what they were saying about their experience with Apex. They introduced themselves as listeners eager to hear honestly the perceptions of customers, needing to hear what would help the client make progress against their situation.

The feedback was disturbing. As a matter of fact, it was so demoralizing Chris went back to customer files from his previous company just to cheer himself up. He read the comments from customers who were delighted with his firm's products and services. One customer said, "they are unlike anybody we do business with in that they think of our contract as a starting point not a rule book. Every firm that sells us on their process brags about the results they get for their customers. Then, when they get the contract, they staff it and move on. If something goes wrong, we feel like we're hearing, 'not our problem, we're doing what we said.' That is usually the beginning of the end but because it is a contract, we have to fight it out." Chris needed to interject a new response to this kind of comment.

He met with small groups of employees all of whom had direct customer contact. He told them stories of how—in his previous experience—so many questions and concerns swirled around in his head. He shared the before and after comments from customers. Then, he asked them: how is my historical experience different from what we are facing here? I can tell you, it's not. We had lots of fear and loathing when we took control of that firm, too.

Then he read part of a letter he received from a customer of his previous firm. "If they get wind something isn't working right, and that is usually the case in the early stages of the business relationship, they run toward the problem with a plate of cookies!" Chris punctuated the statement with one of famous tropes: "When in doubt, better head out." These meetings served to put the issue on the table for all to see and to provide a new response that treated the customer as hero.

He and his team regularly regaled the troops with the successes they encountered. The vp-sales said, "Our customers saw us as out of touch; and we felt pretty much the same about them until we started talking with them about their pain points. We realized we could be different; and it would change everything. And it did. We had a new outlook on reality."

The message resonated and began to alleviate fears when Chris confessed: "As scary as it was leaving the old company behind, it is as just exciting when we look at what could happen when the new Apex representative knocks on the door or rings up the phone."

Chris embraced a selling style that emphasized "how to sell the way people want to buy."[25] This resulted in an uplifting message. He brought a sales trainer into the office after work to create a learning session where the group discussed aspects of the sales strategy, including recognizing selling as a relationship.

FROM *INTEGRITY SELLING,* BY RON WILLINGHAM

- a mutual exchange of value, isn't something you do to people it's something you do *for* and *with* them;
- developing trust and rapport precedes any selling activity;
- people's wants and needs must always precede attempts to sell;
- selling techniques give way to values-driven principles;
- truth, respect, and honesty provide the basis for long-term selling success;
- ethics and values contribute more to sales success than do techniques or strategies;
- selling pressure is never exerted by the salesperson. It's exerted only by customers when they perceive they want or need the item being recommended;
- negotiation is never manipulation. It's always a strategy to work out problems—when customers want to work out the problems; and finally,
- closing is a victory for both the salesperson and the customer.

Used with permission ©2003 Ron Willingham (2003)

Besides the sales training, Chris sent the trainer on sales calls as an observer and personal coach to assure the sales representatives translated their new learning to behavior. Further, he personally checked in with customers to inquire about their satisfaction with how well Apex performed in selling them on its products and services. He was mindful the new emphasis was on walking the customer through the buying process and not selling them what they had in their bag.

Assessing customer needs through good questions helped customers more clearly articulate their expectations. That way both sides win.

This was a drastic departure from the sales tactics of the previous leader. One important component for learning to be effective is that the members share the assumption that "learning is a good thing worth investing in and that learning to learn is itself a skill to be mastered."[26] Chris was fully committed to invest in learning and relentlessly committed to embedding the practice in the hearts and minds of the people at Apex.

Apex invested in training and development. Moreover, the company embedded the training into the culture through active, personal engagement. The management team used the many one-on-one, small group, and all-company meetings to inform learning needs. They discovered that members needed and wanted to learn more about the inner workings of the firm as well as to develop their individual skills and understanding of how to contribute to the success of the organization.

Developing the Individual

Apex' vp-human resources took an entirely new approach to how it would develop employees. It would focus on building individual skills, including people management, with the endgame leading to how the skills transferred deep into the organization. The approach was to inform, educate, and practice all aspects of competency development. As Chris often said, "they need to know what to do and then they need to know when they are doing it. My goal is to catch 'em doing something good!"

The idea began with how Apex would hire the right people, then develop the right expectations, and finally train them accordingly. "People appreciate the honesty of an interview process that tells them who we are, what we expect, and how they will grow. We are best served when we are honest while keeping in mind it is always better when a solution is beneficial to both parties."

In this quest, recruiters often focus on identifying a list of competencies they seek, then hiring the individual who is equipped with those abilities. Zenger and Folkman argue this competency-based approach has failed to deliver desired results. They identify four reasons for the shortfall: It is too complex, based on faulty assumptions, produces unintended consequences, and is often poorly executed.[27] The Apex approach is focused on simplicity, riveted to systemic impact.

Training Is Instruction Aimed at Improving Skills and Competencies

Toward this end, the firm invested in creating a reading library available to all employees, a computer-based log of all jobs within the firm, and the process map for how each was conducted. This knowledge was available to all as a best practices resource. Additionally, the company provided training for everything from how to use Excel software to improving management leadership skills. Skill-specific experts delivered a wide range of training and development programs, including demonstrating how to map processes, teaching supervisors how to deal more effectively with people, developing customer-oriented relationship skills, and as mentioned, training sales personnel on how to sell with integrity. Chris would check out the reading library log and follow-up with people on what they learned from the book. This was a surprise to many, but also a huge message of how Chris valued learning.

Today, training facilitated through technology has exploded within companies. LinkedIn Learning (formerly Lynda) offers a vast supply of online learning videos on its website (www.linkedin.com/learning) offering interactive courses taught by industry experts in software, creative, and business skills. The content is easily searched and grouped into Learning Paths on such topics as digital marketing, becoming a manager, becoming a small business owner, or SEO expert.

Moreover, organizations can contract with the company to administer training and learning programs across the organization to all of its people. The learning paths can be tailor-made by managers to bolster skills and competencies of their workforce so as to align with needs identified in employee evaluations. The platform provides a customized dashboard to track progress including modules completed and grades achieved.

Other platforms that offer a range of effective learning and training from simple skills to advanced degrees from prestigious universities around the world—include Coursera, EdX, Udacity, Skillshare, Code Academy, and Khan Academy.

Apex vp-operations suggested training is intended to raise the overall level of knowledge across the employee base. This required removing obstacles that would prevent the knowledge from taking root in day-to-day practices at Apex: "We have invested so much in training, technology, processes, supervisor training, and leadership training, that it is important that the only thing holding us back is vigorous adoption by the people of Apex and that rears its ugly head when the culture resists."

Knowledge development for the sake of making people smarter was not complete if it didn't have an effect on the business. A newly-hired manager said, "Good people who are well trained can grow the business. But people up and down the organization must be bought in and committed. Middle managers, including me, can be a limiter or a liberator. It feels a lot better to liberate. That's true across the rest of the team under the influence of the new ownership."

To Know Progress, Take a Reading of the Climate?

For people to adopt new behaviors and practices—who intend real change—they have had to confront reality, a concept well covered in the previous chapter. This holds true to the value that success flows from employees feeling satisfaction and enjoyment from their work. Measuring the climate of the organization provides a snapshot of progress. While it was early in its takeover, the top leaders believed it was important to take a reading. Senior managers were prepared if they discovered the results may not be what they hoped, but it would serve as a baseline score and identify specific ways Apex could better its marks.

It commissioned third-party research conducted by *Best Places to Work*, an organization that measured employee responses to a variety of questions about work life, including communication, benefits, belief in management, and perceived opportunity. The standardized survey had been conducted repeatedly against a large national base of employers and reported by size of firm and various cohorts such as top management, supervisory, and line workers.

Firms engage *Best Places* to survey employees and complete a culture brief.[28] The results then are published for all to see, good or bad. The idea is to establish trust and to demonstrate management's sincere desire to become a best place to work; to engage in an informed dialogue about the firm's direction.

Results were eye-opening. Regarding communication, senior managers rated their communication efforts near the top when compared to the national sample, whereas employees registered responses at the lower end of the range. Other measures, such as company vision, were viewed more favorably, whereas pride, respect, and opportunity were worse.

The critical value of the data lies in subsequent year surveys. Did the firm positively affect the climate of the firm? Each year there was significant movement to the upside at the workforce level. While top management assessment remained strong, employee response had improved in ensuing years moving into the middle range of national employee responses. Similar gains were tracked in employee responses to employer support and confidence in management's direction for the firm, and most importantly, in employee perception of employer-provided resources.

In other words, the survey suggested that a well-designed management effort to address the operational needs and reduce cultural barriers was working. By the fourth year, Apex achieved best place to work status in its size category.

To assess progress along the way, Apex used a quick assessment tool called the employee Net Promoter Score (eNPS). Just like the customer NPS is used to answer the ultimate question—Would you recommend this firm to a friend?—the eNPS identifies performance against its goal to serve.

Show Them How and Then Get Out of the Way

Chris advocated a course of action that set expectations for employee engagement and provided them with the tools and knowledge to engage. This action wasn't so much about persuading others to commit, rather, he set a framework for decision making. In metaphoric terms, he didn't seek to micromanage a highly orchestrated strike. Instead, he sought to bring the troops together around a common vision, enabling them to see each individual's role and his or her responsibility to make Apex a means for employees to do what they were capable of doing to create an awesome customer experience.

Younger people in the workforce generally have different priorities than older ones. Bea Bourne, a professor at Purdue University Global, stated: "Millennials [born 1980–1994] are more engaged in an environment where they are evaluated continuously and provided ongoing feedback. Baby Boomers [born 1944–1964] do not share this need. In a learning environment, learners' input must be valued, and individual feedback should be solicited."[29]

Regardless of age, all "people want to work with a person, not for a company."[30] Moreover, they crave consistency to keep them sane, information to keep them in the know, and rhythm to keep them in the loop. Chris instituted practices from management authority Verne Harnish, that established a cadence of communication from top to bottom. Across Apex, front line managers conducted morning huddles, an effective way to expand knowledge, specifically "to increase alignment, strategic thinking, and debate."[31]

The Apex vp-human resources said: "The actual team huddles give everyone a chance to review the current situation. We say here is our performance from yesterday, here is what we have to accomplish today in order to meet customer expectations, here is what our turn times were, etc. and this gives the employees the knowledge to know whether we're succeeding or failing; and what might be holding up progress."

She clarified to managers: "Senior management is not on the front line. You are and your people are, so you are responsible for execution. You are the conduit of communication. Listen to your people. Remove their roadblocks. If those daily huddles identify a bigger problem, table it and get them back to work. Then let's bring that issue forward so we can identify how it holds up our progress and what we have to do to smooth out at the bottleneck." By the way, bottlenecks are usually created at the top.

For Chris, these huddles resolved one major problem. "We were perceived as talking out both sides of the mouth, if you will, as opposed to what our people were trying to tell us. Without daily linkage, facilitated by the manager, top management was perceived as out of touch. Under the old guard, someone on the front would identify a problem, think up a solution, drop it in the suggestion box, and then maybe get a response. Or, worse get a response that looked like it was aimed at the problem, but it wasn't clear. One of the big benefits of the daily huddle was identifying bigger issues and addressing them immediately with the people who knew the issue best."

Employees are commonly subject to lots of mixed signals that are stressful, confusing, and counter-productive—as if the organization is schizophrenic and served to distort individual's view of reality. Without a process like the daily huddles, people feel disconnected, and they eventually disengage, or simply fail to engage. From the top management perspective, Chris observed this reducing understanding of the fundamental skills and quality of people working in the organization. "We found through our exit interviews we frequently lost people because they had great ideas, but we never heard them. Why didn't you tell us? They'd say, no one asked."

Another way to tap into this organizational knowledge is through performance appraisals. They must be timely, honest, and frequent, quarterly if not more often. If people don't know how they are doing, they will rapidly lose interest. Imagine if you were playing a basketball game and there was no scoreboard or coach. Yet, that's the way people are treated on the job at many organizations. And, when they're evaluated, the criteria for performance is squishy, unmeasurable, or glossed over.

The biggest hurdle for the manager is discovering how to coach people to behavior that creates favorable outcomes. This requires training. It takes practice. The daily huddle is a way for the manager to bring these issues of performance to light for all to see. Done properly, these sessions lead to greater clarity of what needs to be done, what stands in the way, and how the individual worker can make a difference. This is supported through diligent training and disciplined management; thrives in an environment that values learning.

Learning Isn't What You Did in School; It's What You Do to Win

The problem with learning is we strive to be too efficient. Nobel prize winning economist Daniel Kahneman wrote "in the economy of action, effort is a cost, and the acquisition of skill is driven by the balance of benefits and costs. Laziness is built deep into our nature."[32] Understanding the value of learning from an economic perspective sheds light on the question, why do people hate learning? Well, it's hard work. It's not fun. Most importantly they ask: why learn?

Students of all sorts experience so many years of structured education, when they think of learning they think of school. Books. Tests. Memorization. Lectures. Sacrifice. Study. Those things aren't what people dream of doing. Often, the only motivator is the piece of paper you get at the end that winds up in a good-paying job. One might ask, "Is it possible to crave learning."

We rarely feel better than when we get a sense of fulfillment or self-efficacy because we have mastered knowledge well enough to teach and inspire our friends and colleagues. Besides, for some careers, continued learning is necessary. Physicians, accountants, lawyers, pilots, and the like must stay current to maintain relevance. For the most part, learning is most cherished by people who

see learning as oxygen, it enables them to feel alive and to accomplish something that makes them happy or proud or better prepared to be safe or happy or
free of pain.

Admittedly, learning is a Sisyphean task and many shy away. Learning is
inherently inefficient. Edward D. Hess[33] says learning new concepts or ways of
doing is a messy process of trial and error and peppered with fits and starts. On
top of that, learning consumes a lot of energy. A brain is only 2.5% of our body
weight but consumes 20% of our energy. He reminds us that Kahneman helped
explain the way our brains work. There's the fast (system 1) and the slow
(system 2). When we are awake, "System 1 runs automatically and System 2 is
normally in a comfortable low-effort mode, in which only a fraction of its
capacity is engaged. System 1 continuously generates suggestions for System 2,
impressions and intuitions turn into beliefs, and impulses turn into voluntary
actions."[34]

Most of the time, we function nicely taking instructions from System 1.
However, if System 1 incurs a problem, it calls on System 2 for deeper analysis
and processing of information. You remember System 2 is slow, right? So,
when we are operating with instructions from System 2, we pause, stare, search
for an answer because System 1 is stumped. As if this heavy lifting wasn't enough for System 2, it also is charged with keeping an eye on our personal
behavior.

System 2 is alerted because it senses something is about to go wrong. System 2
is supposed to think before speaking. These two systems work well together for
the most part, despite that System 1 develops biases over time and simply doesn't
consult System 2. So, when you need it most, System 2 doesn't even get a shot at
the problem. You can imagine then, that if System 2 isn't consulted and System 1
suggests a behavior that it is ill-equipped to direct, the outcome may be less than
optimal.

To the point here, Hess writes: "Another way of explaining it is that System 1
refers to our intuitive system, which is typically implicit and emotional, while
System 2 is reasoning that is conscious, explicit and logical."[35] System 1 relies on
our mental models,[36] and because we favor quick, intuitive processing we "tend
to be confirmation-biased learners."[37]

In keeping with the theme of this book, learning is change. We can't do
unless we know. And that invariably involves change. Yet, we ask why do
people learn and is it fun or is it drudgery? James Zull wrote: "We sense that
suffering and singing are both part of learning. We know that feelings affect
rationality and memory and that these effects can be both bad and good for
learning."[38]

Anthony Di Mello[39] wrote: "… in order to wake up, the one thing you need
the most is not energy, or strength, or youthfulness, or even great intelligence.
The one thing you need most of all is the readiness to learn."

TAKE-AWAYS

- Beyond the old standbys of sight and sound, there's other ways to learn and Howard Gardner presented them in his Theory of Multiple Intelligences (MI). These aren't learning styles—the way one approaches tasks—rather, it is more akin to computing power.
- Different ways of perception create different ways of knowing, and different ways of knowing create greater possibilities for creating buy-in. Leaders must take the initiative to tap into this by reaching out to people one-on-one.
- To leverage knowledge, relentlessly pursue ways to tap into the intelligences of the organization through actions and activities. These planned and spontaneous activities were aimed at keeping energy and engagement at a peak. The activities all tied back to some aspect of organizational goals and performance.
- Daniel Goleman developed a kind of intelligence that ran parallel to the cognitive kind. He called it Emotional Intelligence, and it complements the pure cognitive ability measured by traditional IQ tests. When paired with cognitive intelligence, people become empowered; organizations motivated.
- The pros and cons of IQ testing, including The Wonderlic Test, Myers-Briggs, and Clifton Strengths 34 are identified as tools to help inform us of who we are and how we work.
- With so many learning styles, Chris believed that Apex employees would be a representative sample of the styles and encouraged his human resource people and line managers to find creative ways to infuse learning into the members of the organization.
- Just because a company is profitable does not mean it's a well-oiled machine. Inept management is a systemic disease that yields one disastrous result: disengagement of its people. The solution begins at the frontline, with customer-facing people.
- Turning human potential into organizational performance is accomplished by developing skills through training and absorbing those skills into a variety of organizational contexts through human engagement.
- People crave consistency to keep them sane, information to keep them in the know, and rhythm to keep them in the loop. So, when a firm is planning to adapt, it must have a transition, so members of the organization have context to explain what is happening.
- Teaching the skills that managers need to win the hearts and minds of employees is an ongoing activity. Everyone needs ongoing development to keep the organization attuned to a changing workplace.

- Learning is not easy, so it must be top priority of management. It is simply too easy to slide backward.

Notes

1 Gardner, H. (1993). *Frames of mind: The theory of multiple intelligences.* New York, NY: Basic Books.

2 Coe, F. (Producer), & Penn, A. (Director). 1962) *The miracle worker.* [Motion picture]. USA: Playfilm Productions.

3 Biography. (2020). Retrieved June 15, 2020 from https://www.biography.com/activist/anne-sullivan

4 Gardner, H.

5 Ibid, p. 291.

6 Ibid, p. xi.

7 *Peters, T. & Waterman, R. H. (1982/2004) In search of excellence*: Lessons from America's best-run companies. New York, NY: HarperCollins, p. 289. MBWO is a practice of management when the manager randomly wanders around the business to observe and talk with employees, check on the physical plant, and informal gauge the status of work activity. The emphasis is on unplanned so as to gain a sense of morale, productivity, and general well-being of the organization. While it is informal, it is also an activity the manager can conduct at any time so as to gain a truer picture of the inner workings of the firm.

8 Carnegie, (p. 52).

9 Goleman, (p. 37).

10 Robinson, K. (2014). *Finding your element: How to discover your talents and passions and transform your life.* New York, NY: Penguin Books, (p. 27).

11 Ibid, (pp. 26-7).

12 Goleman, D. (2006). *Emotional intelligence.* New York: Bantam Books, (p. vi).

13 Ibid, (introduction).

14 Ibid, (introduction).

15 Gardner, H. (p. 64).

16 Casserly, C. (February 24, 2012). *Wonderlic test is helpful but not a foolproof test.* [Website]. NFL.com. Retrieved from https://www.nfl.com/news/wonderlic-test-is-helpful-but-certainly-not-a-foolproof-tool-09000d5d82729900.

17 Jung, C. G. (1971). *Psychological Types.* Princeton, NJ: Princeton University Press.

18 Gallup. (n.d.). *Learn how the CliftonStrengths Assessment works.* https://www.gallup.com/cliftonstrengths/en/253676/how-cliftonstrengths-works.aspx

19 Heifetz, R., Grashow, A., & Linsky, M. (2009). *The practice of adaptive leadership: Tools and tactics for changing your organization and the world.* Boston, MA: Harvard Business Press.

20 Schein, E. H. (2017). *Organizational culture and leadership* (5th ed.). Hoboken, NJ: Wiley & Sons, Inc.

21 Bridges, W. (2004). *Transitions: Making sense of life's changes.* Cambridge, MA: DeCapo Press, (p. 7).

22 Ibid, p. 10.

23 Ibid, p. 17.

24 Ibid, p. 17.

25 Willingham, R. (2003). *Integrity selling for the 21st century: How to sell the way people want to buy.* New York, NY: Currency Doubleday.

26 Schein, E. H. (2017). *Organizational culture and leadership* (5th ed.). Hoboken, NJ: Wiley & Sons, Inc., (p. 395).

27 Zenger. J. H. & Folkman, J. (2009). *The extraordinary leader.* New York, NY: McGraw-Hill, (p. 83).

28 See the Best Places to Work website for complete details on how the firm serves to become a best place to work: https://www.greatplacetowork.com/solutions/recognition?utm_source=google&utm_medium=cpc&utm_campaign=recognition&gclid=CjwKCAjwrcH3BRApEiwAxjdPTSktFux_NRk6rJOZy8fc2ob4dcaAk_fpMm9H1KnLMAeEY_ZJI9ns8BoCmZYQAvD_BwE.

29 Bourne, B. (2020). Top of mind. *Chief Learning Officer, 19*(4), 13.

30 Cathy, S. T. (2002). *Eat mor chikin: Inspire more people.* Decatur, GA: Looking Glass Books, (p. 97).

31 Harnish, V. (2002). *Scaling up: How a few companies make, and why the rest don't.* Ashburn, VA: Gazelles Inc., (p. 24).

32 Kahneman, D. (2011). *Thinking, fast and slow.* New York, NY: Farrar, Straus and Giroux, (p. 35).

33 Hess, E. D. (2014). *Learn or die: Using science to build a leading-edge learning organization.* New York, NY: Columbia University Press, (p. 11).

34 Kahneman, D. (2011). *Thinking, fast and slow.* New York, NY: Farrar, Straus and Giroux.

35 Hess, E. D., (p. 11).

36 Senge, P. M. (2006). *The fifth discipline: The art and practice of the learning organization* (Rev. ed.). New York, NY: Currency Doubleday, (p. 7). Senge describes mental models as "deeply ingrained assumptions, generalizations, or even pictures or images that influence how we understand the world and we take action."

37 Hess, E. D. (p. 12).

38 Zull, J. E. (2002). *The art of changing the brain: Enriching the practice of teaching by exploiting the biology of learning.* Sterling, VA: Stylus Publishing, LLC.

39 De Mello, A. (1990). *Conversations with the masters.* New York, NY: Crown Publishing.

4

I GOT YOUR BACK

The idiom, "I got your back" has re-surged in popularity in recent years reflected in its use in a song by the same name released in 2010 by hip hop recording artist T.I.[1] According to The Urban Dictionary, the phrase means, "when life seems to blindside you with undesirable events, they're there for you without complaint, supporting you in your moment of need."[2]

Original use of the term can be traced to World War II, when it meant: supporting or protecting somebody: "As buildings and other defensive positions were cleared by squads, the first soldier to enter would be reliant on others to protect him from the rear as he concentrated fully on what lay ahead of him."[3] It fits with the third element that factor into employee buy-in: creating safety to members taking legitimate bold action.

We'll explore aspects of this statement, in particular, empowerment. When one is empowered, they feel authorized to act, they feel stronger and less powerless. We'll examine how leaders over time have developed the self-efficacy of individuals and organizations by promoting a common vision, creating opportunities to act, and appealing to followers' needs to develop as individuals. From an organizational perspective, maintaining the integrity of the system during a changing environment activates the group to cope, grow, and thrive; to maintain a healthy sense of equilibrium.

They Gotta Know You'll Protect Them

In his book "Leaders Eat Last," Simon Sinek cites a study that states higher performance over time is related to team-learning, coordination, empowerment, and mental model development. "In other words, all of the benefits of higher performing teams are direct results of feeling safe among their own and believing that their leaders have their well-being at heart."[4] Sinek highlights the benefits of the core organizing elements that provide cohesion and direction to a firm.

Organizational guru Edgar Schein advised: "the function of cognitive structures such as concepts, beliefs, attitudes, values, and assumptions is to organize the mass of environmental stimuli, to make sense of them, and to thereby provide a sense of predictability and meaning to the individual."[5] We call this amalgam of "deeply ingrained assumptions, generalizations, or even pictures or images that influence how we understand the work and how we take action"[6] mental models.

This describes how culture lives in an organization. Predominant mental models held by members of the firm will dictate what gets done and what gets ignored. Schein defined culture as *the way we do things around here*, and advised it serves as an unwritten set of rules for members. The power of culture is based upon shared assumptions that assume a set of basic truths. They are in that sense, accepted as the way to think and act.

"A company of strong character will have a culture that promotes treating all people well, not just the ones who pay them or earn them money in the moment. In a culture of strong character, the people inside the company will feel protected by their leaders and feel their colleagues have their backs. In a culture of weak character, the people will feel that any protection they have comes primarily from their own ability to manage the politics, promote their own successes and watch their own backs (though some are lucky enough to have a colleague or two to help)."[7] Conclusion: If you want to create an environment where politics plays heavy and the daggers are at the ready, remove from employees any sense of safety.

Chris obsessed about the looming moment of truth when he would have to tell the client Apex would not provide the quickie product. It was going to have dire consequences.

LESSONS FROM THE BICYCLE

Chris was mindful of the importance that when the time came to tell the client they would not offer the quickie, that members of the new Apex culture would both understand and support the decision. But, what if they didn't?

CHRIS: *I've been thinking all morning about the day Doc took me off the training wheels.*

AGNES: *That is a memorable moment for every child. Always scary but it's got to happen.*

CHRIS: *I did not feel that way at the time. As much as I wanted to, I did not share his confidence that I was ready. After all, he didn't live through the several dozen "Uh-oh" moments when I fell in complete support of the wheels to save me from an embarrassing and painful crash!*

AGNES: *Somehow, this fits into work, right?*

CHRIS: *Yep. (Chris took a big slurp of coffee, swallowed then continued). Remember when we talked about Doc holding back on truth about Janie Gunderson's calf?*

AGNES: *Yes, sometimes it's better to swallow the truth and let things play out.*

CHRIS: *But you always worry if people can handle the truth. That's where I am now. I have a sinking feeling something bad is going to happen in the mortgage market. Our biggest customer is so caught up in getting the biggest share of this over-heated market that they are asking us to hold back the truth, so to speak. They want reports that gloss over the risk yet permit them to write loans.*

AGNES: *But you'll lay it out honestly, right?*

CHRIS: *Yes, but they don't want to hear it any more than Janie Gunderson wanted to hear what she knew to be a fact, her calf was dying.*

AGNES: *When Doc told you it was time to take the training wheels off, he was speaking the truth. You have two issues. One is that you must tell the client the truth. Your firm can't deliver reports that are really representing the truth.*

CHRIS: *Yes, and that will surely lose us the business we can hardly afford to lose.*

AGNES: *And the second problem is that you're worried if your people have the confidence to take off the training wheels!* analogy).

CHRIS: *It is going to be a disaster and while I am ready for the wheels to come off, I am not sure my peeps are willing to take on the eventual burden of losing a big piece of business.*

AGNES: *Well, if it means anything, Doc was right, you didn't need those training wheels. You got along quite well without 'em.*

CHRIS: *But I did fall!*

AGNES: *We all fall. You just have to get back up.*

Chris drove home with a sense of relief that he knew he was going to have to rely on his team to confront a difficult obstacle, and he knew down deep that people take about anything if you just tell them the truth and have a plan to deal with it.

A Strong Culture, Well Adapted, Is an Extraordinary Asset

Culture is a powerful driver of behavior. Apex had developed a 20-year history of culture under the previous leader and founder of the firm. Management at the time considered obedience to be a stabilizing factor. Keep your head down and follow orders. This explains why getting people to adopt new behaviors is not a simple matter.

New owners and new CEOs are often tested when their call for change conflicts with deeply held assumptions. So, when people resist the new way of doing things, leaders re-double their push for acceptance of their plan. That's wrong-headed. More pressure and more communication advocating the virtues of the new plan will only reinforce opposition. If you want to re-direct the behavior of people, showing the error of their ways won't warm them to your ideas; it will convince them the ignorance of yours. Leaders need to find more effective ways into the psyche.

Since ancient times, Aristotle's three elements of persuasion have proven effective. Ethos, exhibiting trustworthiness; logos, offering a logical argument; pathos, delivering the message with passionate belief[8] is the trifecta for winning hearts and minds. However, the most effective way to deal with the power of culture is to re-design, re-orient and re-acquaint members of the firm. When members of the organization are able to grow and develop leadership skills, they are able to confront the adaptive challenge.

Chris saw the current situation with the quickie loan as a means to develop adaptive capacity. That is defined as the "resilience of people and the capacity of systems to engage in problem-defining and problem-solving work in the midst of adaptive pressure and the resulting disequilibrium."[9] In other words, Chris needed to re-develop cultural norms to effectively deal with its changing environment. That called for a shift from obedience to engagement.

He sought to inspire members to raise their game. To these apply the old proverb, it wasn't about giving people fish, it was about teaching them to fish. The objective was for Apex to be remarkably adaptable and scalable and require minimal reinforcement by management. A well-adapted culture responds positively to novel new external challenges. Chris knew that by teaching people about adaptive challenges, he would legitimize their need to learn new ways of doing things, identify losses they'd need to accept so as to advance, and shift their mindset from avoiding conflict to resolving conflict.

Functional Familiarity

Schein advises the key to this effort lies in members seeing the wisdom of the new leaders. If an organization is successful in fulfilling its mission, it will mature and grow. However, the new leader must consciously focus on how to mold the culture to serve a new set of rules to deal with its changing environment.

Specifically, Schein advises new leaders to establish functional familiarity, that is, make it a priority to know what people do in a face-to-face manner, where they can internalize "tone of voice, pacing, and other cues needed to sense emotion in communication."[10] In this way, personal commitments become deeper testable propositions for employees. It begins at the top. When the leader keeps his word, trust is generated, and all members sense the support.

Consider these actions leaders take to re-shape culture:

- Integrate and align functions and groups through effective methods of coordination;
- Establish measurement of effectiveness that is considered fair and equitable to all;
- Standardize ways of doing things as much as possible to reduce complexity;
- Resist the reduction of performance to numbers. It may help to focus on actions that lead to the desired numbers, not using accounting nuances to arrive at the desired posting;
- Understand who is accountable (held to outcomes) and who is responsible (held to execution leading to outcomes);
- Clearly define the roles of central functions and support services within the firm. Know the roles of management, operations, and support as this knowledge will clarify differences and surface biases;
- Identify growth opportunities and show the path for advancement in the firm; and
- Keep decision-making clear and grounded in strategically sound criteria.

These entries identify areas that Schein considers important to shaping the culture to serve the strategic intent of leaders.

This chapter is dedicated to identifying, explaining, and understanding why people accept and willingly support and participate in an idea, a practice, or a behavior, what we call buy-in. The key message to leaders is if you want to win the hearts and minds of people in the organization appeal to their sense of self-efficacy, how they can increase their capacity to rely on their self and their colleagues to thrive.

It's Just Common Sense

In his landmark book, "How to win friends and influence people," Dale Carnegie shared this wisdom regarding the motivations of people: "In every work of genius, we recognize our own rejected thoughts; they come back to us with a certain alienated majesty."[11] This quote originally from Ralph Waldo Emerson raises the power in awakening the greatness within each of us. When leaders seek to find a way to understand and support the thoughts of others, they get more good feedback from them, call it a dividend of engagement.

Consider the wisdom in Philosopher John Dewey's observation: "the deepest urge in human nature is to be important."[12] Having a grasp of fundamental drivers of human nature enables leaders to move people to action. Appealing to their core desires is primal, as is the emotional task of a leader: "It is both the original and the most important act of leadership."[13] So, it's prudent to devise a time-tested persuasion strategy. Straying from Aristotle's three-part formula is fraught with uncertainty because we know people see trust (ethos), logic (logos), and passion (pathos) as the time-tested formula for effective persuasion.

The "Burning Platform" Will Initiate a Response; But Not Always as Planned

Most everyone knows this story. A new owner or leader or consultant comes into the organization. They declare, "a part of our company is on fire and we must act now, or it will burn to the ground!" Labeled the burning platform argument, it's favored by many leaders because they see how prominently the fear of loss resides in human beings. Yet fear has an unintended consequence, too. It tends to paralyze people. If an unsettling event is about to occur, leaders must know how to deal with the response as it is a turning point.

Upon acquiring Apex, Chris faced a group of people about to experience significant change in their daily routine. The acquisition introduced fear of the unknown; quickly followed by fear of the known (which may be even worse). Apex had entered a transition stage in its life. During such times, we have learned that even the best laid plans are met with skepticism as members experience a break in the setting in which members know themselves.

Pulling Back the Curtain

An invisible curtain forms around the members that puts the new leaders responsible for leading change management, into a state of confusion followed by frustration. What might ordinarily be accepted as logical and necessary actions to adapt to a challenging environment, are seen as potentially threatening to the way of life in the firm. In reacting to this resistance, the new management team will likely find their plan fall on deaf ears resurfacing a familiar management lament: "They are not team players!"

Yet, the reality is if a culture functions, it attempts to maintain the status quo. If a single member is pushing back—either actively or passively—aren't they the single gene that may attempt to protect the group from a bad move? In a sense, aren't they the definition of team player? After all, in many cases, none of what is recommended in the new plan looks like what got the members to their present position. In an effort to keep the team together, they pull away from the Kool-Aid being offered by the new leaders. Driven by the cultural beliefs, they don't have what is needed to successfully adapt; they simply see their nest being disassembled and that is too risky.

Complicating this even more, people often see many change efforts over time and become a bit fatigued by the latest "fix" to the allegedly broken system. So, just as the body's immune system protects it from undesirable pathogens, so too, does the culture when it senses something incongruous with the group's shared assumptions about the organization.

Writing in the Harvard Business Review, Michael D. Watkins makes the case for the body's immune system analogous to an organization:

> The function of the human immune system is to distinguish between "self" and "not-self." It's there to protect the body from foreign organisms. To accomplish this, the immune system must remain poised on a tight-rope between under- and over-reactivity. If it is damaged or weakened, it may fail to mount an effective response against a virus or permit a damaged cell to grow into a cancerous tumor. If this happens, you die. On the other hand, if the immune system is over-reactive, it can mount an attack against the body, producing allergies or auto-immune conditions such as rheumatoid arthritis and multiple sclerosis. Once again, you can die or be severely disabled.[14]

If we accept this rationale, we would dismiss the idea that resistance to change in organizations is not the product of naysayers, it's the warning from real "team players" who see a threat to the life of their team. This is contrary to what Chris has heard and felt as an instigator of change in an organization. As such, leaders don't see culture as protective to the group, they see it as resistance to their change effort. To Chris, it's a familiar lament he heard from bosses in his early career: "We made our case, we told them the storm was coming. We showed them what they need to do. Why are they fighting this?"

On the employee side, change is threatening and almost always considered the wrong thing to do. They think, "While business could be better, the place is still open, and we've still got a job." As is often the case, employees don't have a clear picture of the financial health of the firm because they have no access to the P&L and balance sheet, two important indicators of financial health. Moreover, many companies employ poor employee evaluation processes that often are conducted infrequently, if at all. Further, the nature of the review is not based on key performance indicators (KPIs) as much as anecdotal evidence, like personal incidents or relational observations.

Given the nature of these two perspectives, it's understandable that conflict is likely to erupt with each side believing they're on the high, moral ground. When the conflict devolves to this, people will never see themselves as the weakest link. Just the opposite, they see themselves as part of a chain of custody for the culture that must endure; they are poised to literally defend the high ground; they *do things around here* that have worked to preserve us all.

Roots of a Remedy

Kurt Lewin provided an early conception of how organizations respond in his theory of fields.[15] He wrote, "In discussing the means of bringing about a desired state of affairs one should not think in terms of the 'goal to be reached' but rather in terms of 'change from the present level to the desired one.'"[16] He theorized that organizations have forces that both resist change and push for change. When in balance, "an organization is in the state of inertia and does not change."[17] This is counterintuitive for many who believe balance is the state in which people will address change.

Disequilibrium is the state described above when people are suspicious that the forces of change are attempting to disrupt the status quo. Kurt Lewin advised that "because of some type of 'inner resistance' to change ... a force sufficient to 'break the habit,' to 'unfreeze' the custom"[18] was necessary. Schein states Lewin means that significant disconfirming data would cause enough "disequilibrium to force a coping process that goes beyond just reinforcing the assumptions that are already in place"[19]

Expanding on this, Schein advised for organizations to substantively change, they need: "(1) enough *disconfirming data* to cause serious discomfort and disequilibrium; (2) the connection to the disconfirming data to important goals and ideals, causing *anxiety and/or guilt*; and (3) enough *psychological safety*"[20] to overcome the paralyzing anxiety. While this makes sense, many change management schemes seem to fail at a point where they need to succeed the most: supporting members executing the change. Rather, too often change efforts take a toll on the members because the members get caught in the middle without support. The result is they are unproductive.

Consider Figure 4.1 that shows the organizational response to two types of organizational challenges: technical and adaptive. Technical problems are seldom the kind that incite resistance. They "can be diagnosed and solved, generally within a short time frame, by applying established know-how and procedures."[21] In the figure, the anxiety of the technical problem is high at first (represented by the dotted line over time), but when the known solution is put into place, members move out of the productive zone of disequilibrium (PZD) and regain confidence and balance.

The challenge of change is typically found in adaptive problems where there is no known solution. Rather, there is "a gap between the values people stand for (that constitute thriving) and the reality they face (their current lack of capacity to realize those values in their environment)."[22] The solid line represents the typical state of people as they advance through the challenge over time. When members of the firm recognize there is a real threat to survival of the organization, they

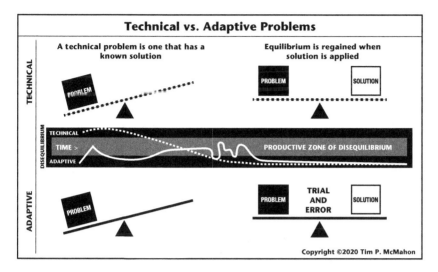

FIGURE 4.1   A matter of balance (disequilibrium) to be resolved over time.

enter into the PDZ. As Schein discovered this is triggered by the discovery of disconfirming data.

The fluctuating nature of the solid line reflects the concern of members as the plan to address the problem unfolds. Since there is no known solution, the team is in trial-and-error mode to test various actions that may resolve issues. During this time, the anxiety can often force some members to disengage. Others may attempt to reduce the urgency, minimize or confuse the effort to stall or abandon the effort.

Operationalizing Adaptation

Leaders walk a tender balance between creating urgency for members to act and paralyzing their actions. In his best-selling book, "Leading Change," John Kotter wrote of the challenge that faces leaders who must disrupt the status quo that prevents the organization from making progress against its external threats. "They become paralyzed by the downside possibilities associated with reducing complacency: people becoming defensive, morale and short-term results slipping. Or, even worse, they confuse urgency with anxiety, and by driving up the latter, they push people even deeper into their foxholes and create even more resistance to change."[23]

Heifetz, Grashow, and Linsky offer a different course. In their thesis on adaptive leadership,[24] they assert leaders have three core responsibilities to the members of the organization: (a) direction, (b) protection, and (c) order. In other words, they must identify roles and responsibilities that offer a compelling vision of the organization's direction. Leaders must make sure the group isn't vulnerable and can survive the external threat, and they must maintain stability in the organization.

They must distinguish between technical challenges—problems that can be easily diagnosed and solved—and adaptive problems—those challenges members of the firm haven't encountered, and therefore, must develop some capacity in diagnosing and solving problems. As we saw in Figure 4.1, adaptive challenges are fraught with uncertainty and hover in the area labeled "productive zone of disequilibrium" where even if the challenge is eventually resolved; members of the group at some point disengage from the challenge through work avoidance.

This happens because "there is no clear, linear path to resolution ... [they not only] need a plan, but ... also need freedom to deviate from the plan as new discoveries emerge, as conditions change, and as new forms of resistance arise."[25] The authors identify such circumstance require "an iterative process involving three activities: (1) observing events and patterns around you; (2) interpreting what you are observing ...; and (3) designing interventions based on the observations and interpretations to address the adaptive challenge you have identified."[26] Success in leading in this model is dependent on leaders actively engaging followers in the challenge and building their adaptive capacity—the resilience of people needed for the journey.

Fear Has Left the Building

Amy C. Edmondson defined psychological safety "as the belief that the work environment is safe for interpersonal risk taking.... when colleagues trust and respect each other and feel able—even obligated—to be candid."[27] Perhaps, there's no better way to elicit trust and respect than through dialogue. Dialogue, not merely conversation, moves past informational interchange to exchange between two people. "When it comes to risky, controversial, and emotional conversations, skilled people find a way to get all relevant information (from themselves and other) out into the open."[28] We ask: how does it lead to success and what can one do to create the free flow of meaning?

Here's six points to remember in creating productive dialogue. Success is created when:

- We remind ourselves the goal of the conversation. What do you want? What does the other person want? Come to agreement and stay on path;
- Manage stress. Watch for signs that people are withdrawing and shutting down. Then step back. Regroup. You're trying to create shared meaning;
- Give yourself options. It seems we often default to dichotomies. Life is not binary—you'll always find multiple options. Seek ideas from others. Open up the possibility;

- Check how you see others. Don't make leaps of abstraction from a single raised eyebrow. Allow people to work out the clarity of their thought. If they shut down. You must restore safety;
- Show respect. Validate. Remove defensiveness. Show genuine care; and
- Creating safety. Start softly. Be genuine and honest. Employ the devil's advocate. Dialogue has the power to liberate people.

People in organizations facing change or adaptive challenge, must be liberated from organizations built on control, manipulation, and intolerance. Even strong-willed leaders recognize the need to liberate people if empowerment is the goal: "The old organization was built on control, but the world has changed ... moving at such a pace that control has become a limitation."[29] Yet old habits die hard. Leaders are still dealing with the challenge of resistance from people as they are presented with a new vision as a means to adapt to change.

External Change Demands Potent Internal Integration

Whether you call them basic values or basic assumptions, Schein stated the culture of a group can be defined as a pattern of shared basic assumptions learned by a group as it solved its problems of external adaptation and internal integration, that has worked well enough to be considered valid and, therefore, to be taught to new members as the correct way to perceive, think, and feel in relation to those problems.

If one accepts that culture is a powerful mechanism of organizational intent, isn't it essential to know what the culture intends to accomplish? Asked in a more personal way, what motivates you more: winning or not losing? Not losing is often the choice. Culture by definition favors the behavior history has produced. Yet, most organizations embark on change by discarding the definition as a means to adapt to a changing environment.

As Schein wrote, culture holds the basic assumptions that have solved the problems of external adaptation through internal integration. The workplace landscape is littered with organizations that failed to adapt. Think Blockbuster, Kodak, and Borders. They didn't effectively address the threat at their doorstep, and they're gone.

John P. Kotter wrote: "... people who are making an effort to embrace the future are a happier lot than those who are clinging to the past. That is not to say that learning how to become a part of the twenty-first century enterprise is easy. But people who are attempting to grow, to become more comfortable with change, to develop leadership skills—these men and women are typically driven by a sense that they are doing what is right for themselves, their families and their organizations."[30]

At the heart of the issue is fear. Many unspoken fears inhabit the hearts and minds of members of an organization. If the company experienced a history of autocratic management, or if led by a "my-way-or-the-highway" leader, or people were dismissed (either officially or symbolically) for speaking out, then fear drives behavior. Survival is paramount.

Schein spoke to the need for individuals in a firm to provide sufficient psychological safety in the "sense of being able to see a possibility of solving the problem and learning something new without loss of identity or integrity."[31] Ample evidence shows Chris had an advantage inherent in his natural communication skills. He demonstrated natural charismatic traits and behaviors that transformed followers.

Study Charisma; Know Commitment

When studying effective leaders, charisma rises as extraordinarily effective at empowering followers and generating their buy-in. So, we review its traits and organizational characteristics as a means to understand these components in Chris' work at Apex. In Greek, *charisma* means "'divinely inspired gift,' such as the ability to perform miracles or predict future events"[32]

The famous German sociologist Max Weber pioneered the study of charisma in the mid-1940s and concluded it was powerful and should be considered a form of authority, along with traditional and rational. Weber's characterization of charisma was theological in nature and considered it a gift of grace.[33] To explain this phenomenon, Edward Lawler expressed successful charismatic leaders as having vision, being good communicators, and using symbols effectively.[34] For Weber, these traits provided a path to moral authority, and followers complied with the leader's direction.[35]

Based on German sociologist Max Weber's studies, Trice and Beyer[36] developed a list of criteria for charismatic leadership: (a) a person with extraordinary gifts and qualities, (b) a social crisis or situation of desperation, (c) a radical vision or set of ideas promising a solution to the crisis, (d) a set of followers who are attracted to the charismatic leader, and (e) the validation of the person's extraordinary gifts and the radical vision by repeated successes in dealing with the perceived crisis.

Leaders Lay It On the Line

Alan Bryman reflected on Conger and Kanungo's conception of charismatic leadership as followers attributing it to leaders who: (a) present an idealized goal; (b) engage in personal risk to achieve the vision; and (c) engage in unconventional methods to achieve the vision.[37,38] Crisis, an event in the life of an organization that presents the need for a significant or radical change, is a breeding ground for a charismatic leader to emerge as the person who sees the situation clearly, knows the path to safety, and is able to articulate it clearly so that people are compelled to follow.[39]

Charisma was considered an emotional play and a precursor to transformation. Believing that the subject had become overworked, re-named charisma in more romantic terms, *heroic leadership* and wrote, "The heroic, transcending leader excited and transforms previously dormant followers into active ones. For example, leaders of an exodus heighten the followers' motivation, purposes, and missionary zeal. Followers become proselytizers, who, in turn, act as leaders as a consequence of their exalted awareness."[40] Yet, Bryman pointed out such leaders are more effective in the role of change agent, because "if they act as administrators or managers, their charisma fades."[41]

In the chart below, we map charismatic behaviors exhibited by Chris and how they theoretically lead to desired outcomes in the group and individual. It is important to note that Chris has not been deemed charismatic[42] but does have mastery of the behaviors shown in Figure 4.2.

Chris exhibited many charismatic "change agent" traits, in three behaviors in particular. He developed a common vision expressed in a set of business goals that would bring revenue into the firm; he presented members with a picture of their role in the vision; and, in so doing, made members feel stronger and less powerless. He laid a charismatic leadership foundation that enables people to see the deficiencies in the status quo; moved to formulate and articulate a course that may be highly discrepant yet within the latitude of acceptance.[43] We learn

Where the Leader Drives the Bus, the Organization Follows

Leader Behavior			Hypothesized Outcomes
Stage 1: Evaluation of Status Quo	**Stage 2:** Formulation and Articulation of Organizational Goals	**Stage 3:** Means to Achieve	Organizational or Group Level Outcomes:
■ **Assessment of environmental resources / constraints and follower needs** - Effective articulation - Realization of deficiencies in status quo	■ **Formulation of environmental opportunities into a strategic vision** - Effective articulation of inspirational vision that is highly discrepant from the status quo yet within latitude of acceptance	■ **By personal example;** risk taking; and countercultural empowering, and impression management practices, leader conveys goals, demonstrates means to achieve, builds follower trust, and motivates followers.	■ *High internal cohesion* ■ *Low internal conflict* ■ *High value congruence* ■ *High consensus* **Individual (Follower) Outcomes:** ■ *In creation to the leader* - Reverence for the leader - Trust in the leader - Satisfaction with the leader ■ *In creation to the task* - Work group cohesion - High task performance - High level of empowerment

©1998 Sage Publications

FIGURE 4.2   Behavior related to outcome.

that charismatic leaders like Chris are exceptionally talented at impression management.

Chris delivered streams of knowledge creation to all hands in the organization. This included training and development of technical and interpersonal skills, the means by which members would devise actions to deal with the reality of a marketplace under distress. He also provided psychological safety for people to choose discrepant yet effective courses of action. Above all, he established fair and equitable terms for team membership and stood hard and fast on these judgments. He altered follower perception of work, offered an appealing vision for the future, established an organizational identity for people, and heightened self-efficacy by putting the ball in the employee's court.

One of the more effective ways a leader provides safety for members of the organization to take bold action is in removing obstacles. Chris recognized that often the obstacle to people taking bold action is other people in the organization. He demonstrated repeatedly that he wouldn't tolerate individuals to stand in the way of other people's bold actions. Chris met with managers frequently and they would discuss expectations. He repeated himself often and in many different contexts, including in coaching sessions where he clarified roles and outlined definitions.

Are You Responsible or Accountable?

For example, Chris found that people often used terms they didn't entirely understand. "You can't be expected to be held to standards or actions if you do not fully know their meaning. For example, what is the difference between *responsibility* and *accountability*?" In almost every management situation, people assume at least one of these two roles. And consider them interchangeable. People believe they should know these roles, and they may, but they can't always define them. So, Chris moved to providing a definition.

"Maybe this will help. Responsibility is an obligation to do something or perform according to direction or instruction. Accountability is to answer for the work performed." He then showed a photo of a field-level scene from a baseball game where the baserunner is rounding second base and heading for third. The point-of-view of the photo is from behind the third base coach.

Chris asks, "Who here is *accountable* and who is *responsible*? The question was met with a gaze of confusion mixed with anxiety."

Then, one young lady said, "The baserunner is responsible. If the coach waves him on, he must go or the whole thing falls apart."

Chris acknowledged the comment and then asks, "What whole thing?"

Another manager shot out, "the plan, the game plan falls apart if people don't do what they are supposed to do."

Chris smiled and confirmed, "Yes, you are both are right. The baserunner is responsible to do what the base coach instructs." Chris turned to another manager, "Bill, you played baseball, did you always do what the third base coach told you?"

Bill's extended pause drew laughter, then he said, "No! It depended on who was coaching third base. If I trusted him and his judgment, then yeah, I'd do what he said,"

Chris interrupted, "And if not?" Looking a little sheepish Bill said, "I'd be responsible to myself!"

Chris used the moment of brutal honesty about decisions as a means to make a point about human nature, "People *want* to be responsible and know they *should* be responsible but aren't *always* responsible, especially when they are in the moment of truth. When you are rounding second base, you are not thinking, you are acting, it is an instinctive moment of truth, not unlike any moment in a day at work. Sometimes, we just act, or react, according to our gut feel. As Bill said, if he trusted the coach, then yes, he'd follow the order. If not, then he acted on his own … and he would not be responsible to the boss." Chris then paused and said, "So, let's finish the lesson."

"The coach is accountable. What that means is that he will be held accountable for the outcome of the baserunner's actions, whether the baserunner is responsible or not in following his instruction. How do you feel about that?" After a long pause, one manager answered, "I think that is what was meant by the whole thing falls apart. There is no responsibility. There is no accountability." Chris pressed the others, "Is that all? Anything else missing?"

One quiet fellow said, "If there is no trust, there is no team."

Chris asked, "Without trust, does the team win?" A quick response, "maybe, maybe not. Without trust, there is no predictable response. Maybe the runner gets to base safely, maybe not. It has nothing to do with the interaction between coach and runner. You'd have to question if coaching was ever in play."

Chris wrapped up by saying, "We should be in control of our own destiny. It works when we all feel like we have something to do with the outcome. We all assume our responsibilities and accountabilities to make that happen. That is how we earn our salaries and our bonuses as a team."

One of the key findings Chris and the management team had learned in their initial assessment of the firm was that good ideas, often discrepant from the status quo, were stubbed off at some level of the company. Either clear direction was not sent down nor were productive thoughts sent up. People were sometimes responsible and sometimes accountable and sometimes not.

Accountability and Responsibility in Practice

Top-down and mechanistic environments are two characteristics of the inherited culture at Apex. Managers hand down marching orders to the rank-and-file and sometimes they acted appropriately, and sometimes not.

The vp-human resources said, "We had a difficult time getting people to think about what they were doing. We would say, 'Is there a better way? Tell us,' but seldom got any feedback." She added that at first, the management team thought that maybe people simply didn't have any ideas. However, in exit interviews and other employee outreach efforts, they heard the previous owner placed restrictions on people thinking or suggesting new ideas. If Apex was to realize a vision of the firm as a highly competitive meritocracy, this had to change.

Chris and his team concluded that many people reporting to supervisors held back on their ideas, observations, and actions for fear the supervisor would penalize for speaking or acting out. To break this unwritten rule, Chris needed to create more productive dialogues about responsibility and accountability.

In retooling the front-line manager position, Chris saw a more serious impediment to people speaking out and acting in bold, effective ways than simply encouraging them to talk. He needed a measure of customer satisfaction, so he introduced the Net Promoter Score (NPS) system to keep a finger on the pulse of customers' and employees' on-the-spot answer to a single question: "*On a zero-to-ten scale, how likely is it that you would recommend us (or this product or service) to a friend or colleague?*"[44] A 9 or 10 is a *promoter*; 7–8 is a *passive*; and 0–6 is a *detractor*. There's one follow-up question: What is the primary reason for your score? The fundamental benefit is that it provides quick feedback on how well the efforts of the firm are working to get and keep employees and customers. Satisfying customers, knowing that they deal out the dough, hits home with people.

The NPS is based on the idea that a meritocracy is all about merit! It shuns hierarchy that impedes performance and disdains complicated performance reports that did not provide actionable information. Chris adopted a set of management principles originally introduced in a book called *The Rockefeller Habits*. The book was so successful its author, Verne Harnish issued a re-tooling of the book and called it "Scaling Up." It provided a full set of workable documents that provided everyone in the organization at all levels the meaningful data that's both fresh and accurate, and measurable.

Our Goal: World Dominance!

Chris set the example of his commitment to Apex and its people over an extended period of time. He demonstrated this by working on weekends, serving without pay during lean times (as you will soon discover), and in risking personal wealth to both remove constraints and provide the tools and resources for people to accomplish what was expected of them. Under the previous autocracy, power (authority) was formal and delegated to a few who were loyal to the owner.

Chris pushed authority (along with responsibility and accountability) down the line. As one of the legacy employees said, "I think our people see conflict melts away when being held responsible and accountable. That is because when we know what is expected of us and what power we had to make things happen for the customers people feel empowered. It becomes a better place to work."

Under stress, people do mask their thoughts and actions. In controlling environments, they either accept or change. If employees recognize they can't succeed, they withdraw and protect themselves because they don't want conflict. People are better able to work through challenges where conflict is dealt with openly and honestly and without emotion. One supervisor said, "we love it that the big boss tries to find you doing something good. And, they tell us how to do that and expect us to do that."

In characteristic charismatic style, Chris articulated a big idea, held it forth as a strategic vision, and tied job descriptions to it so people could see and know what to do to win. With a big smile on his face, Chris routinely spoke of Apex achieving world dominance. He displayed "world dominance" as a caption on the cover of the strategic planning document. Chris regularly encouraged employees to divulge the plan, even brag about it, exhibiting his attitude toward transparency of information.

Further, he expected bold action. It is a statement that "leadership is a property of a social system ... [and when] usefully framed ... in terms distinctly and qualitatively differing shared meaning making principles,"[45] members understood thinking big is dependent on all members of the organization having the freedom to perform leadership tasks in response to their collective social meaning making. Simply put, *no guts, no blue chips.*

Peter Drucker asserts an effective leader follows eight practices:

- They ask: "What needs to be done?";
- They ask: "What is right for the enterprise?";
- They develop action plans;
- They take responsibility for decisions;
- They take responsibility for communicating;
- They focus on opportunities rather than problems;
- They run productive meetings; and
- They thought and said "we" rather than "I."[46]

When Warren Bennis examined the question: *Are leaders born or made?* He determined they were made, and more often than not, *self*-made.[47] However, he warned not every one of them will become a leader, some will become bosses. Bosses are focused on power; whereas, leaders are focused on transforming themselves, their workers, and their organization. In this sense, they desire to develop the innate abilities of the people in their organizations. These leaders have a growth mindset.

If there was any kind of behavior that is certain to destroy the positive karma that may be operating in an organization, it is destructive behavior listed in Figure 4.3.

BUY-IN CRUSHERS

- Poor management of people networks, especially superiors and peers
- Unconventional behavior that alienates
- Creation of disruptive "in group/out group" rivalries
- An autocratic, controlling management style
- Claims of responsibility for innovative products and ideas when in reality the sources are the other individuals
- Alternation between idealizing and devaluing others, particularly those who report directly
- Creation of excessive dependence on themselves among subordinates
- Failure to manage essential details and to act as an effective administrator
- Attention to the superficial
- Absence from operations
- Failure to develop successors of equal ability

©1998 Sage Publications

FIGURE 4.3   Always root out the bitter from the sweet

Psychologist Carole Dweck is known for her work on the mindset psychological trait. She identified some leaders believe their qualities immutable. Dweck discovered that such a mindset, "creates an urgency to prove yourself over and over. If you have only a certain amount of intelligence, a certain personality, and a certain moral character—well, then you'd better prove that you have a healthy dose of them. It simply wouldn't do to look or feel deficient in these most basic characteristics."[48] This idea is self-limiting.

The key finding for individuals is the view you decide to hold affects the way you lead your life. It can determine if you can become the person you want to become.

Chris was keenly aware of his mindset. He was all about growth. Moreover, it worked so well for him he wanted it for his loved ones and the members of the organization. Chris, like so many leaders of his kind, was what Dweck described as being on "an inclusive, learning-filled, rollicking journey."[49]

TAKE-AWAYS

- A culture is a statement of the "way we do things around here." Cultures are the shared assumptions member hold about the way the organization survives (or as we shall see, thrives).
- The most effective way to deal with cultures is to re-design, re-orient and re-acquaint members of the firm to increase adaptive capacity, how it can become more self-efficacious.

- When a firm must adapt to a change in its environment, it is prudent to have a transition plan in mind, or people won't see what you're showing and won't hear what you're saying. A transition breaks down the expectations so members can understand and accept.
- Leaders lay it on the line and invite members to accept big challenges. They provide the understanding they'll be safe in finding the solution.
- The concept of the "burning platform" has been long used by management to move people to action. However, what management says is not necessarily what the people of the organization hear. Address the issue relentlessly through integration and alignment of the organization, its systems for doing things, the means by which it measures progress against desirable outcomes, and the organizational structure of the many units and functions working to accomplish the firm's mission.
- By virtue of the way they're created, cultures have a built-in immune system that rejects new ideas as a potential threat to its existence. Just as an immune system protects the human body from, members of the culture will sense outsiders as a threat.
- There's a long history of theory that supports the need for an informed approach to dealing with internal integration (response) to an external threat (environmental change) in organizations. This plays upon mutual identification and acceptance of the real threat that creates a need to adapt. However, it requires a mix of disconfirming data, tied to important goals and ideals, along with enough psychological safety for members of the organization to act.
- Leaders are expected to provide direction, protection, and order to members of the organization. For this to happen, leaders must confront the threat. While this is inherently uncertain, the exercise can be a tremendous engagement generator because a lot is on the line and by involving members of the firm in creating the solution, leaders empower individuals and groups.
- Groups can face two types of challenges: technical and adaptive. Technical problems are recognizable and can be readily resolved. Adaptive problems are not, and there's no clear, linear path to resolution. You need a plan, but you also need freedom to deviate from the plan as new discoveries emerge from the process.
- The deepest urge in human nature is to be important. The challenge to getting the most out of people—true buy-in—is to appeal to their basic needs in a persuasive, meaningful manner. This requires productive conversations and the knowledge of how to create and manage them. Further, it demands that leaders recognize the limits of group productivity when the group is resolving adaptive challenges, what is known as the Productive Band of Disequilibrium.

- Charisma is a powerful way to engage followers, especially when a problem defies conventional logic. By showing the discrepant (alternate) path during times of crisis, charismatic leaders demonstrate high internal cohesion, low internal conflict, high value congruence, and high consensus.

Notes

1 T. I. (2010). Got your back [Song]. Om. *No Mercy* [Digital Download]. Grand Hustle.
2 Urban Dictionary. (2014). Got your back. In *Urban Dictionary*. Retrieved June 24, 2020 from https://www.urbandictionary.com/define.php?term=Got%20your%20back
3 Idiomic.com. (n.d.). (I've) got your back. In *Idiomic.com*. Retrieved June 24, 2020 from http://idiomic.com/got-your-back/
4 Sinek, S. (2014/2017). *Leaders eat last: Why some teams pull together and others don't.* New York, NY: Penguin Books, (p. 211).
5 Schein, E. H. (2017). *Organizational culture and leadership* (5th ed.). Hoboken, NJ: Wiley & Sons, Inc., (p. 320).
6 Senge, P. M. (2006). *The fifth discipline: The art and practice of the learning organization* (Rev. ed.). New York: Currency Doubleday, (p. 8).
7 Sinek, (p. 163).
8 Throughout this text, Aristotle's theory of persuasion is referenced. To review, the three appeals are Ethos (Appealing to ethics, morals, and character); logos (appealing to logic); and pathos (appealing to emotions). Having an ethical position (ethos) provides a sense of trustworthiness. Presenting a logical argument that will pass through the brain without question presents the desired response, and it will take the passion of a leader to excite the follower to act.
9 Heifetz, R., Grashow, A., & Linsky, M. (2009). *The practice of adaptive leadership: Tools and tactics for changing your organization and the world.* Boston, MA: Harvard Business Press. The authors provide this definition of adaptive capacity in the glossary. It serves as a way to think about how a firm can test and implement interventions that the firm's members can test and determine its viability in helping members thrive, (p. 303).
10 Schein, (p. 208).
11 Carnegie, D. (1981). *How to win friends and influence people.* New York: Simon & Schuster, (p. 199).
12 Campbell, J. (1995). *Understanding John Dewey.* Chicago, IL: Open Court Publishing, (p. 45).
13 Goleman, D., Boyatzis, R., & McKee, A. (2002). *Primal leadership: realizing the power of emotional intelligence.* Boston, MA: Harvard Press, (p. 5).
14 Watkins, M.D. (2007). Organizational immunology (Part 1: Culture and change). *Harvard Business Review.* Retrieved June 25, 2020 from https://hbr.org/2007/06/organizational-immunology-part-1.
15 In the 1940s, Psychologist Kurt Lewin developed Field theory, an examination of the patterns of interaction between the individual and the environment (field).
16 Lewin, K. (1947). Group decision and social change. In T. N. Newcomb & E. L. Hartley (Eds.), *Readings in social psychology* (pp. 340–344). New York: Holt, Rinehart and Winston, (p. 341).
17 Jones, G. R. (2001). *Organizational theory: text and cases.* Upper Saddle River, NJ: Prentice-Hall, (p. 138)
18 Lewin, K. (p. 327).
19 Schein, E. H. (2017). *Organizational culture and leadership* (5th ed.). Hoboken, NJ: Wiley & Sons, Inc., (p. 320).

20 Ibid, (p. 320).
21 Heifetz, et al., (P. 307).
22 Ibid, (P. 303).
23 Kotter, J. P. (2012). *Leading change.* Boston, MA: Harvard Business Review Press, (p. 4).
24 Ibid, Adaptive leadership is the activity of mobilizing the work necessary to close the gap between the values people stand for (that constitute thriving) and the reality that they face (their current lack of capacity to realize those values in their environment).
25 Ibid, (p. 31).
26 Ibid, (p. 32).
27 Edmondson, A. C. (2019). *The fearless organization: Creating psychological safety.* Hoboken, NJ: Wiley & Sons, Inc.
28 Patterson, K., Grenny, J. McMillan, R. & Switzler, A. (2012). *Crucial conversations.* New York, NY: McGraw-Hill, (p. 23).
29 Tichy, N. M., & Sherman, S. (2001). *Control your destiny or someone else will.* New York: HarperBusiness, (p. 32).
30 Kotter, J. P. (2012). *Leading change.* Boston, MA: Harvard Business Review Press, p. 286.
31 Schein, E. H. (2017). *Organizational culture and leadership* (5th ed.). Hoboken, NJ: Wiley & Sons, Inc., (p. 320).
32 Yukl. G. (2006). *Leadership in organizations* (6th ed.). Upper Saddle River, NJ: Pearson Prentice Hall, (p. 249).
33 Weber, M. (1963). *The sociology of religion.* Beacon, NY: Beacon Press (Originally published in 1922).
34 Lawler, E. E. (1982). Increasing worker involvement to enhance organizational effectiveness. In P. S. Goodman (Ed.), *Changes in organizations.* San Francisco: Jossey-Bass.
35 Weber, M. (1947). *The theory of social and economic organization* (A. M. Henderson & T. Parsons, Trans.). New York: Free Press (Originally published in 1924).
36 Trice, H. M., & Beyer, J. M. (1986). Charisma and its routinization in two social movement organizations. *Research in Organizational Behavior, 8,* 113–164.
37 Bryman, A. (1992). *Charisma & leadership in organizations.* London, UK: Sage Publications, (p. 102).
38 Ibid, (p. 102).
39 Bass, B. M. (1990). *Bass and Stogdill's handbook of leadership: Theory, research, and managerial applications.* New York: Free Press, (p. 192).
40 Burns, J. M. (1978). *Leadership.* New York: Harper & Row, (p. 243).
41 Bryman, (p. 102).
42 Noted charismatic leadership scholars Conger and Kanungo (1998) developed the Conger-Kanungo Charismatic Leadership Questionnaire to be administered to followers of a leader that would determine the presence of charismatic leadership. (pp. 251–253).
43 Bryman, (p. 102).
44 Reichheld, F. (2011). *The ultimate question 2.0.* Boston, MA: Harvard Business Review, (p. 138).
45 Drath, W. (2001). *The deep blue sea: Rethinking the source of leadership.* San Francisco, CA: Jossey-Bass, (p. 26).
46 Drucker, P. F. (2004). *Managing oneself and what makes and effective leader.* Boston, MA: Harvard Business Review Press.
47 Bennis, W. (1989/2003). *On becoming a leader.* Cambridge, MA: Perseus Publishing.
48 Dweck, C. (2006, 2016). *Mindset: The new psychology of success.* New York, NY: Random House, (p. 6).
49 Ibid, (p. 125).

PART III
The Essentials of Leadership

In this section, you'll see a deeper dive into the challenge of obtaining buy-in from members of the organization. Many texts exist on communication and a good lot focus on persuading people to buy-in to the mission, goals, and purpose of the organization. This book looks at some nontraditional kinds of communication that leaders might use to generate buy-in based on our working definition of leadership.

We've established the definition of leadership contains four essential elements: (a) influence, (b) relationship, (c) real change, and (d) mutual purposes. When all four elements are present, leadership forms. The effectiveness of leadership—leaders and followers acting within the elements above—is determined by how well it navigates the factors that must be present for an organization to thrive.

In this section, we explore four elements that leaders and followers can use to inform the leadership potential of their organization: (a) direction, (b) culture, (c) renewal, and (d) learning. These elements probe historic and contemporary thought in the areas of leadership, power and authority (Chapter 5), persuasion and influence (Chapter 6), change and adaptation (Chapter 7), and individual/ organizational purposes (Chapter 8).

5

WHERE ARE WE HEADED?

Harry Truman was an unlikely choice for president. He wasn't a man of physical stature. He didn't have a history of success in business. He became president by the death of a powerful and popular president who was just three months into his fourth term. And think about this: barely seated comfortably in the Oval Office, he would wipe out two cities in Japan with an epochal weapon he knew nothing about when he took office.

The man known for a desk sign that read, "The buck stops here!" did not have the appearance of a leader. Commentators regularly referred to him as "the little man." However, those close to him saw a leader of large stature. While serving in France as a captain in World War I, his superiors witnessed something in Truman that he didn't see in himself and put him in charge of "the most mischievous, unpredictable, and difficult-to-handle unit in the entire AEF [American Expeditionary Forces]."[1] Though only 5'9" Truman stood tall and provided his troops with direction, protection, and order, the three core responsibilities of leaders.[2] In return, they collectively created leadership.

Scholars have examined leaders for decades with the goal of trying to understand how and why leaders are effective getting people to follow. From management theories about the division of work to theories of the Great Man to contemporary thoughts on follower-centered models, the field's been thoroughly hypothesized, analyzed, tested, and inspected, yet there's no single answer or solution.

That's probably because there's so many circumstances of varying shades that demand an efficacious organizational response. For our purposes, this chapter probes the many dimensions and nuances of power and authority. In other words, what a leader does, she does it in the scope of engaging people to accomplish change that's necessary for the members of the group to thrive.[3] Therefore, she must deftly manage the conditions from which members of the organization authorize, and thus, buy-in, to the direction it must move in to thrive.

It Starts at the Top

Studying presidential leadership is productive in unveiling the secrets of getting folks to follow, to understand, and accept direction established by leaders. First, it is a robust field that is widely published. Second, the position itself is a publicly visible daily manifestation of leaders challenged with "getting someone else to do something you want done because he wants to do it,"[4] and third, because the lessons learned are reality-tested, vetted, and validated. Consider what some believe to be our most accomplished president, Abraham Lincoln.

The role of the leader is often a lonely one. People default to some sense of distancing when in the midst of a person of formal authority and the president is the ultimate authority for many. Yet, when a leader erases this distance by making themselves readily accessible, she opens the door to generating informal authority. Informal authority is people-driven. It is in leaders because they inspire people to follow, or buy-in.

In his book "Lincoln on Leadership," Donald T. Phillips wrote: "If subordinates, or people in general, know that they genuinely have easy access to their leader, they'll tend to view the leader in a more positive, trustworthy light. 'Hey,' the followers think, 'this guy really wants to hear from me—to know what I think and what's really going on. He must be committed to making things work!'"[5] Setting direction is a principal responsibility of the leader. She does so with the understanding that the direction must be compatible with the values, perceptions, and trustworthiness they express in their leader.

James McGregor Burns offered this test of a leader: Ultimately, they "will be tested by the achievement of purpose in the form of real and intended social change"[6] He adds, leaders creatively combine ideological and charismatic qualities in creating a relationship between leader and follower. Burns referred to Chinese leader Mao Tse-tung "fulfilling his necessary role as hero, father figure, cult object, idol."[7] as possessing an extraordinary relationship with his people. Burns described a cult-like relationship suited for the cultural challenge at the time he ascended to power.

Burns wrote that it's "needed at certain times, for in human affairs one thing will always exist: 'the desire to be worshipped and the desire to worship.'"[8] Toward our purpose, a leader-follower relationship validates and energizes both leaders and followers. Consequently, it's necessary to establish shared values as they serve as determinants of human behavior.

Shared Values Provide Compelling Guidance for Members

Value is a heavy word in that it is laden with strains of meaning determined by context. One's values can contribute to the value one provides. Values can be both *goals* and *standards*—both the *end* of the journey and *benchmark* by which to measure the quality of the journey.

Further, a value can be the mode of behavior, as in one who values fairness treats others as he would like to be treated. Burns summarized its various applications wisely: "a test of adherence to values is the willingness to apply principles or standards to oneself as well as others." When this occurs, values are shared and serve to influence behavior with or without penalties being imposed for violation.[9] In other words, people's needs are evoked in their values.

Social psychologist Milton Rokeach wrote: "A person's individual needs somehow become cognitively represented as values, and so also do societal goals and demands. Thus, we may come to view the value system that each person internalizes to be just as much a reflection of individual needs as of societal goals and demands—a resultant of internal psychological and external sociological forces acting upon the person."[10] Needs and values align as humans minimize their differences. Leaders who can effectively align values with purpose have the power to move people's hearts and minds.

One can think of a value in an intrinsic sense, as an end in itself; or extrinsically, as a means to achieving an end-state. Burns cited the example of a person going to college to get a job but who also *values* educating one's self. That same individual considers high grades as validation of learning, as well as a means to be selected for a job. In this, a value is both a goal and a standard of performance. Repeat: values are both end-state goals and standards of behavior.

Zenger and Folkman submit "that it is virtually impossible for an organization to change its culture until its leaders' behavior is consistent with the values of the culture,"[11] explaining their conviction that actions speak louder than words. For the leader, understanding the full meaning of values and how to command them, presents a powerful tool in shaping organizational commitment.

Since values truly matter, it should be a primal consideration for the leader. Goleman, et. al. remind "to achieve improved business performance, leaders need to be emotionally engaged in their self-development."[12] That means as leader you must listen to your heart, regularly assessing what matters in the moment.

Chris was a seasoned leader. He had experienced the growing pains of a young leader testing his bounds. He had a longer and deeper view, the kind driven by strong personal beliefs. Apex wasn't his first rodeo. The company wasn't another stop on his career path; for Chris, it was another phase of his life to be executed more perfectly than in his younger days.

Power and Authority

One of the headier challenges for a leader is to apprehend a deep understanding of power and authority. Power is the ability to act or have influence over others. For our discussion here, let's refer to Ronald Heifetz' definition of authority "as conferred power to perform a service."[13] Interpreting it strictly, Joseph Rost wrote: "Authority is a contractual (written, spoken or implied) relationship wherein people accept superordinate or subordinate responsibilities in an organization.... [and] wherein certain people control other people by rewards and/or punishments."[14]

This definition implies coercion—the use of threat or force. In certain circumstances, coercion is necessary to exercise power. For example, imposing fines for traffic violations as a means to enforce compliance with traffic safety laws. However, coercion is seldom the preferred practice. The use of coercion is often counterproductive in influence relationships because people in influence relationships are free to exit the relationship.

Think of authority as followers engaged with leaders in an agreement: "Party A entrusts Party B with power in exchange for services.... 'I look to you to serve a set of goals I hold dear.'"[15] The follower agrees to follow in exchange for the leader tending to his or her needs, which are mutually desired. When this occurs, the firm is vitalized to deliver an effective response to external challenges.

The complicating factor is when the follower believes the leader's practices don't lead to the desired outcome. In this situation, the authorizer withdraws their authority. This is particularly applicable when leadership is facing an adaptive challenge, when a gap exists between the values people believe constitute thriving and the reality they face.

Authority Incubated in a Holding Environment

Authority, whether formal or informal, is a resource the leader uses to mobilize organizational response to an adaptive challenge. Heifetz identified capabilities that flowed from leaders entrusted with authority, in an influence relationship. He held that leaders benefit by providing a "holding environment for containing the stresses of the adaptive efforts."[16]

If the leader owns the burden, followers reciprocate with support. Think of the PZD (Figure 4.1), where the leader will protect followers from harm to safely discuss values, perspectives, ideas, and assumptions held by the members. The PZD and the holding environment are one in the same. Beneficial results can emerge if leaders and followers engage in this safety zone to work through possibilities.

- The leader can fully expect to direct attention based on the leader's observations of the challenge;

- Information is provided to the leader to inform decisions; coming in form of follower comments and observations;
- As a result, the leader exerts control over the flow of information, doling it out in a manner that will shape follower perceptions;
- Information is power that enables the leader to frame issues, an effective tool to focus the attention of followers in a manner that supports the leader's point-of-view;
- In such relationships, the leader is implicitly expected to maintain order and shape conflict in a favorable light; and
- In the role of preserving order, the leader may choose how decisions are made—consultative, autocratic, consensual, or some combination or refashioning.

The idea of a holding environment springs from psychotherapy and the relationship between the therapist and the patient. Just like between a mother or father and a child, the leader becomes a conduit for learning what needs to be known to address the adaptive challenge. In a holding environment, individuals form bonds of trust, fear, threat, and need. Even holding environments that emanate from conflict may serve to transform stresses into adaptive change as witnessed in war and conflicts in history, yielding a mutual desire for peace.

Trust and Trustworthiness

In his study of trust, David de Steno wrote, "Your mind intuitively shifts from using signals of affiliation and integrity to using signals of competence to determine trustworthiness as needed."[17] In other words, context matters when it comes to attributing trustworthiness to others. In the circumstance in which you must determine if another is trustworthy, one must ask, "Am I seeking competence or honesty? Whichever is sought, body language is often a reliable influencing factor."

De Steno identified four reasonably reliable body language "tell" signs in both perception (what we see) and behavior (what they do). The more a subject engaged in these four cues the less likely they were trustworthy. The gestures are crossing arms, leaning away, face touching, and hand touching. As it turns out, the experiment yielding the findings determined that if all four cues were present, "observers dialed back expectations for fairness and loyalty."[18]

Chris bought Apex because he saw the organization's potential to be much more successful. Though it was profitable, its profits weren't predictable possibly because its people weren't alive with each day's possibility. His vision was not some machination inspired by an income statement. Chris had real-life experience with teams who succeeded in winning business by creating awesome customer service.

He had a track record of developing lasting personal relationships by identifying the inherent traits of people; bringing to the surface the hidden talents of
unsuspecting followers, all in the name of awesome customer service. He
bought in wholly that making a profit was a requisite (or you couldn't stay in
business) but the real fun was watching people develop and become the best
version of themselves and contributing extraordinary value to get and keep
customers.

How do Chris' personal values populate his vision? When a leader is authentic
and honest with himself and others, people deem him trustworthy. When his values
are inextricably tied to the vision, followers begin to feel safe in being themselves,
particularly if they see their personal values align with the leader's values.

Publicly Exhibit Values to Create Affiliation, Community

> Kouzes and Posner advise: "Leaders are their organizations' ambassadors of
> shared values. Their mission is to represent the values and standards to the
> rest of the world, and it's their solemn duty to serve the values to the best of
> their abilities. People watch your every action, and they're determining if
> you're serious about what you say. As leader, you need to be conscious of
> the choices you make and the actions you take because they signal priorities
> that others use to conclude whether you're doing what you say."[19]

Chris considered himself a role model. He acted the way he believed everyone
should act. His messages were focused on the two most important constituents to
Apex' success: employees and customers. He saw them tied together, what was
good for one was good for the other. This was a foreign thought to members of
Apex when Chris assumed control. The hierarchy at that time was (in descending
order of importance) boss > boss' chosen people > big dollar customers > the
rest. While not published anywhere, this was emblazoned on the minds of all.
The way Chris saw it, Apex was ready for a change of leadership, but it required
getting some of the "chosen" off the bus.

Max De Pree wrote: "Instinctively, most of us follow a leader who can
transform ... [our] vision into a meaningful and hopeful strategy.... People with a
vision [are prepared to] inject ambiguity and risk and uncertainty into our lives.
They embark on voyages to new worlds. Without the vitality and strength of an
organization, a vision wastes away."[20]

In times when people felt uncertainty or fear, Chris was quick to brush away
the self-doubt: "Be somebody!" he'd snap, and then brandish a big victorious
Churchill-like grin often with a cigar clenched between his jaws. When a leader
demonstrates conviction, people are emboldened. For employees of Apex, the
20-year formation of the culture had come to an inauspicious end, ill-prepared
for challenges it may face. Launching into a new world may be just what the
doctor ordered, and Chris was prepared to lead.

What Do Leaders Do?

In this text, we've meted out over the pages various perspectives of the job of leadership and how we recognize when leadership is present. Heifetz, Grashow, and Linksy tell us three core responsibilities of the leader are to provide followers with direction, protection, and order.[21] Wilfred Drath has a similar take that leadership arises to accomplish these tasks: direction, commitment, and adaptation.[22] Figure 5.1 combines the two viewpoints into one comprehensive list of leader tasks and leader/follower actions.

Leaders Draw Out Collective Authority

In a popular leadership tale, Ernest Shackleton set out to walk across Antarctica during the Heroic Age of Antarctic Exploration, which began at the end of the 19th century. In textbook fashion, Shackleton set a mission, established goals, communicated the vision, and embedded purpose and compassion in his followers, who he carefully selected for their unique talents, optimism, and cheerfulness. Richard Danzig, U.S. Secretary of the Navy, said, "He is not the complete leader, but he is an exceptional example of a set

LEADER TASKS	
The Tasks	**Leader / Follower Actions:**
DIRECTION	▪ **Set mission, establish goals, communicate vision, embed purpose** ▪ **Articulate strategy, business model and operating plan**
COMMITMENT	▪ Create alignment, Inspire team work, employ intrinsic motivation ▪ Reward intended accomplishments ▪ Drive upward spirals of emotion
ORDER	▪ **In stable mode,** – Define roles, provide clarity of duty/functions – Create and monitor meaningful evaluation criteria – Identify gaps in individual/team performance ▪ **In adaptive mode,** – expose conflict – challenge status quo
PROTECTION	▪ In stable mode, protect people from external threats ▪ In adaptive mode, mobilize people to respond to external threats ▪ Always provide psychological safety for people to act boldly
ADAPTATION	▪ Inspire innovation to address customer need to make progress against their situation ▪ Relentlessly eliminate costs that do not create value
	Copyright ©2020 Tim P. McMahon

FIGURE 5.1   The business model gives structure to the mission

of traits we highly value … Warfare constantly requires adaptation and innovation, and he was extraordinary in those."[23]

It is refreshing to hear about a man who did great things yet may not be considered complete. Few human beings are completely endowed with all the skills they will need for every occasion. This is one reason they reach out to find others who will supplant and enrich the collective abilities of the group. However, setting direction, especially preparing people to adjusting along the way, is an essential task. As it turns out, Shackleton's heroic tale was *not* on the setting of direction and reaching it at all costs, it was about course correction and persistence to thrive in dire conditions, actions which kept people headed in the right direction.

Vision and values are statements to the members of the organization to convey the purpose of the group. The goal is to develop a *shared* sense of purpose, a portrait of an ideal future.[24] Evidence shows shared vision boils down to shared purpose. Specifically, "a large amount of vision imagery combined with a small number of values—will boost performance more than other combinations. This triggers a shared sense of the organization's ultimate goal, and, in turn, enhances coordination."[25] Further, researchers hypothesized that leaders veer from effectiveness when they communicate visions without imagery and rely on overuse of value-laden rhetoric.

The Power of Verve

To communicate vision and values in a compelling way so that followers get a clear picture, leaders must appeal to one's senses through language that depicts objects, actions, and events. Moreover, true empowerment comes when people see themselves in the vision, when they've activated a sense of verve. When President John Kennedy delivered his message at Rice University in Houston on May 12, 1961, he said: "We choose to go to the moon."[26] Further, he established a deadline, "in this decade."[27] And further, he said, "… not because they are easy, but because they are hard, because that goal will serve to organize and measure the best of our energies and skills, because that challenge is one that we are willing to accept, one we are unwilling to postpone, and one which we intend to win, and the others, too."[28]

Kennedy's message was clear to everyone through their senses. His words depicted objects (USA), actions (go to the moon), and events (NASA launches). The purpose, understood by all, gives the essence of the word vision as we use it with respect to leadership. Further, it stood as a driving force through setbacks and miscues as the mission proceeded. This provided a means for leaders to course correct—like after the initial Apollo 1 explosion on January 27, 1967—yet remain committed to mission (purpose).

Direction is a Guided Mission

A second aspect of direction lies in creation of a specific strategy to accomplish the mission and live the purpose of the firm. Leaders must provide a strategy and a business model. It matters not whether you're working in a profit or not for profit structure, both are required to make money—take in more than you send out! The way firms accomplish this, is to acquire and keep customers.

Weintraub Austin & Pinkleton defined goals (what direction we need to move), and objectives (how we will know we have arrived), and strategies (how we get to our destination).[29] Chris takes business seriously but has fun with words. When he refers to how we get to our destination, he calls it *strategery*—a reference to a 2000 "Saturday Night Live" sketch where Will Ferrell played George W. Bush in a debate with his rival Al Gore. When asked by a mock debate moderator to sum up his candidacy in a single word, replied *strategery*.[30] Chris found the word to have a softening effect on people. Strategy is not friendly, whereas strategery is met with a smile. It is not threatening.

When Chris set out to devise a strategy, he was keenly aware its success depended on constructing a business model that would support the vision and customer proposition. A business model describes how the company works to achieve its goals. How does it create, capture and sustain value on behalf of its customers and itself? It is the fundamental statement of internal integration (e.g., common language and concepts, boundaries, duties and responsibilities, responsibilities and accountabilities, recognition and rewards) that must accompany execution.

Bossidy & Charan described the business model as the environment, financial targets, and activities of the business. The leader's role is to "harmonize the three components by repeatedly reviewing them as you add new information and analyzing the subsequent changes in relationships among them."[31] Like all purposeful structure, a building begins with a blueprint as seen in Figure 5.2.

Depending on how well the members of the firm link the various aspects of the three critical components (assumptions, financial targets, adjustments) will determine how well the business model works to accomplish goals, serve the firm's purpose, and execute its strategy. The operating plan lays out the day-to-day tasks for various people and functions. This is a means of operationalizing the culture.

The reality of performance is that we truly *learn* when we *do*. Buckminster Fuller said: "If you want to teach people a new way of thinking, don't bother trying to teach them. Instead give them a tool, the use of which will lead them to new ways of thinking."[32] While values can articulate purpose, the most effective way to ensure adoption of values is to embed them, that gives members strength.

Moving Individuals to Team Commitment

Peter Drucker made famous the phrase: "Culture eats strategy for breakfast." That means no matter how strong your strategic plan is, members of your team

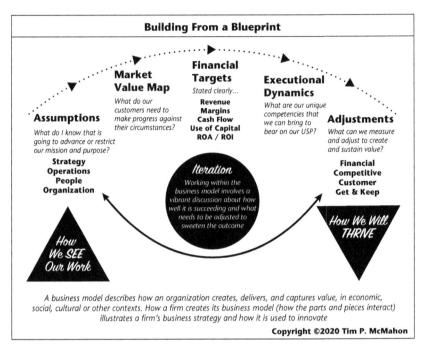

FIGURE 5.2 The business model gives structure to the mission

will reject it, if they don't share the cultural values to support it. Mike Tyson has become a cult hero and is famous for his line: "Everyone has a plan until they get punched in the mouth." People understand these phrases. They ring true. For leaders attempting to get people on the same page with a strategy, this is wise advice.

David Maister warned, "The problem is that many change efforts are based on the assumptions that all you have to do is explain to people that their lives could be better, convince them that the goals are worth going for, and show them how to do it."[33] This addresses the central question in this book, how to get buy-in? Creating a vision can be compelling, but people need to know there is a plan because, as Maister reminds, the pain and discomfort associated with executing a strategy is immediate, yet the rewards are in the future. Without a plan, there is no evidence of direction and eventual payout; therefore, no future.

Chris knew he needed all his people transitioning from the old Apex to the new, needed to re-think the way they did business. He also knew people act according to what they believe. Their beliefs "are conditioned by training, experience, what people hear inside or outside about the company's prospects, and perceptions about what leaders are doing and saying."[34] That is why Chris ramped up training and knowledge creation across the firm; why he put financial incentives in place. Chris said, "I want them to know this is a great place to work and we are going places. World Dominance!" This conveys a sense of vitality.

Chris had a winning formula—intrinsic and extrinsic rewards—combined with a vision and a plan. All they needed now was an environment that provided order in times of stability and in times of chaos, because Apex would inevitably face both. Scholars have written extensively about management and leadership.

Perhaps the best distinction is that management produces order and stability; whereas leadership produces change and movement.[35] We naturally associate order with stability. However, there is order in chaos, too. Chaos theory posits that within the randomness of chaos there are underlying patterns of inter-connectedness. It is along this line of thinking that we see order in non-linear thinking; there're multiple starting points to apply logic.

Create Order in Both Turbulent and Calm Seas

Remember Ernest Shackleton, the South Pole explorer who set out with his men to walk across the continent? It never happened. They never crossed the continent. Despite meticulous planning, their ship, the Endurance, became mired in pack ice just two days into the journey.

One of the leadership lessons from his experience is the advice: "Give your staff an occasional reality check to keep them on course. After time, people will start to treat a crisis situation as business as usual and lose focus."[36] With their ship hopelessly locked in frigid temperatures, it would be quite normal for Shackleton's crew to obsess about how they got into their mess. Such periods are paralyzing. But it's the leader's duty to prepare people to handle business as usual and business in crisis; more importantly, to recognize the difference.

Apollo 1 was planned to be launched on February 21, 1967. It didn't happen. During a rehearsal test on January 27, a cabin fire killed all three astronauts—Gus Grissom, Roger Chaffee, and Ed White. Deputy flight controller Gene Kranz recalled the moment: "At 5:31:04 Houston time a brief voice report jolted the launch and flight teams. It was perhaps the defining moment in our race to get to the Moon. After this, nothing would be quite the same, ever again."

"Fire!"

"We've got a fire in the cockpit!"

"We've got a bad fire ... get us out. We're burning up ..."

The last sound was a scream, shrill and brief. The elapsed time of the crew report: twelve seconds. Kranz wrote: "There was a gallant but futile effort to rescue the trapped threesome. The pad rescue team as well as crewmen from North American, mechanics and technicians, grabbed fire extinguishers and rushed toward the inferno. At least twice, shock waves and secondary explosions drove them back, knocking many to their knees.... But it was too late."[37]

In his post investigation meeting with the team, Kranz declared: "We were the cause. The simulators weren't ready, our software in mission control didn't function, procedures weren't complete, nothing we did had any shelf life, and no one stood up and said, 'Dammit Stop!'" Kranz's lament that day accepted full responsibility for the three lost lives. It brought him to conclude: "From this day forward, mission control will be known by two words: tough and competent."[38] Kranz summed up these two words in straight-forward language: "tough meaning we will never again shirk from our responsibility ... and competent, we will never again take anything for granted, we will never stop learning."[39]

Your Opportunity to Create Leadership

While it's difficult to top that story in drama; something just like it happens every hour of every day somewhere, and the outcome, depends on teams recognizing when its business as usual and when it must act in crisis mode. If we truly are looking for engagement, to get buy-in, there is no better time to create the conditions for it to happen than during a crisis. The guidance is clear.

During times of stability, leaders must define rules and provide clarity for people, so they are prepared in times of trouble. Chris spent every day surveilling his people in his daily walks through the company. He monitored performance, eavesdropped on their daily interactions and poured over daily, weekly, and monthly data that reported their actions and outcomes. Chris kept an eye on the firm and its environment. He trained himself to recognize early indicators that predict what the firm may soon face and quickly find a way to respond.

The question all leaders must regularly ask is: Does the team measure up? Figure 5.3 is a concise tool to visualize and measure your team's performance. Do they have the skills and abilities empower themselves?

In the next chapter, we will take a look at the research that produced this chart. This is based on team performance research conducted by Richard Hackman.

A Misunderstood Word

When you hear the word *discipline*, do you get excited, depressed, or disinterested? Since we were children, the word has been connected to notions of punishment, deficiency, or obedience. Until human beings gain some sense of joy flowing from discipline, they're not likely to sign up for it. What if someone presented it as focusing on something wildly important? What if they told you discipline was about doing less, not more? These are two suggestions made by the authors of a book titled, *The 4 disciplines of execution*. With respect to results, there are two items a leader can influence: strategy and execution of that strategy.

DOES YOUR TEAM MEASURE UP?

On a scale of 1 (worst) to 5 (best), rate your team on these criteria:

OUTPUT	COLLABORATIVE ABILITY	INDIVIDUAL DEVELOPMENT
Are our customers happy with our output—with its quality, quantity, and delivery?	Do our team's dynamics help us work well together?	Are individual team members improving their knowledge, skills, and abilities?

Then score your team on the following aspects of the conditions for effectiveness:

COMPELLING DIRECTION	STRONG STRUCTURE	SUPPORTIVE CONTEXT	SHARED MINDSET
Do we have a common goal that is clear, challenging (but not impossible), and consequential?	Down have the right number and mix of members? Are people responsible for tasks from beginning to end? Do we have clear norms for acceptable conduct?	Do we have the resources, information and training we need? Are there appropriate rewards for success?	Do the team members have a strong common identity? Do we readily share information with one another and understand one another's constraints and context?

FIGURE 5.3   Three criteria; four conditions

The authors, McChesney, Covey, and Huling begin by making a distinction among measuring points. Lag measures and lead measures. A "lag measure tells you if you've achieved the goal, a lead measure tells you if you are likely to achieve the goal. While a lag measure is hard to do anything about, a lead measure is virtually within your control."[40]

Chris used measures to assess the ongoing viability of the Apex strategy. In his mind's eye, Chris would challenge the status quo. He would run scenarios, anticipate the good and bad outcomes and then assess the need to tell others, keep it in the back of his mind, or dismiss it out-of-hand.

In this daily assessment, Chris could see potential danger to his people. He adopted the posture of Shackleton and Kranz in being keen to recognize stability and threat and know the difference.

Protect Members; Promote Resilience in Disequilibrium

Resilience is the ability to bounce back, that is, at a moment's notice cope with a crisis or return to stable mode. We've discussed that instability in organizations thrusts its people into crisis, such as Apollo 1. It was a return to discipline that put the mission back on track. While disequilibrium elicits a response that motivates people to regain balance, extended disequilibrium, such as when a firm undergoes an ownership change, may force people to escape and stop working, and check out.

Moreover, disequilibrium can cause conflict, panic, frustration, and worse, personal loss. Members of the organization who aren't prepared for that will withdraw their authorization for you to lead them. A firm that has failed to develop adaptive capacity—resilience—won't thrive. Since sometimes the firm will live in disequilibrium, it's advisable for leaders to build resilience, the capacity to define and effectively resolve problems.

Each year, Chris assembled his senior management team, and they reviewed the Apex SWOT analysis.[41] This tool helps management determine if its strategy is on point. Besides an annual two-day deep dive, the Apex team met quarterly for a brief check-up to take vital signs and assess executional issues.

The number one concern on the list of threats was the long-term viability of its largest client who absorbed 50% of the firm's revenues and even more of its resources. When presented at the SWOT meeting, Chris smiled and quipped, "If that elephant hiccups, we'd be thrown into the bushes." In Chris' dialogue, he even responded to threats in a jovial tone. Apex needed to get its act together—a fact not lost on the team. This issue is what Chris was obsessing about. One response to this dilemma might be the way the firm developed new products. Either way, he had to get more of the right people in the right places doing the right things. Apex had to build its products more efficiently.

Roles and responsibilities needed better understanding by all to accommodate smooth hand-offs and reduce redundancy. Yet, operations must be nimble enough to pivot from customer-to-customer so it could improve response times and identify potential bottlenecks. Finally, it needed to widen its circle of clients, which meant salespeople would need to become more efficient and fleet-of-foot in recognizing and responding to the needs of clients—both existing and new. Awesome customer service would begin with the mindset that Apex would anticipate what customers needed to make progress against their situation and specifically identify the specific job the customer wanted performed.[42]

Perhaps the biggest need to protect people in the firm is in recognizing changes in the environment or enfeeblement of the firm's internal capabilities. To avoid mission drift, and to *keep the main thing the main thing*, Chris reminded himself of the importance of recapturing for all members the firm's strategy. "One prime suspect behind execution breakdown was clarity of objective. People simply don't understand the goal they were supposed to execute."[43]

YOU CAN'T HANDLE THE TRUTH

CHRIS: *Craziest thing. I have been obsessing about this problem with our customer getting sucked into asking us for this quickie report. They want it to cover their behind so they can issue approvals faster!*

AGNES: *So, what's the crazy thing?*

CHRIS: *Last night I am dialing around and land on the old movie with Jack Nicholson and Tom Cruise …*

AGNES: *A few good men.*

CHRIS: *And it comes to that famous scene where Cruise's character, the JAG prosecutor, questions Nicholson's character, the Marine commander. He pins him down and gets him all worked up and finally, the colonel, screams out: "You can't handle the truth!" Then the commander goes on to describe that the young lawyer could never imagine the quandary of the real world.*

AGNES: *I loved that scene. Why has that stuck in your mind?*

CHRIS: *Because it made me realize in a small way I am in the same position as that colonel. I am so sure I have some closer view or deeper understanding about our customer that I don't think my peeps can handle the truth.*

AGNES: *But they can.*

CHRIS: *Yep, sometimes it's okay to brush over the truth ...*

AGNES: *Like when Doc did with Janie's calf.*

CHRIS: *Yea. But that was harmless. If I don't level with my peeps about what I am thinking ... and trust them to respond properly ... I am no better than that colonel leading his troops into trouble.*

Chris finished his coffee, talked a bit about weekend plans, and headed back to the office for some serious discussions.

Thriving Begins With Taking Care of Yourself and Your Customer

Chris opened his next meeting reminding everyone of their purpose. "Our everyday work is to gather information from sources in all 3,141 counties in America. We then pick and cull the key data that will enable our clients to make decisions swiftly, easily, and confidently. Any company can do that."

If we want to dominate, if we want to be around for a long time, we must embed the idea we're here to do for our customer what they may not be able to do for themselves: provide what they need to create competitive advantage without losing sight of the inherent risk of approving a high-risk loan. If we're simply making new products, anyone can do that, and when you do, you'll be copycatted overnight. We must be building an organization that knows how to create an *experience*—much more difficult to copy. When they experience a relationship that anticipates problems and protects them from loss, we win."

The ongoing challenge at Apex centered on "Creating the right experiences and then integrating them to solve a job. This is critical for competitive advantage. That's because while it may be easy for competitors to copy products, it's difficult for them to copy experiences that are well integrated into your company's processes."[44]

TAKE-AWAYS

- Leaders who are approachable, yet resolute, are likely to draw followers into a relationship. The nature of the relationship will ultimately shape its ability to face its challenges. The relationship may range from cult-like to simply effective in all events causing the organization to thrive.
- When the people of an organization share values, they attain both goals and standards—both the end of the journey and a benchmark to denote progress. This will influence behavior in an affirming way without penalties being imposed for violation.
- Leaders are role models. This isn't a burden; it's an opportunity to model the way for followers and for followers to demonstrate the way to their customers. Sometimes, it's necessary to get the people off the bus that willfully choose not to embrace the idea.
- Power and authority represent the measure of influence a leader can exert and the degree to which followers can acquiesce and affirm the direction and means by which a firm pursues its goals, strategies, and overall purpose.
- Since leadership is an influence relationship involving leaders and followers, authority is recognized as a contract—explicit or implicit—in which the two parties agree to exchange services, actions that embellish a firm's ability to confront external challenge with effective internal integration.
- Leaders are empowered to mobilize organizational response to adaptive challenges (ever-present change in the environment) when followers entrust them with authority when leaders embody a holding environment wherein the leader becomes a conduit for members of the organization to learn.
- Trust is rooted in trustworthiness and the recognition that it exists in the individuals engaged in the relationship and balances on what each is seeking in the other, usually competence or honesty, the choice of which rests in the need at the time.
- The tasks of leading are manifold. However, five stand out. Leaders must provide direction, create commitment, establish order (in good times and bad), provide protections, and lead the organization to thrive.
- Direction is accomplished when members of the organization have a shared sense of purpose, a portrait of the ideal future. Research suggests, leaders are best served when they communicate a large amount of vision imagery on a small number of values. Imagery is far more important than fuzzy rhetoric, though rhetoric is a powerful tool of influence.
- When a firm has an actionable strategy, it will likely have clarity of

mission, and clarity is a powerful motivator. People need to know what to do when they come to work every day.

- Strategy is composed of a firm's environment, its financial targets, and the activities of its business. The leader's role is to harmonize the three by repeatedly reviewing them as you add new information and analyzing the subsequent changes in relationships among them.
- Moving people to commitment revolved around free flow of information, a healthy combination of intrinsic and extrinsic rewards that support the vision and purpose of the organization.
- Thriving means living up to people's highest values. This requires adaptive capability that distinguish what is essential from what is expendable. This makes innovation essential. When people are healthy in body and mind, they can grasp a growth mindset that feeds on what matters most in organizations—getting and keeping customers. To make money is a requisite. The firm accomplishes that by getting and keeping customers.
- Growth of people is the result of growing their minds and equipping then with not just a sense of what to do but how to do it in a manner that distinguishes them from competitors.

Notes

1 Baime, A. J. (2017). *The accidental president: Harry S. Truman and the four months that changed the world.* Boston, MA: Mariner Books, (p. 56).

2 Heifetz, R., Grashow, A., & Linsky, M. (2009). *The practice of adaptive leadership: Tools and tactics for changing your organization and the world.* Boston, MA: Harvard Business Press.

3 Ibid, *The practice of adaptive leadership: Tools and tactics for changing your organization and the world.* Boston, MA: Harvard Business Press. In their book on adaptive leadership, the authors provide this definition of thrive: To live up to people's highest values. Requires adaptive responses that distinguish what's essential from what's expendable, and innovates so that the social system can bring the best of its past into the future.

4 Dwight D. Eisenhower Quotes (n.d.). BrainyQuote.com. Retrieved July 1, 2020 from https://brainyquote.com/quotes/dwight_d_eisenhower_112040.

5 Phillips, D. T. (1992). *Lincoln on leadership: Executive strategies for tough times.* Illinois, USA: DTP/Companion Books, p. 18.

6 Burns, J. M. (1978). *Leadership.* New York, NY: Perennial, (p. 251).

7 Ibid, (p. 251).

8 Ibid, (p. 251).

9 Rokeach, M. (1973). *The nature of human values.* New York, NY: The Free Press, (p. 3). The Rokeach Value Survey is a values classification tool developed by social psychologist Milton Rokeach. It is designed to rank-order 36 values, 18 terminal and 18 instrumental. Terminal values refer to desirable end-states, goals a person may hold; instrumental values refer to modes of behavior, or a means to achieve terminal values.

10 Rokeach, M. (1979). *Understanding human values: Individual and societal.* New York, NY: The Free Press, (p. 4).

11 Zenger. J. H. & Folkman, J. (2009). *The extraordinary leader.* New York, NY: McGraw-Hill, (p. 201).

12 Goleman, D., Boyatzis, R., & McKee, A. (2002). *Primal leadership: realizing the power of emotional intelligence.* Boston, MA: Harvard Press, (p. 119).

13 Heifetz, R. A. (1994). *Leadership without easy answers.* Cambridge, MA: Belknap, (p. 57).

14 Rost, J. C. (1993). *Leadership for the 21st century.* Westport, CT: Praeger, (p. 106).

15 Heifetz, R., Grashow, A., & Linsky, M. (2009). *The practice of adaptive leadership: Tools and tactics for changing your organization and the world.* Boston, MA: Harvard Business Press, (p. 24).

16 Heifetz, 1994, (p. 103).

17 deSteno, D. (2014). *The truth about trust: How it determines success in life, love, learning, and more.* New York, NY: PLUME, (p. 180).

18 Ibid, (p. 162).

19 Kouzes, J. M. & Posner, B. Z. (2017). *The leadership challenge* (6th ed.). Hoboken, NJ: Wiley & Sons, Inc., (p. 73).

20 De Pree, M. (1992). *Leadership jazz: The essential elements of a great leader.* New York, NY: Dell Trade Paperback, (p. 40).

21 Heifetz, et al. (p. 28).

22 Drath, W. (2001). *The deep blue sea: Rethinking the source of leadership.* San Francisco, CA: Jossey-Bass, (p. 18).

23 Morrell, M. & Capparell, S. (2001). *Shackleton's way: Leadership lessons from the great Antarctic explorer.* New York, NY: Penguin Books, (p. 47).

24 Rafferty, A. E., & Griffin, M. A. (2004). Dimensions of transformational leadership: Conceptual and empirical extensions. *The Leadership Quarterly, 15*(3), 329–354. Retrieved July 3, 2020 from https://doi.org/10.1016/j.leaqua.2004.02.009

25 Carton, A. M., Murphy, C., & Clark, J. R. (2012). A (blurry) vision of the future: How leader rhetoric about ultimate goals influences performance. *Academy of Management Journal.* Retrieved July 3, 2020 from https://journals.aom.org/action/fedSearchRedirect?doi=10.5465%2Famj.2012.0101

26 NASA Archives. Retrieved July 3, 2020 from https://er.jsc.nasa.gov/seh/ricetalk.htm

27 Ibid.

28 Ibid.

29 Weintraub Austin, E. & Pinkleton, B. E. (2015). *Strategic public relations management* (3rd ed.). New York, NY: Routledge – Taylor & Francis Group, (p. 17).

30 Despite his occasional gaffes, George W. Bush a gifted speaker because he had found his voice. It was not polished and erudite. It was quite the opposite, folksy, self-deprecating. What made it endearing is that Bush owned it. He made no airs of being anything but what he was; it drew people closer to him. In the 2000 election "W" stood in stark contrast to the effete-appearing Al Gore, the opponent he defeated.

31 Bossidy, L., & Charan, R. (2004). *Confronting reality: Doing matters to get things right.* New York, NY: Crown Business, (p. 79).

32 Goodreads [Website]. N.d. Buckminster Fuller. Retrieved July 3, 2020 from https://www.goodreads.com/quotes/467583-if-you-want-to-teach-people-a-new-way-of

33 Maister, D. (2008). *Strategy and the fat smoker.* Boston, MA: Spangle Press, (p. 4).

34 Bossidy, L., & Charan, R. (2004). *Execution.* New York, NY: Crown Business.

35 Kotter, J. P. (1990). *A force for change: How leadership differs from management.* New York, NY: Free Press, pp. 3–8.

36 Morrell, M. & Capparell, S., (p. 152).

37 Kranz, G. (2000). *Failure is not an option*. New York, NY: Berkley Publishing Group, (p. 197).
38 Jovanovic, N. (June 29, 2014). *Gene Kranz – Tough and competent (NASA Speech)*. [Video]. YouTube. https://www.youtube.com/watch?v=9zjAteaK9lM&feature= emb_logo.
39 Ibid
40 McChesney, C., Covey, S., & Huling, J. (2012). *The four disciplines of execution: achieving your wildly important goals*. New York, NY: Free Press, (p. 45).
41 A SWOT is a business tool designed to identify in a glance the Strengths, Weaknesses, Opportunities, and Threats the firm faces.
42 Christensen, C. M., Hall, T., Dillon, K., and Duncan, D. S. (2016). *Competing against luck: The story of innovation and customer choice*. New York, NY: HarperCollins, (p. 28).
43 Ibid, (p. 5).
44 Christensen, C. M., Hall, T., Dillon, K., and Duncan, D. S. (2016). *Competing against luck: The story of innovation and customer choice*. New York, NY: HarperCollins, (p. 16).

6

CULTURE IS THE PEARL

Southwest Airlines is a trailblazer in the way it chooses to run an airline. From its founder, the charismatic and colorful Herb Kelleher, to its break-the-mold approach to its business model, the firm is built on extraordinary relationships up and down and side-to-side throughout the organization. The result: a durable firm with low turnover, steady profits, and a well-adapted culture.

Judy Hoffer Gittell studied the airline in the creation of her theory of relational coordination, which is rooted in "relationships of shared goals, shared knowledge, and mutual respect [that] contribute substantially to effective coordination and therefore to quality and efficiency performance."[1] The power of relationships is when they cause leaders and followers to be in sync, or resonant.

"The men and women we call resonant leaders are stepping up, charting paths through unfamiliar territory, and inspiring people in their organizations, institutions, and communities....These leaders are moving people—powerfully, passionately, and purposefully."[2] How is this state achieved? Fundamentally, by creating a potent, yet nurturing culture.

Our ever-present goal in this book is to address the challenge of creating buy-in; in this chapter, we focus on how and why some leaders get their teams to muster collective resolve while others cannot. We'll investigate the role that culture, the nature/nurture of the leadership relationship, the many forms of influence that persuade members of the firm, and a variety of theories that provide insight into how people work and perform in the organization of the 21st century.

The Roles of the Leaders and Followers in Creating a Leadership Culture

In the last chapter, we learned it's nearly impossible to change the culture of an organization if the leaders don't live and breathe the values that underpin the firm. As Edgar Schein taught, leaders shape and influence the culture of a firm through the way they direct resources, influence actions, reward behavior, and model values. In other words, a significant part of dealing with culture lies in influence, defined as "the process of using persuasion to have an impact on other people in the relationship."[3]

Schein also advised, "the function of cognitive structures such as concepts, beliefs, attitudes, values, and assumptions is to organize the mass of environmental stimuli, to make sense of them, and to thereby provide a sense of predictability and meaning to the individual."[4] This describes how culture lives in an organization. The simple definition of culture is *the way we do things around here*, and is described as "learned patterns of belief, values, assumptions, and behavioral norms that manifest themselves at different levels of observability."[5] The power of culture is based upon shared assumptions, that is, members assume a set of basic truths. We accept culture as the way to think and act. Additionally, culture inoculates the organization from destructive forces that threaten survival, like ill-conceived ideas in management initiatives.

Culture serves to sustain survival. While that addresses the primary levels of Maslow needs, organizations are better served when they seek to thrive. For individuals and organizations, "thriving means growing and prospering in new and challenging environments."[6] Thriving is dependent on the individuals maintaining their health and avoiding burnout, effectively accomplished by establishing a strong holding environment.[7] Maintaining a holding environment is a practice used in psychology and sociology to create a frame in which treatment may take place positioning the therapist as a reliable and consistent individual. This is necessary because as explained in Chapter 2, friction (conflict) creates the pearl; the pearl is the culture.

Influence as Persuasion: Multi-Faceted

In explaining the role of persuasion in his definition of leadership as we use it in this text, Joseph Rost wrote "along with rational discourse, influence as persuasion involves reputation, prestige, personality, purpose, status, content of message, interpersonal and group skills, give-and-take behaviors, authority or lack of it, symbolic interaction, perception, motivation, gender, race, religion, and choices, among countless other things."[8] That's a lot to chew on, so let's break it down.

As stated, the role of influence seems to live without bounds except the fences provided by the scope of the relationship. Yet, not all members of the firm participate in the leadership relationship either as leader or follower. Many good people in an organization lack motivation to develop the skills and use the power resources to attain a role in leadership. The basic requirement to be a part of leadership—whether leader or follower—is to be active. Figure 6.1 depicts leadership as an influence relationship.

The premise: leaders and followers are the players in leadership and must be active. It illustrates a view of leadership as a multidirectional influence relationship between leaders and followers participating in a rational discourse where persuasion—moving parties to a course of action—is the goal. The discourse incorporates power resources. See the sample list of 16 items below Rational Discourse in the chart below. These are the many sources of influence people use to persuade others. The diagram depicts a fluid relationship where leaders and followers may assume alternate roles which enable the definition of leadership used in this text. With this, we can imagine influence emanating from daily acts, formal and informal, intentional or unintentional.

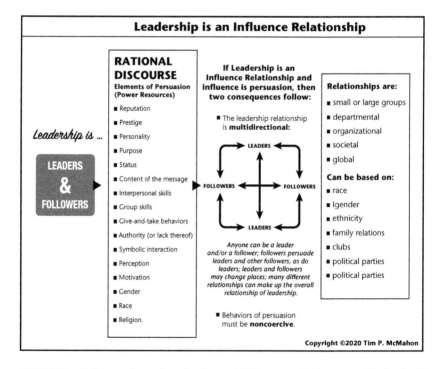

FIGURE 6.1 Influence flows from leaders and followers actively engaged in leadership

THE HASSLE OF DETASSELING IS A LESSON FOR LIFE

Chris barely got a sip of his coffee down before he asked his mother something that gnawed at him all morning—something he observed happening at work he needed to discuss.

CHRIS: *I've been working professionally ever since I graduated from college. I know not everyone is a leader. Some people just don't want to be, but some people don't really want to be a follower either. It seems that no matter what you do, they remain passive. They come to work, go through the motions and go home. I wonder how much that hurts the business? What I really want to know is can I accept that and still keep everyone else engaged?*

AGNES: *Actually, you've been working professionally all your life, Chris. Remember the summer after 8th grade?*

CHRIS: *Detasseling.*[9]

AGNES: *Yes, and boy, how that job opened your eyes. You had to get up with the chickens, make your lunch, then drag yourself down to school to catch your ride to the fields. You'd work all day in the heat and humidity, eat your lunch, finish up in the hotter afternoon, then come home, eat dinner and go to bed.*

CHRIS: *And all for $1.15 an hour*

AGNES: *I remember you talking about some of your buddies who didn't really take to that work very well.*

CHRIS: *Some did. It's not pleasant work.*

AGNES: *There's a lot to be learned, and you discovered a lot more that summer than how to top off a cornstalk.*

CHRIS: *Yes, like how to get through the day doing something that isn't much fun.*

AGNES: *But you made it better.*

CHRIS: *You're talking about the soda pop contests?*

AGNES: *Yep!*

CHRIS: *Actually, that happened because it was me and a couple of guys trying to figure out how we could get Boss Bob to spring for some cold soda pops at the end of the day.*

AGNES: *So, you talked him into giving pops to the team that detasseled the most tassels at the end of the day. You turned work into fun. Every place you have worked people would come to you and ask you about something about the job. From that first job, you didn't know squat on your first day, but you knew how to get people involved in something they could see as fun or created a little competition. You learned you didn't have to be an expert. It was more important to get people involved.*

CHRIS: *I also learned it was hard work and that was not the way I wanted to earn my living the rest of my life. It wasn't much money and the only way to make the most out of it was to keep my costs down. I made my own lunch, skipped the snacks on the way home and put my money in the bank.*

AGNES: *You did. That helped you find ways to serve everybody's own interests. You were a leader at an early age; you went out to detassle and you dehassled!*

CHRIS: *The crew could care less about plucking every last one, but it made a difference to the seed corn company. Boss Bob understood that!*

AGNES: *That's right. You created teamwork. You did it well. Lots of people don't become bosses so well. People have to like you, respect you and know you have their interests in mind. That's the magic.*

CHRIS: *It's that simple, isn't it?*

AGNES: *Yes, Chris. It's that simple. What you took with you that summer was self-confidence. Self-confidence is earned, no one gives it to you. Yet, it can leave as fast as it comes. Leading people is not a game of solitaire ... they need you and you need them.*

Chris left his mother's that day and went back to work with a different attitude. He thought leading is a tough thing to do and it is so easy to lose sight of the important little things. That's why he always turned to Agnes to bring him back and put the little things into perspective; to help him re-discover his self-confidence. As he pulled into the parking lot, he reminded himself he needed to encourage his work family to do the same ... build a support team and free themselves from the stuff that moved people off the front line and into a box of bureaucratic safety. He needed to let people know they could have a voice and it would be heard.

Case in Point: Work-Out®

Charged with developing a program to spark a revolution at GE, Noel Tichy and Stratford Sherman wrote about the challenge to change the culture by knocking down the walls between entities within the firm, a concept dubbed boundarylessness. They aimed to re-kindle competitive advantage by tapping into positive emotional energy.

Their plan for setting off a revolution within GE relied on three acts of the play, as they described it: awakening, envisioning, and rearchitecting. They asserted: "Revolutions are predictable. The pain, the resistance, the breakthroughs and joys of successful passage from one phase to another can be understood and mastered."[10] The authors claim corporations are not machines, they are "really more like theatrical troupes: Ideas, dialogue, and actions flow among the cast. Managers in the company are part of the ensemble cast demonstrating their skills and magnetism as they perform."[11]

Integral to this revolution was a process dubbed Work-Out. Typically consisting of five sessions over the course of several days, participants from all levels and perspectives of the problem are briefed and provided a road map for the journey. This is followed by people breaking into multiple teams each tackling various aspects of the issue, each creating 10 ideas for achieving a solution.

Each team presents its work before the larger group in what was termed a Gallery of Ideas. The larger group then voted to narrow down the list to 3–4 worth implementing. Then, teams prepared presentations, with supporting data, requesting approval from the Sponsor at the final Town Hall Meeting of all participants. During that final session, the Sponsor dialogues with the teams and all participants with an eventual yes/no vote on the spot.

This process is three decades old, yet it's fundamentally sound in that it focuses on the three-pronged idea of speed, simplicity, and confidence. Too often, CEO's attempt to engage their people through delegation. It goes like this: CEO identifies an issue holding back the organization. The CEO then frames the problem and delegates members of the organizers to resolve the issue. Too often, the terms of the problem—dictated by the CEO—fail to empower the team with the responsibility to develop a solution. No one can see themselves in the picture.

The magic of Work-out shows the conception of the problem, allowing the elements of the potential solution to bubble up from the front-line workers and leaders, in their terms, and in their realm of understanding. This unleashes their critical thinking. Over time, their individual and collective confidence emerge as an organizational asset.

In a speech to shareholders in 1989, GE's Welch seized on the elements of success in the Work-Out process: "If we're not simpler we can't be fast and if we're not fast, we can't win…. But just as surely as speed flows from simplicity, simplicity is grounded in self-confidence. Self-confidence does not grow in someone who is just another appendage on the bureaucracy … whose authority rests on little more than a title. Bureaucracy is terrified of speed and hates simplicity. It fosters defensiveness, intrigue, sometimes meanness. Those who are trapped in it are afraid to share, can't be passionate and … won't win."[12]

The converse is also true. If you free people from their little box in the organization, their status relies on the value they generate through applying their competencies and skills to the challenges facing the firm. This presents risk to top management; but a CEO cannot dole out confidence, she can only put people in a situation where they can grow their knowledge, skills, and subsequently, develop self-confidence.

Optimal Relationships are in Sync

If culture is as Peter Northouse defines: "the learned beliefs, values, rules, norms, symbols, and traditions that are common in a group of people…. [and] Culture is dynamic and transmitted to others"[13] then it's informative to further understand the nature of the relationship.

In its most productive form, leadership is a relationship where leaders and followers are in sync, or resonant. To realize and maintain that state, leadership must deal with everyday challenges that can be stressful. "Sometimes we attempt to deal with sacrifices and stress by oversimplifying our tasks, doing the minimal required to get the job done. Maybe we get tunnel vision and focus on the technical approach to getting results, to the exclusion of the heart, body, spirit and relationships. Maybe we just tune out any messages that do not jibe with our sense of what needs to happen."[14]

Moreover, "power creates distance between people"[15] and to bridge the gap, Rost advocates the influence relationship between leaders and followers must be multidirectional and noncoercive. In this view, anyone can be a leader at any given time and influence flows in multiple directions—leader to follower, follower to follower, and follower to leader—and if this doesn't exist, we question if leadership is operating. How does a leader nurture the culture, and empower leaders and followers?

This chapter began with recognizing the extraordinary performance of Southwest over a sustained period of time. While keen attention focused on the unique operational aspects of the firm, Kelleher's successor at Southwest Airlines, Colleen Barrett, chose to place equal emphasis on developing a culture, or spirit of the company, that emphasized respect and compassion for one another.

When leaders and followers corroborate on developing culture, good things happen as studies show culture accounts for as much as 30% of organizational performance.[16] Southwest attributes a significant amount of its success to its emphasis on relational competence—the "ability to relate effectively with others."[17]

In a conventional construct of leadership, leaders tend to be drawn from the ranks of the elite—those with the pedigree, wisdom, knowledge, social status. However you choose to define it, this tends to further distance leaders from followers. Looking back on Rost's conception of leadership, he summarily dismisses the notion that leadership is limited to leaders. Rost identifies five measures that illustrate follower substance and clarity.

- A role in leadership—either leader or follower—is contingent on activity, not passivity. Being active means, one chooses to be involved;
- Active people may be either highly involved and commensurately influential or minimally active and minimally influential. This recognizes that at any given time activity may be greater or lesser depending on the situation;
- The roles of leaders and followers are interchangeable. In other words, the mantle of leadership may be passed from leader to follower and vice versa;
- Depending on their given role at any time, people can be leaders or

followers. For example, the staff accountant may be substantively a follower in the workplace, but a leader on her recreational basketball league; and lastly
• Followers do not do followership, they do leadership!

We'll focus on influence among leaders and followers in a relationship where any member can be a leader and/or a follower; where leaders persuade followers, and vice-versa; where they may trade places based on the skill or knowledge needed at the time; and where leadership may come in duos, triads, teams, or groups of any size, which may be under one roof, or at any location dispersed or digital. We make the distinction that we are operating under the idea that leadership, not management, is at work.

Management vs. Leadership

According to Northouse, management "is a unidirectional authority relationship. Whereas leadership is concerned with the process of developing mutual purposes, management is directed toward coordinating activities in order to get a job done."[18]

The distinction is that under leadership, leaders and followers work to address real change; whereas management is about coordinating actions to do a job. We make this distinction because it allows us to see clearly there's a place for each. We conclude leadership seeks adaptive and constructive change such as the case of a firm that faces an external threat, what we call, an adaptive challenge. So, it is leadership where we direct our attention.

We often say leadership is a relationship. We now elevate the relationship to include the adjective *resonant*. The distinguishing feature is resonant leaders are in sync with those around them. "The men and women we call *resonant leaders* are stepping up, charting paths through unfamiliar territory, and inspiring people in their organizations, institutions, and communities. They are finding new opportunities within today's challenges, creating hope in face of fear and despair. These leaders are *moving people*—powerfully, passionately, and purposefully."[19]

This manifests in people working with each other, in tune with each other's thoughts (what to do) and emotions (why to do it). In most cases, they have an understanding of Ryan and Deci's self-determination theory. For large scale change in organizations, leaders must address three basic psychological needs. In their self-determination theory, Ryan and Deci enumerate these conditions: (a) they need to feel *competent*, (b) they must sense a feeling of *relatedness*, connection with others, and (c) they must have *autonomy*, knowing that they are in control of their own lives.[20]

In the theory of relational coordination, "relationships of shared goals, shared knowledge, and mutual respect contribute substantially to effective coordination and therefore to quality and efficiency performance."[21] Among the important practices guided by the theory are robust and frequent communications among the functions within the organization that's both frequent and timely; an emphasis on problem-solving, rather than focus on blame, and the operationalizing of shared goals, shared knowledge, and mutual respect.

Moreover, we know buy-in is fueled when teams together, specifically how and why they collaborate. J. Richard Hackman who has studied teams for 50 years, concluded "[what] matters most to collaboration is not the personalities, attitudes, or behavioral styles of team members. Instead, what teams need to thrive are certain 'enabling conditions.'"[22] Specifically, high performance hinges on four factors that have a sizable effect: (a) compelling direction, (b) strong structure, (c) supportive context, and (d) shared mindset.[23]

Fuel on the Fire Deep Within

The ultimate fuel for the fire of persuasion is motivation. Daniel Pink distinguished the evolution of motivation over the years. He articulated three upgrades of motivation. From the very early Motivation 1.0, survival was paramount in an untamed world. It worked until societies became more complex. Motivation 2.0 addressed our needs beyond survival, to a "second drive—to seek reward and avoid punishment more broadly."[24] Finally, Motivation 3.0 supplanted the inadequacies of the carrot and stick approach by appealing to one's need to create and innovate. Pink identified three key elements to operationalize Motivation 3.0, specifically, autonomy, mastery, and purpose.

Related to this, we look into a means by which we understand leadership is happening "when people who acknowledge shared work use dialogue and collaborative learning to create contexts in which work can be accomplished across the dividing lines of differing perspectives, values, beliefs, cultures, and more generally ... differing worldviews."[25]

This principle of leadership assumes leadership is a property of a social system. Leadership happens in collaborative forms of thought and action. Leaders actions are an aspect of participation in the process of leadership. "Leadership tasks ... center on three kinds of tasks related to direction (mission, goals, vision, purpose), commitment (alignment, motivation, spirit, teamwork), and adaptation (innovation, change, dealing with paradigm shifts)."[26] There is much to consider. So, let's proceed to presenting the case for how organizations can leverage the concepts in these thoughts to create resonant relationships that create buy-in.

A Review of Associated Theories

While not all theoretical research can be applied to the real world, the theories presented here align to create outcomes favorable to creating organizational resolve of its members.

Goleman: Emotional Intelligence

We now recognize if the goal is to create resonance—where leaders and followers are in sync with one another with what they do (cognitive) and why they do it (emotional), then ramping up emotional intelligence is beneficial. Chris' extensive reading on leadership led him to understand people held a bias toward the belief the leader is the primary focus of the relationship between leader and follower. Chris viewed that influence in the leader-follower relationship wasn't one-way. Rather, it connected as depicted in Figure 6.2, leading to mutual relationship management.

Chris saw that "[f]ollowers have great capacity to influence the ultimate outcome through the relationship. Just as leaders influence the actions and performance of followers, so followers influence their leaders."[27] Leaders make followers better by drawing out their individual strengths and raising them up; followers make leaders better by helping them course-correct and refine their visions.

In this relationship lies the ultimate reality test, particularly when the relationship is a partnership in which leaders and followers are proactive and engaged. So, the organization is then better prepared to deal with a volatile external

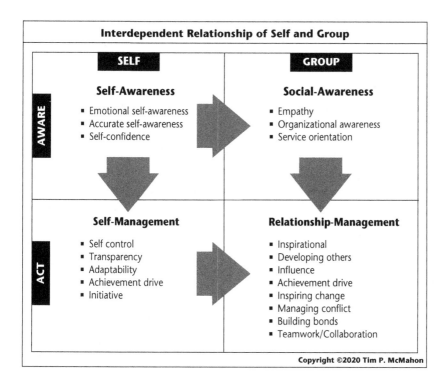

FIGURE 6.2 Move to bottom right together

environment because it is able to execute more potent, internally integrated action as an effective response to external challenge. This is an example of *friction creates the pearl* introduced at the outset of this book.

Ryan and Deci: Self-Determination

Chris believed that a boss is not likely to influence behavior by manipulation, at least not in a healthy way. Instead, he believed as Ryan and Deci stated: "behavioral outcomes are most easily changed by appealing to the person's motives, goals, and expectations or by altering the proximal features of social environments that give rise to them."[28] Labeled self-determination theory (SDT), it hypothesizes that an individual's behavior is self-motivated and self-determined. SDT states human nature can be active and social or derailed and fragmented, the direction of which is determined by the environment in which the person inhabits. SDT makes "the assumption that there is a human nature, which is deeply designed to be active and social and which, when afforded a 'good enough' (i.e., a basic-need-supportive) environment, will move toward thriving, wellness, and integrity."[29]

Similar to Pink's findings, the researchers identified three basic psychological needs that, depending on the degree to which they are fed or starved, determine the quality of wellness. These needs are autonomy, competence, and relatedness. Autonomy surfaces many interpretations, but in this case, it means "one's behaviors are self-endorsed, or congruent with one's authentic interests and values.... [so that] when acting with autonomy, behaviors are engaged wholeheartedly."[30] Competence stems from feelings of mastery and effectiveness which is self-motivating.

However, competence may be derailed when the challenge is intimidating, criticism by others is felt, or when confidence in one's mastery is diminished or undermined. Relatedness, as we've explored, emerges when one feels socially connected with others and feels a sense of being cared-for or belongingness. We can conclude that "aspects of a social context that are likely to support satisfaction of the fundamental psychological needs are predicted to promote effective functioning."[31] No doubt, Chris fostered the proper context for this to occur at Apex.

Gittell: Relational Coordination

Like most business people, Chris admired actions he observed in organizational life. He remembered a trip he had made years ago when fuel prices were skyrocketing. Waiting for a flight to board, he engaged a Southwest Airlines agent. He was making small talk about the rising fuel prices at the time.

"Those fuel prices must be eating into your profits, eh?"

Anticipating a blank stare in response, Chris was quite surprised when the agent said, "Not at Southwest. We hedged fuel prices about two months ago."

Pleasantly surprised that a gate agent knew the firm's policy on fuel acquisition, Chris later discovered the airline was fully engaged in the theory of relational coordination, developed by Jody Hoffer Gittell. As referenced earlier, she discovered interdependent work is most effectively coordinated by frontline workers engaging each other, their customers, and their leaders, through relationships of shared goals, shared knowledge, and mutual respect.

Colleen Barrett, who followed Herb Kelleher at Southwest Airlines, directed her attention to developing a culture of interdependence throughout her tenure. The effect of that effort on SWA workers was illustrated through stark comparison of Southwest to a larger competitor, American.

The two carriers were quite different. "Interviews with frontline employees at American revealed that they had little awareness of the overall work process, and instead had a tendency to understand their own piece of the process to the exclusion of the rest [of the employees],"[32] wrote Gittell. "By contrast, interviews with Southwest frontline employees revealed that they understood the overall work process—and the links between their own jobs and the jobs performed by their counterparts in other functions."[33] The takeaway is simple: when asked to describe their job, they did so in relation to the other functions. Employees understood the puzzle and what piece they owned.

Early on, Barrett "began organizing systems, processes, and rituals that would essentially create and preserve what we now call resonance. She took charge of many of the processes that guided people's behavior within the company and with customers."[34] This is an example of what Schein calls the inculcation of *basic taken-for-granted assumptions*. "The earliest shared learning provides meaning and stability and becomes, in a sense, *the cultural DNA*: the beliefs, values, and desired behaviors that launched the group and made it successful."[35]

So as Chris installed a new culture at Apex, he examined what was already present at the company.[36] His ongoing discussion with employees revealed the pain points and incongruences that workers experienced day-to-day. Acknowledging the dynamics of the inherited culture is the first step to effectively shaping the desired future culture. After his conversation with his mother, Chris realized reading all the books on leadership doesn't really mean much if you don't have the presence of mind to put that knowledge to use when it is most needed. He convened Apex people to ask the simple question, "Should we provide the quickie report requested by the customer?"

Chris recognized that over the term of his career, some 30 years, the workplace had changed. Teams were different. His observations are supported by researchers as well, "They're far more diverse, dispersed, digital, and dynamic (with frequent changes in membership)."[37] As we've witnessed, Chris is committed to creating a collaborative workplace where work bridges the many functions and levels in a firm. As the leader, he sees his duty to create a high-performance environment. That means dealing with the truth, expanding the knowledge to confront challenges, and create safety for members taking bold action, the sum and substance of Part II.

When it comes to teamwork, he learned it works best when people have clear, compelling direction; with the right mix and number of members well designed with productive processes in place. They have the information and sufficient rewards and are supported fully, in some cases, even when working remotely or from the road. Often, the only impediment is an us vs. them mindset, a conflict that must be put to rest. Chris saw his role was to orchestrate a response, not dictate the response.

The upgrades of motivation over time have advanced from mere survival to extrinsic to intrinsic. We learned simple tasks with a clear path to a solution can be positively affected by extrinsic rewards. However, they may also have detrimental effects on intrinsic motivation, performance, and creativity. This may even create ethical concerns and short-term thinking. These issues all run counter to Chris' mode of operation. He prefers to motivate people by appealing to what they enjoy or find interesting, their natural inclinations.

Chris has always held a Theory Y mindset. He believes people generally like work, are self-directed, seek and accept responsibility, are motivated by the desire to realize their own potential and are creative, though not recognized as such.[38] For this reason Apex values included meritocracy, proactivity, and teamwork. Pink's thesis on motivation fits with Apex, especially in the intrinsic sense. This informed Chris that going deep on extrinsic motivation may not be a good fit for Apex due to its emphasis on "carrots and sticks." Pink's research showed tangible rewards work in performing technical challenges but are counterproductive to moving people to buy-in on an adaptive challenge.

Experiments suggested contingent rewards—"if, then"—had a negative effect because such offers cause people to forfeit their autonomy, and essentially snuff out the power of their natural curiosities. "Rewards, by their very nature, narrow our focus ... and blinkered the wide view that might have allowed ... [people to see] ... new uses for an old object."[39] In a world where seeing new possibilities produces innovation, Motivation 2.0 is an inadequate motivator; whereas Motivation 3.0 hits the sweet spot.

Drath: Relational Dialogue

Chris had a sixth sense, call it intuition, that one always had to keep vigilant, even in the best of times, especially in the best of times. He considered it healthy paranoia. He'd say, "The problem with having a lot of success is you begin to believe you're successful!" While it may sound like false humility to some, to Chris, it reminded him you're only as good as your last act. If you think you can't fail, you'll probably become complacent, or worse, arrogant. Chris believed falling into such a state makes one blind to threats and dangers. He frequently warned, "Win one, then pop off!"

No wonder Chris favored a leadership model that rejected strict reliance on the principles of leader dominance or leader influence. While dominant leaders were effective at setting direction and causing people to passionately pursue a vision, their dependency on the enigmatic personality—the power of the persona—had a vulnerability. What if the vision, the direction, following the leader failed to deliver followers to the promised land? "When the leader's personal direction proves to be less than effective, the basis of leadership itself is undermined."[40] Chris couldn't afford this to happen.

For similar reasons, Chris viewed leader influence in a similar vein with parallel concerns. Leaders who chose to exercise interpersonal influence as the determining factor to buy-in run the risk of defining leadership as a "negotiated outcome, a vector of differing perspectives resolved in the vision of the leader—the person who emerges as having the most influence."[41] In his mind, influence had to be multidirectional.

While soliciting the perspectives of the entire group is a good practice, how are the tasks of leadership—direction, commitment, and adaptive challenge—discharged? Does the process of interpersonal influence yield leadership? Or, is it a contrivance "composed of the convergence of parts, the revitalizing of differing perspectives into a whole"?[42] The principle of interpersonal influence may have the appearance of leadership, but it contains none of the sum and substance such as commitment and resolve, that leadership must deliver to generate buy-in.

While all members may benefit when the leader creates a climate of free expression, if the tasks of leadership are contingent on interpersonal influence, then leadership fails to reap the benefits that come from "embracing the differences, [establishing] an openness to the continuous unfolding of possibility."[43]

Thus, Chris believed the principles of leader dominance and leader influence fail to imbue members of the organization with compelling drive and sustainable energy—the kind of buy-in that emerges with commitment and eagerness to pursue the desired outcome. Remember, Chris saw the firm as a meritocracy, where people advanced in the firm not through persuasive rhetoric, rather they earned it in deeds or actions that created value for the organization. He had seen leaders who attempted to create win-win scenarios accomplishing little more than convincing themselves that buy-in had been secured by portraying it as a transactional arrangement.

It is important to note that governing structures of businesses may have significant impact on their performance. In a capitalistic society in particular, meritocracy advocates claim it's not only the best way to organize but is the only way to fairly reward individuals. Critics rightfully warn that managers operating in a meritocracy may exhibit a paradoxical behavior. See Figure 6.3 illustrating the good and the bad.

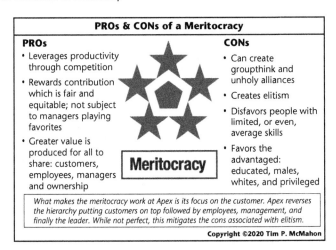

FIGURE 6.3 There is no perfect governing system for a business, reversing the order, putting customer on top, helps

Lest we think it is a panacea, let it be known that there is significant research that points to ill effects of a meritocracy. For example, in conducting three experiments with a total of 445 participants, Castilla and Benard discovered, "the main finding … consistent across the three studies: when an organization is explicitly presented as meritocratic, individuals in managerial positions favor a male employee over an equally qualified female employee by rewarding him a larger monetary reward."[44]

The researchers suggest it might be productive to study the effect of increasing transparency or accountability in the workplace, which "have been shown to reduce the expression of bias both experimentally (e.g., Lerner & Tetlock, 1999) and in field studies (e.g., Castilla, 2008)."[45] Suffice to say, Chris's prioritization of customer at the top of the pyramid indicates the beneficiary of managerial decisions defaults to creating value that will manifest in competitive advantage; and not, in biased behavior if managers were the ultimate deciders.

As detailed above, Chris embraced a third option, relational dialogue, as a means to accomplish the tasks of leadership, with special attention to the creation of buy-in—"the acceptance of and willingness to actively support and participate in something (such as a new plan or policy)."[46] Commitment is generated through shared creation. Leadership is not something *out there* that's objectively waiting to happen. Instead, it's something intersubjective, the product of relationships.

This concept is essentially socially constructed; embraces four assumptions to help us understand the thinking which drives social construction. They are (a) letting go creates new possibilities, (b) relationship creates meaning, (c) we can fashion our future, and (d) reflection hones our assessment. Kenneth Gergen wrote, "As we animate these assumptions in our work and our lives more generally, they may have significant if not dramatic potential."[47]

TAKE-AWAYS

- Culture is a broad bucket that serves as a receptacle for a variety of organizational challenges. Culture is the learned beliefs, values, symbols, artifacts, traditions, and general way members of an organization choose to adopt and preserve. It is both intangible and real. It's a set of unwritten rules held by long-term members and taught to new members as a way to think and act. It will serve an organization to adopt a holding environment
- Influence is more than reasoned argument, as persuasion involves reputation, prestige, personality, purpose, status, content of message, interpersonal and group skills, give-and-take behaviors, authority or lack of it, symbolic interaction, perception, motivation, gender, race, religion, and choices, among countless other factors.
- Leadership is an influence relationship. Active leaders and followers are the components of leadership. This role of leadership exercises power and authority to accomplish organizational goals and objectives.
- Since leadership is leaders and followers in an influence relationship, they use the power resources available to them to persuade one another to accomplish what's necessary for the organization to thrive.
- The most effective way to activate leaders and followers is to entrust them to solve a problem that affects the ability of the firm to deliver value. This is critical to turn the entire process from identification to implementation over to the people most responsible. It works because people activate when they see genuine purpose and value in themselves. Solving problems creates self-confidence.
- Bureaucracy is the obstacle to getting and keeping customers. To eliminate bureaucracy, speed up, and simplify. What's more, the outcome is more than getting and keeping customers it's also the self-confidence that grows in people and teams.
- A culture that develops a strong bond between leaders and followers also builds the connections to keep the organization energized and immune to the deleterious effects of a workplace lost in a bureaucracy, incapable of facing external challenges.
- It's important to distinguish between management and leadership. The distinction is that under leadership, leaders and followers work to address real change; whereas management coordinates actions to do the job. We make this distinction because it allows us to see clearly there's a place for each. Formal authority has a critical role in keeping the firm focused on execution. Leadership is about seeking adaptive and constructive change.

- Six theories inform the concept of influence in relationships that creates understanding and resolve. They are Goleman's emotional intelligence, Ryan & Deci's self-determination, Gittell's related coordination, Hackman's, Haas & Mortenson's theories on teamwork, Pink's motivation 3.0, and Drath's relational dialogue.

Notes

1 Gittell, J. H. (2003). *The Southwest Airlines way: Using high power of relationships to achieve high performance*. New York, NY: McGraw-Hill, (p. 26).
2 Boyatzis, R. & McKee, A. (2005). *Resonant leadership: Renewing yourself and connecting others through mindfulness, hope, and compassion*. Boston, MA: Harvard Business School Press.
3 Rost, J. C. (1993). *Leadership for the 21st century*. Westport, CT: Praeger, (p. 105).
4 Schein, E. H. (2017). *Organizational culture and leadership* (5th ed.). Hoboken, NJ: Wiley & Sons, Inc., (p. 320).
5 Ibid, (p. 1)
6 Heifetz, R., Grashow, A., & Linsky, M. (2009). *The practice of adaptive leadership: Tools and tactics for changing your organization and the world*. Boston, MA: Harvard Business Press, (p. 295).
7 Willingham, R. (2003). *Integrity selling for the 21stcentury: How to sell the way people want to buy*. New York, NY: Currency Doubleday. Willingham refers to the loving arms of a mother holding a new-born infant as the original holding environment. Expanding on the metaphor, Willingham wrote: "The relationship of the individual to his or her internal objects, along with confidence in regard to internal relationships, provides of itself a sufficiency of living, so that temporarily he or she is able to rest contented even in the absence of external objects and stimuli Maturity and the capacity to be alone implies that the individual has had the chance through good-enough mothering to build up a belief in a benign environment." (p. 32).
8 Heifetz, et al., (p. 105).
9 Detasseling. (03/04/20). In Wikipedia. Retrieved November 16, 2020, from http://en.wikipedia.org/wiki/Detasseling. Detasseling corn is a farm chore. It is used to produce hybrid seed corn. Hybrid corn is a specialized crop produced when two different variety seeds are planted and crossed-pollinated to produce a third variety. The process requires tassels on top of the plant to be removed from one variety leaves the grain growing on that plant to be fertilized by the tassels of the other variety. Seed corn growers usually use teenagers to physically remove the tassels and place them on the ground. Typically, a machine removes the majority of tassels. However, it may only remove between 30 and 90%. For effective uniformity, 99.7% of the tassels must be removed, so the remainder are detasseled by hand.
10 Tichy, N. M., & Sherman, S. (2001). *Control your destiny or someone else will*. New York: HarperBusiness, (p. 586).
11 Ibid, (p. 586).
12 Ulrich, D., Kerr, S., & Ashkenas, R. (2002). *The GE Work-Out: How to implement GE's revolutionary method for busting bureaucracy and attacking organizational problems—fast!* New York, NY: McGraw Hill Education. [Kindle Edition], (loc. 3711).
13 Northouse, P. G. (2019). *Leadership: Theory and practice*. (8th ed.). Thousand Oaks, CA: Sage, (p. 434).
14 Ibid, (p. 18).
15 Boyatzis & McKee, (p. 6).

16 Ibid, (p. 21).
17 Gittell, (p. 85).
18 Ibid, (p. 13).
19 Boyatzis, & McKee, (p. 132).
20 Ryan, R. M. & Deci, E. L. (2017). *Self-determination theory: Basic psychological needs in motivation, development, and wellness*. New York, NY: The Guilford Press.
21 Gittell, J. H. (2003). *The Southwest Airlines way: Using high power of relationships to achieve high performance*. New York, NY: McGraw-Hill, (p. 26).
22 Haas, M., & Mortensen, M. (June 2016). The secrets of great teamwork. *Harvard Business Review*. [Reprint R1606E].
23 Ibid
24 Pink, D. H. (2009). *Drive: The surprising truth about what motivates us*. New York, NY: Riverhead Books, (p. 18).
25 Drath, W. (2001). *The deep blue sea: Rethinking the source of leadership*. San Francisco, CA: Jossey-Bass, (p. 14–15).
26 Ibid, (p. 19).
27 Chaleff, I. (1995). *The courageous follower: Standing up to and for our leaders*. San Francisco: Berrett-Koehler, (p. 23)
28 Ryan, R. M. & Deci, E. L. (2017). *Self-determination theory: Basic psychological needs in motivation, development, and wellness*. New York, NY: The Guilford Press, (p. 3).
29 Ibid, (p. 3).
30 Ibid, (p. 3).
31 Ibid, (p. 3).
32 Haas & Mortenson, (pp. 31–32).
33 Ibid, (p. 32).
34 Boyatzis & McKee, (p. 21).
35 Schein, E. H. (2017). *Organizational culture and leadership* (5th ed.). Hoboken, NJ: Wiley & Sons, Inc., (p. 6).
36 Ibid, Schein points to these powerful means to embed their own assumptions. They include: what they pay attention to and reward, through ways in which they allocate resources, through their role modeling, through the manner in which they deal with critical incidents, and through the criteria they use for recruitment, selection, promotion, and excommunication.
37 Haas, M., & Mortensen, M. (June 2016). The secrets of great teamwork. *Harvard Business Review*. [Reprint R1606E].
38 Dating back to the 1950s, MIT professor Douglas McGregor developed two theories (X and Y) to describe how people responded to motivation. It describes two contrasting sets of assumptions that managers make about their people: Theory X suggests people dislike work, have little ambition, and are unwilling to take responsibility. Theory Y states the opposite: people like to work under their own initiative, want to be a part of decision making and generally take ownership of their tasks. Theory Y managers (those who lean that way) are more likely to relinquish control and hold people accountable for their actions.
39 Pink, D. H. (2009). *Drive: The surprising truth about what motivates us*. New York, NY: Riverhead Books, (p. 38).
40 Drath, (p. 23).
41 Ibid, (p. 24).
42 Ibid, (p. 24).
43 Ibid, (p. 24).
44 Castilla, E. J. & Benard, S. (December 2010). The paradox of meritocracy in organizations, *Administrative Science Quarterly, 55*(4), 543.
45 Ibid, (p. 571).
46 Buy-in. (2018). In *Merriam-Webster's collegiate dictionary*. [Pro App].
47 Gergen, K. J. (2007). *An invitation to social construction*. San Francisco: Sage, (p. 47).

7

REAL CHANGE IS IN RENEWAL

Leadership expert James McGregor Burns described authority as legitimated power rooted in tradition, rights of succession, and even religious sanction and not by a mandate of the people. He wrote it was quite one-sided: "Rulers had the right to command, subjects the obligation to obey."[1] Burns asserted this remained uncontested because people had a need for order and security and in exchange offered their obedience. Yet, Burns questioned why "humankind should have made such limited progress in developing propositions about leadership—propositions that focus on the role of the ruled, the power recipients, and the followers."[2] Burns wrote: "If we see leaders as interacting with followers in a great merging of motivations and purposes of both, and if in turn, we find that many of those motivations and purposes are common to vast numbers of humankind in many cultures, then could we expect to identify patterns of leadership behavior permitting plausible generalizations about the ways in which leaders generally behave?"[3]

Scholars have pursued that hypothesis for four decades. What we ask now is: How can leaders and followers working in unison develop "a capacity for renewal: an organization's ability to understand, interact with, shape, and adapt to changes in its situation and the external environment."[4]

The idea of renewal suggests bringing something back to life. It lends itself to reconceiving organizations as vibrant places of collaboration and collective accomplishment. This chapter is dedicated to pursuing how renewal is the wellspring of real change.

Emphasis on "Intend"

Burns recognized, "The leadership process must be defined, in short, as carrying through from decision-making stages to the point of concrete changes in people's lives, attitudes, behaviors, institutions."[5] Burns identified the "test is purpose and intent, drawn from values and goals, of leaders, high and low, resulting in policy decision and real, intended change."[6]

To clarify, Rost stipulates that "leadership is a relationship of leaders and followers who *intend* real changes, not who *produce* real changes."[7] Underpinning this distinction is his assertion that an effective outcome is not part and parcel of the existence of leadership. He wrote: "A relationship wherein leaders and followers intend real changes but are unsuccessful or ineffective, or achieve only minimum changes, is still leadership. Leaders and followers can fail to achieve real changes and still be in a relationship called leadership."[8]

On its surface, this idea will strike many as heresy, or simply futile. Failure to pay homage to what many believe is the very measure of leadership—the desired result—will surely create suspicion. Yet, therein lies the red flag. When we revert to a definition that mandates a specific result, we shift our focus from process to outcome. While it may feel right to tie actions to outcome, by doing so, it's easy for a leader to get caught up in pursuit of the goal vis-à-vis pursuit of the *right* goal through a process that is adopted by members of the organization.

Adopting a way to pursue intentions of the firm is far more valuable than obtaining a result. Pursuing the result often leads to unintended consequences such as an ethical lapse, a default to coercion, or worse, the dissolution of leadership.

The Fuel of an Ethical Lapse?

Kenneth Goodpaster warns of the seductive power of goals. Specifically, he states when people become fixated on goals, "they tend to rationalize or even deny responsibilities and realities that might impede the accomplishment of those goals and purposes ... [and they often demonstrate] a general separation of the ethics of business goals from the ethics of everyday life, leading to emotional *detachment* regarding the full human implications of pursuing these goals."[9]

Goodpaster dubbed this phenomenon *teleopathy* and considers it exists in an unbalanced pursuit of the goals at the expense of moral considerations "about means, obligations, and duties."[10] See the three symptoms of teleopathy in Figure 7.1.

In such circumstances, the voices of dissent are hushed. Hopefully by now, the value of loyal opposition has been established, so you'll recognize any attempt to snuff it out will be seen for what it is—a buy-in crusher. In enlightened organizations like the new Apex, people must challenge in order to be good followers and must listen to be good leaders. As Chris often reminded, "If you don't speak up when I am being foolish or ill-informed, you're undermining the whole place,

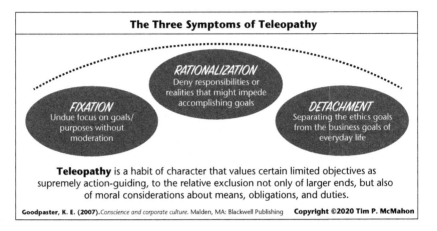

FIGURE 7.1 Teleopathy rises from an unbalanced pursuit of goals

especially me!" This is an unexpected response to someone who typically sees dissent as a roadblock, not a guide rail.

Detrimental Effects of Coercion

While we speak often about leadership with respect to adaptive challenges, *management* is an effective method to resolve technical challenges.[11] The distinguishing feature of management is the basis of authority. "Authority is a contractual (written, spoken, or implied) relationship wherein people accept superordinate or subordinate responsibilities in an organization."[12] The transactional nature of management includes both coercive and noncoercive actions. For example, when a manager tells an employee to perform a specific task, she is exerting her will on the subordinate, the very definition of coercion. Not all management actions are coercive, but all will be viewed by followers as part of the implied contract.

"While subordinates may resent some coercive behaviors—for instance, a police officer giving a person a ticket for running a red light—most subordinates accept the general pattern of coercive action in the management of organizations—for instance, a law requiring everyone to stop at red lights and police officer enforces the law."[13] Since we value our safety, we have laws that provide for sanctions against behavior that threatens our well-being. However, coercive tactics can be detrimental in situations that call for adaptive leadership.

In adaptive situations, followers and leaders are far better served to employ influence, not coercion. Each aims to move people to an action. Coercion employs force, demands obedience, threatens dire consequences for failure to comply, or psychologically intimidates; whereas influence is aimed at persuading one to adopt, or at least consider, an alternate point of view. This is why having a vision and understanding a firm's purpose is necessary.

The chief difference between coercion and influence is that the latter affords personal choice. An individual in an organization may choose to buy-in or not. With choice, the individual has the freedom to dissent. So, it is incumbent on leaders to provide for people to question, or to borrow a colloquialism, be the devil's advocate. This inspires meaningful dialogue while sidestepping the air of personal attack and leads a robust understanding of the issues and clear view of the direction of the firm.

Dissolution of Leadership

The most injurious result of suppressing dissent is that leaders nullify the benefit of inspiring new possibilities through vigorous debate. The definition of leadership used here is premised on leaders and followers being in a relationship. Make no mistake in this book, it does not occur in a democracy. Rather, it's a meritocracy.[14] The relationship is a means to invigorate, not enfeeble or placate. Confining individuals to accomplish a pre-determined outcome—especially in a situation where certainty of the action is questionable—undermines leadership as members know it. Further, by relentlessly pursuing the goal—especially in light of legitimate contrarian concern—they douse the energy and commitment that followers may have embraced in their role in articulating the leadership relationship.

Leadership Reset

From the opening words from Burns, the roots of leadership have been called into question. As long as we retain a romantic image of an action figure riding in to save the day, the more we entertain the notion that authority springs from social position or arbitrary tradition. If life is pre-ordained, or fatalistic, we are less likely to surrender the power of individual choice and freedom to pursue ennobling possibilities. After all, in such a world, there is no personal choice. What will be will be.

Similarly, continuing to believe that there is a solution flowing from the magic wand of the leader is foolish optimism. In the business of change management, this is often the culprit inspiring failure. In reality, it has been long accepted that "we no longer live in a world where we have the right to expect authorities to know the answers [except for technical challenges]. The adaptive challenges facing businesses demand [more] … ongoing changes in habits, attitudes, and values of people high and low in the workplace."[15]

Chris was committed to maintaining a mindset that leadership is a relationship, free of coercion, and relentlessly open to confronting the truth, as terrifying as it might be. Chris relied on a time-tested truth: take your orders from the situation and that undoubtedly involves the customer!

A VISIT WITH MOM TO REAFFIRM CONVICTIONS

CHRIS: *I think the peeps are beginning to understand that I really expect to hear their concerns about the direction of the business.*

AGNES: *You know, Chris, people don't like to argue with the boss ...*

CHRIS: *Well, some do! (hearty laugh) But, yea, it is difficult to make them understand, I mean it when I say, they need to be the eyes and ears of the customer. Listen to the customer. Act on their behalf and all will be well.*

AGNES: *But you call on customers all the time don't you?*

CHRIS: *But they're at the top of the house. We need customers feedback from top to bottom. We should be better at understanding the customers issues than they do. When we do our jobs right, and that means listening and observing at every step and every level, we see a picture of our customer's organization that's better than they could see themselves!*

AGNES: *What's your plan for making that happen?*

CHRIS: *Same as always. Do what I expect them to do and always keep on task if we intend real change, and we do. Great places are always evolving and renewing.*

Chris was a "do-as-I-do" kind of guy. He believed the boss makes the weather. If the top guy is concerned about something, everyone ought to be concerned. If someone, and it could be anyone, has a key observation of a customer thought or action, he or she must bring it forward. Air it out. Chris believed the more snapshots his people could collect about a customer, the better they could make sense out of the changing customer needs and wants ... the better they could diagnose exactly where Apex needed to help them make progress against their situation.

It's Like Making a Movie

The challenge humans and organizations have with commitment is that for them to buy-in they must first understand. Did you ever notice that trying to make sense out of a situation can be very difficult? For example, it's difficult to see patterns in behavior over time. Patterns are composed of thousands of snapshots. Seeing behaviors of co-workers that might bring clarity to a situation may not happen every day or may occur only under certain circumstances. So, if reality cannot be experienced, the situation is not readily understood, or is understood in a less than clear manner.

Think about going to a movie. In a couple of hours of uninterrupted viewing, characters are revealed, schemes are unveiled, and motives identified. However, life plays out in bits and pieces over time, it can be difficult to see all the pieces of the puzzle, let alone make sense of it all. Further, the actors may be more or less candid depending on the contest, who is present and with that which they are engaged. In other words, not always transparent.

For leaders to construct an understanding of what is happening, it is necessary to collect those snapshots, store them in collective memory, and allow the subconscious to let the patterns emerge. It's just like it happens in the movies: frame-by-frame, scene-by-scene in a revelatory manner. To catalyze this process, individuals may engage in relational dialogue.

Organizations face adaptive challenge in one of three ways: the leader identifies the challenge and solution through her eyes; through a negotiation of leader influence; or through dialogue. Leaders and followers need to engage in an exchange that will "organize truths capable of making sense of leadership in a context of an enduring difference, of unity in embracing diversity."[16]

Optimizing Diversity

Diversity—envisioned as many voices in the choir—optimizes the power of the organization. Members embrace the idea that the "interconnection of the world is not just global. It is also local. Just as different parts of the world re interconnected, so are different parts of communities, and different parts of organizations, and different groups of people."[17]

With respect to Apex, Chris recognizes that there is institutional knowledge, an asset, held by members. Through their shared work and mutual respect for each member's perspective, the firm can apprehend a deeper understanding of the adaptive challenge the firm faces. Wilfred Drath hypothesizes the elements of relational dialogue are:

- People holding differing worldviews are involved in mutually acknowledged shared work;
- The differing worldviews are held as if they were equally worthy, true, real;
- The leadership tasks are relevant but not capable of being accomplished across worldviews; and
- No person can be the leader and create leadership without giving up the equal gravity of differing perspectives.

It must be noted that conflict will certainly arise in an environment of different and many opposing views. This too, is good, as long as the leaders and followers involved are able to amiably resolve conflict. To resolve conflict parties must identify the issues to be clear that a problem exists. By understanding interests of all, it is possible to generate possible solutions that will appeal to factions so as to construct a foundation for resolution.

Roger Fisher and William Ury[18] warned against entrenchment: "The more attention that is paid to positions, less attention is devoted to meeting underlying concern of parties. Agreement becomes less likely."[19] Each side holding dearly to their positions and offering little concession will result in a potential stalemate. Parties will stall, stonewall and object or stall, in an effort to prevail.

The negotiation experts offer a concept of principled negotiation to accomplish resolution. The negotiation experts recommend parties not bargain over positions. Rather, it is best to separate people from the problem, focus on interests, not positions, invent options for mutual gain, and insist on using objective criteria.

When leaders and followers are able to "organize common sense and common experience in a way that provides a usable framework for thinking and acting … the more consistent these ideas are with your knowledge and intuition …"[20] the more likely a firm can turn differences into opportunities.

The Quandary

Chris faces a looming problem in that Apex' largest client is asking for a product that he believes will not supply sufficient information to mitigate lending risk. This is an example of a clash of worldviews. Think of it in terms of a challenge for principled negotiation where seeing the problem through the other's eyes is the starting point. Consider these differing points-of-view (POV):

> From the client's perspective, if they don't shorten the interval between loan application and approval, they will lose significant market share to competitors who are providing such products.

> From the inside Apex, the sales force believes their duty is to help their client make progress against their situation, which at this point is about cutting time to issue approval. If they will not meet the clients' needs, they will lose the business.

> From the operations perspective within Apex, such a product would reduce cost significantly—an ever-present objective—while generating revenue. If we can make money, we should provide it.

> From competitor point-of-view, competition is brutal so what must be done, must be done, they'll offer the product.

Chris sees it from a different worldview. If Apex provides this product; they will sacrifice their ethical beliefs and may still lose the business. If Chris unilaterally denies the product, certain doom awaits. Scenarios indicate as much as 50% of revenue and 40% of employees would be lost. The brutal reality of these events creates anxiety, both in leaders and followers, leading each to entrenchment within their POV. However, failing to deal with the truth of the matter, may cause short-term pain, but long-term extinction when it abandons its values.

The True Test of Leadership

A fundamental theme in this book is that leadership flows from meaning, not the reverse. That is, members remain open and aware and take their direction from the situation. For this to happen, members must be engaged, aware of their surroundings, and in sync with one another. Dialogue helps create the snapshots of reality that once arranged in a coherent pattern produce the movie in Technicolor clarity. Members of the firm in dialogue present a meeting of the minds where everyone cannot only see what's happening (understanding multiple POVs exist) but may also suggest ways to address the challenge.

The leader has several paths she may take. However, even the best conceived solution will crumble under the weight of member skepticism and accompanying uncertainty and anxiety. When a mastermind writes up the marching orders, as if carefully choreographing the movements of the orchestra, the missing element is human response. If employees, customers, regulators, shareholders, and myriad stakeholders—who hold the success of the plan in their hands—fail to see themselves in the solution, the energy behind execution dissipates and the solution ultimately rests in peace as yet another failed attempt at managing change.

There is another way. Specifically, it permits all parties to see themselves in the solution, that is recognize their position has been acknowledged and incorporated into alternatives for discussion. Chris said, "This is negotiation. It's part of any selling scenario inside or out. I read this line in a book on negotiation that summarizes the way we should treat each other. It is about 'being hard on the issues and soft on the people.'[21] Instead of attacking each other, you attack the problem."

Conducting the Orchestra

We learned in Chapter 2 that it pays to vigorously confront reality. Putting spin on the hard facts serves only to distort and confuse. The leader must clarify the challenge and unite the troops behind a plan to deal with the truth.

In all movements, there's a vision, at least there should be. It serves to provide direction, energy, and engagement. "But such a vision doesn't belong only to the leader. It must be shared. Everyone has hopes dreams, and aspirations. Everyone wants tomorrow to be better than today. Shared visions attract more people, sustain higher levels of motivation, and withstand more challenges than those exclusive to only a few. You must make sure what you can see is also something that others can see."[22] Developing an environment where people can see ennobling possibilities is highly compelling.

Consider a symphony leader choosing to play to the most prestigious audience ever, and deciding it was acceptable to play with inferior instruments, or the lower level of accomplished musicians. This is unthinkable. For such an occasion, everything must be optimal and must draw upon the exceptional abilities, not the pedestrian. The leader is the conductor. In Figure 7.2, you see she doesn't play all

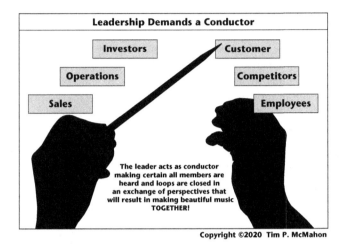

FIGURE 7.2 Leader as conductor

the parts but masters the ability for all to play to their fullest in concert with one another. Recognize that there are many players contributing to the final performance. So, how does a firm appeal to the greatest potential in each member?

Expand and Enable Personal Control: Autonomy

Unless people feel some comfortable level of control in making a decision, they seldom fully buy-in to the execution of the decision. The primary problem lies in the anxiety human beings have in events not in their control. If people are unable to plan, they are less likely to fully buy-in to the execution of the decision. Planning is dependent on future conditions and events, often unpredictable.

"The greatest achievement of the human brain is its ability to imagine objects and episodes that do not exist in the realm of the real, and it is this ability to think about the future."[23] Daniel Gilbert believes there're at least two ways in which humans construct concepts of their future. The first is basic and is inherent in nearly every creature; constructing that concept is based on experience.

For example, wild rabbits often make their nests in the open spaces, hidden in plain sight, so to speak. They have learned predators seldom hunt in open spaces, so their bunnies are safest out in the open. Rabbits, and "other machines and invertebrates prove that it doesn't take a smart, self-aware conscious brain to make simple predictions about the future."[24] They're not predicting so much as they're *nexting*. Nexting describes the continual process of predicting what is likely to happen next, based on external stimuli. Not predicting, nexting. It is about reading the situation and responding intuitively.

That brings us to the second means of creating a future view. This one is the sole purview of the human brain. In a strange turn of events, prominent scientists discovered a couple of observations about our brains, specifically, the frontal lobe of our brain. In examining patients with frontal lobe brain damage, scientists discovered patients were in a calm state. Learning this, medical researchers found that severing the two hemispheres of the frontal lobe—called a frontal lobotomy—produced beneficial treatment outcomes for anxiety-ridden patients.

The procedure was so effective at reducing the disruptive effects brought on by anxiety and depression that physicians began to perform frontal lobotomies on patients they diagnosed with such maladies but continued to suffer from disruptive symptoms.

The Fly in the Ointment

In observing these patients post-op, researchers determined they were normal in every way. They could feed themselves and engage in light conversation. However, they demonstrated another behavior that had become associated only with patients who had the frontal lobotomy: they had no ability to plan. They couldn't say what they were doing next week, or even the coming afternoon. "For instance, when given a maze or puzzle whose solution required that they consider an entire series of moves before making their first move, these otherwise intelligent people were stumped."[25]

What we can draw from these two discoveries—the calming effect and the loss of planning ability? People exercise their frontal lobe when they look into the future to predict an outcome. As a matter of fact, this is the only part of the brain that permits us the luxury of envisioning a future state. Humans are the only beings with this ability. Studies show we spend about 12% of our time peering into future events. If you have tried to meditate, or tune into the present in a deep way, you know how difficult it is to stop thinking about the future. Why? What causes humans to exercise their frontal lobe and step into the future?

Chris would often allow himself a little time for daydreaming. He said it was a way to escape into a big pleasurable thought. Call it positive thinking, that's what Norman Vincent Peale labeled this exercise in envisioning your future. Considered controversial to many, because he had little substantive evidence to support his claims, Peale nonetheless developed a legion of followers. And why not, he was appealing to our innate desire to imagine our future and plan accordingly to make it happen.

The message here is that unless one can see themselves in the future, they are not likely to be exhilarated by it coming to fruition. People will follow your dream if they can be made to see themselves as an active participant in bringing it to life. It is the vision that compels us to embrace the plan to make the future happen. It is fundamentally about bringing predictions to life.

Predictions permit us to do something about our current state of affairs that might provide us happiness or allow us to avoid loss. Think of how nice it would be if you could predict with certainty how a game might end or how the stock market may perform. To use a popular phrase: it's a game-changer! We are so attached to this need to create our imagined future, that experiments have proven that from birth to death. If people lose "their ability to control things at any point between their entrance and their exit, they become unhappy, helpless, hopeless, and depressed."[26] But control is elusive. Effectively planning a future for one's self is difficult enough, how does a leader engage followers in the dream?

Don't Just Shout, Talk it Out

Our thesis in this chapter is people can be more effective if leaders and followers influence one another in relational dialogue, a principle that "recognizes leadership as an embracing of differences, an openness to the continuous unfolding of possibility."[27] People become empowered when they cultivate a course of action together. This is a daring departure for leaders who fear taking *their eyes off the prize*, so to speak, when they defer to rapidly deploying *their* gut instinct in favor of members committing to "the process of crafting a future in which individuals have no way of knowing what the personal outcome will be. Commitment is to transformation toward an unknown future."[28]

The assumption is that when leadership is recognized as leaders and followers, "crafting of a sensible but unresolved whole out of differing and even conflicting worldviews, its capacity for flexibility of understanding in the face of an adaptive challenge is great."[29] This demands trust, emboldened by an atmosphere of trustworthiness. Moreover, the leader must know when the problem is technical or adaptive. If technical, a leader may allow her well-honed intuition to kick in and rule the day since follower's likely share the intuitive instinct.

Technical problems are swiftly resolved when known solutions are proven and a quick outcome is achieved. Adaptive problems demand an *all-hands-on-deck* approach where the solution will bubble up from the group through collaboration that plays out in widespread member understanding and commitment. Adaptive problem solving is transformative over time as the vision sharpens and values become ingrained in the individual and the collective.

Lest we think this is a process that's simply self-affirming—everyone feeling good about the workplace—be certain that leaders must always keep the evolving organization foundation intact through these practices:

- Sharpening the focus on vision and values as the bedrock of the organization;
- Maintaining strict adherence to customer-centricity;
- Remaining nimbleness and adaptive capacity through flat structures;
- Demonstrating ongoing respect for employees; and
- Committing to individual and organizational growth and development.

Effective Change Flows Through Healthy Organizations

Scott Keller and Colin Price conducted extensive research to understand why change initiatives frequently fail due to poor organizational health. Drawing on access to McKinsey & Co. to thousands of clients in 57 countries, the pair consulted experts in three areas—business colleagues, senior executives, and leading academics—to frame their query of global clients. Three themes of inquiry emerged: internal alignment, quality of execution, and capacity for renewal.[30]

From this framework, the researchers set out to collect data to investigate their hypothesis on organizational health. They developed a simple three-step process to diagnose, design, and deliver a program to perform against the plan. The diagnosis was two parts: to set a performance aspiration, and to assess the organization's readiness for change. They determined the delivery step should be focused on: (a) delivering against the plan, and (b) making a transition from a transformation program to a "state where continuous improvement is part of the organization's whole way of life."[31]

After reading about it, Chris considered this approach made sense. Researchers define organizational health as an organization's ability to function effectively, to cope with change, and grow internally through member behavior. Keller and Price quantified the improvement in performance through an instrument called the Organizational Health Index (OHI), that measures firms commit to alignment, execution, and renewal. The determined to gauge the effectiveness of their approach through the McKinsey-developed (OHI) that identifies the relationship between healthy organizations and their financial performance.

It turns out the OHI is a reliable predictor. "The proof is strong—the top quartile of publicly traded companies in [the OHI] … delivers roughly three times the returns to shareholders as those in the bottom quartile."[32] McKinsey recommends that corporate leaders "start managing your organizational health as rigorously as you do your P&L, providing pathways for leaders at all levels to take part and embedding and measuring the new ways of working."[33] Chris saw this as making sense but struggled to find a way to easily incorporate onto an increasingly complicated dashboard[34] of KPIs at Apex.

Keller & Scott identify nine elements of organizational health: direction, leadership, culture and climate, accountability, coordination and control, capabilities, motivation, external orientation, and innovation and learning. In Figure 7.3 the elements are arranged along the three themes: internal alignment, quality of execution, and capacity for renewal. The final dimension, renewal, is a measure of how effective a firm deals with understanding, shaping, and adapting to external challenges.

This chapter began with the idea that leadership is best served when it develops capacity for leaders and followers to contribute inspiration and perspiration to resolution of adaptive problems. We've learned organizations are able to

FIGURE 7.3 These nine elements are bound and driven by leadership at the center of organizational health

address the real change they intend when they focus members attention on the external environment and ways to shape and activate internal capabilities through innovation and learning.

TAKEAWAYS

- People turn to their leaders for order and security. Historically, followers surrendered their freedom by committing to obedience with leaders' commands. While appropriate when a firm is faced with a technical problem, adaptive challenges require collaborative response facilitated through dialogue.
- Again, related to adaptive challenges, leaders are best served to develop a process for problem identification and solving rather than insisting on strict adherence to execution defined in the language of the leader.
- When leaders remain inflexible, they surrender any chance of engendering buy-in from the members of the firm thereby forfeiting the unique perspective of workers on the front lines who are in daily contact with customers.
- By too rigidly focused on outcome, the leader is more vulnerable to unintended consequences such as an ethical lapse, a default to coercion, or worse, the dissolution of leadership.
- The challenge is to permit members of the firm to take their orders from

the situation as it's the direct path to health and well-being of the organization. This flourishes in an environment where dialogue among members is robust and non-threatening.

- While it all begins with a common vision and shared values, the leader must orchestrate members as if she were conducting a symphony, thereby, drawing upon the exceptional abilities unique in each member.
- Expanding personal control and responsibility appeals to workers who want to be a part of something bigger than self. Repeated experiments and studies show we're gratified when we exercise control and, to some degree, become inextricably through the personal benefits self-control permits.
- When leadership is recognized as leaders and followers collaborating to resolve the issues they face, people are empowered individually and collectively. Technical problems are recognized as such, and are quickly dispatched, while the thornier adaptive problems get the attention of the group in an all-hands-on-deck mentality with each individual holding a piece of the solution in hand.
- An organization is healthy when it functions effectively, copes well with change, and grows it members to effectively perform. Three themes come together to create a prescription for health: internal alignment, quality of execution, and capacity for renewal.
- The final theme—capacity for renewal—has been the overall theme of the chapter. Firms

Notes

1 Burns, J. M. (1978). *Leadership*. New York, NY: Perennial, (p. 23).
2 Ibid, (p. 23).
3 Ibid, (p. 30).
4 Keller, S., & Price, C. (2011). *Beyond performance: How great organizations build ultimate competitive advantage*. Hoboken, NJ: John Wiley & Sons, Inc., (p. 80).
5 Burns, (p. 414).
6 Ibid, (p. 415).
7 Rost, J. C. (1993). *Leadership for the 21st century*. Westport, CT: Praeger, (p. 118).
8 Ibid, (p. 116).
9 Goodpaster, K. E., (2007). *Conscience and corporate culture*. Hoboken, NJ: Blackwell Publishing, (p. 28).
10 Ibid, (p. 16).
11 Technical challenges are those we have experienced before and have known solutions that can be implemented with current know-how.
12 Rost, J. C. (1993). *Leadership for the 21st century*. Westport, CT: Praeger., (p. 146).
13 Ibid, (p. 146).
14 Cooper, M. (December 1, 2015). The false promise of meritocracy. *The Atlantic*. Retrieved October 20, 2020 from www.theatlantic.com/business/archive/2015/12/

meitocracy/418074. Meritocracy has been well accepted in business because it is aimed at rewarding performance. In this book, Chris leans away from autocratic and democratic organizational conceptions, and favors meritocracy because the latter presents the opportunity for any member of the organization to have an impact on the firm. Sadly, there has been significant documentation that along with a full-throated meritocracy comes a bias toward rewarding males for meritorious contributions more than females. Critics of meritocracy call this "the Paradox of Meritocracy" and the author of this publication fully recognizes this unfair result in compensation bias is unacceptable. Yet, it remains the preferred organizational structure because the power lies in the situation which under the Apex mission lies in defaulting to the customer. Secondly, it recognizes the boss' role is that of a coach and mentor. See Figure 1.2 in Chapter 1.

15 Conger, J. A., Spreitzer, G. M., & Lawler III, E. E. (1999) *The leader's change handbook*. [Kindle version]. San Francisco, CA: Jossey-Bass.

16 Drath, W. (2001). *The deep blue sea: Rethinking the source of leadership*. San Francisco, CA: Jossey-Bass, (p. 126).

17 Ibid, (p. 126).

18 *Getting to Yes*, by Roger Fisher & William Ury, was originally published in 1981 as an outgrowth from the Harvard Negotiation Project. In 1991, the book was issued in a second edition with Bruce Patton, an editor of the first edition, listed as a co-author. The book became a perennial best-seller. By July 1998, it had been appearing for more than three years on the *Business Week* "Best-Seller" book list. As of December 2007, it was still making appearances on the list as one of the "Longest Running Best Sellers" in paperback business books. The third edition was published in 2011.

19 Fisher, R., Ury, W., & Patton, B. (1991). *Getting to yes: Negotiation agreement without giving in*. New York, NY: Penguin Books, (p. 5).

20 Ibid, (p. 17).

21 Ury, W. (1991). *Getting past no: Negotiating your way from confrontation to cooperation*. New York, NY: Bantam Books., (p. 5).

22 Kouzes, J. M. & Posner, B. Z. (2017). *The leadership challenge* (6th ed.). Hoboken, NJ: Wiley & Sons, Inc., (p. 96).

23 Gilbert, D. (2006). *Stumbling on happiness*. New York, NY: Alfred A. Knopf, (p. 4).

24 Ibid, (p. 6).

25 Ibid, (p. 14).

26 Ibid, (p. 22). For a fascinating study on the effects of control and purpose see *Helplessness: On depression, development, and death*. San Francisco, CA: Freeman. "In one study, researchers gave elderly residents of a nursing home a houseplant. They told half the residents that they were in control of the plant's care and feeding (the control group), and the remaining group that a staff person would take responsibility for the plants well-being. Six months later, 30 percent of the residents in the low-control group had died, compared with only 15 percent of the residents in the high-control group. A follow-up study confirmed the importance of perceived control for the welfare of nursing home residents but had an unexpected and unfortunate end. Researchers arranged for student volunteers to pay regular visits to nursing-home residents. Residents in the high-control group were allowed to control the timing and duration of the student's visit ('Please come visit me next Thursday for an hour'), and residents in the low-control group were not ('I'll come visit you next Thursday for an hour'). After two months, residents in the high-control group were happier, healthier, more active, and taking fewer medications than those in the low-control group. At this point the researchers concluded their study and discontinued the student visits. Several months later they were chagrined to learn that a disproportionate number of residents who had been in the high-control group had died. Only in retrospect did the cause of this tragedy seem clear. The residents who had been given control, and who had

benefited measurably from that control while they had it, were inadvertently robbed of control when the study ended/. Apparently, gaining control can have a positive impact on one's health and well-being, but losing control can be worse than never having had any at all."

27 Drath, W. (2001). *The deep blue sea: Rethinking the source of leadership.* San Francisco, CA: Jossey-Bass, (p. 25).

28 Ibid, (p. 25).

29 Ibid, (p. 26).

30 Keller & Price, (p. 80).

31 Ibid, (p. 84).

32 Gagnon, C., & Theunissen, R. (September 7, 2017). Organizational health: A fat track to performance improvement. *McKinsey Quarterly.* Retrieved November 22, 2020, from https://www.mckinsey.com/business-functions/organization/our-insights/organizational-health-a-fast-track-to-performance-improvement#.

33 Ibid.

34 A dashboard is a graphical interface that pools together relevant measures of a firm in a single view. Hence, the name dashboard.

8

LEARNING TO LEARN

Zappos sells shoes online. Like many firms with seemingly unlimited growth in committing to commerce on the internet, Zappos has grown at an annual rate of six percent over its 20-year life and has rewritten the rules of employee culture every step of the way. How does a firm like Zappos use learning to drive its business? In unconventional ways.

This chapter is dedicated to providing some insights into how people learn—in unconventional ways—to embrace corporate values to fulfill the organization's purpose?

Igniting Engagement

Zappos founder Tony Hsieh was fearless when it came to making significant and norm-shattering business moves and along the way built a culture around WOW, a concept that encompasses many factors, but always tied to serving the customer. "To WOW, you must differentiate yourself, which means do something a little unconventional and innovative. You must do something that's above and beyond what's expected. And whatever you do must have an emotional impact on the receiver."[1]

This culture doesn't happen by accident or through kismet though it feels like it does. It's very purposeful. Shieh said: "We thought that if we got the culture right, then building our brand to be about the very best customer service would happen naturally on its own." It begins with how the firm recruits and treats its people. To begin with, the company has dual job interviews: one for business and one for culture; they hold equal importance in determining an offer. "The business interview ensures the candidate has enough talent and proficiency to do the job. The culture interview ensures they'll fit in with the rest of the Zappos family."[2] It is a philosophy inspired by Hsieh but embodied by Zappo's people who believe if the recruit comes into the firm the right way, they stay for all the right reasons.

The firm has conducted a new-hire boot camp for more than 15 years, called, of course, customer service boot camp. The camp never strays from its prime focus on the customer. During the first three weeks, new employees soak up the culture; learn the customer service program; familiarize themselves with the inventory management system; and work with seasoned employees in the customer contact center. This is a deep indoctrination.

With a strong foundation knowing values, direction, and operating style, employees work in the primary job: picking, packing, and shipping orders. Now, here's the WOW part. Each new employee is offered a month's salary to quit. Originally it was $100 but bumped up because employees saw the long-term value in rooting out people who won't be a long-term fit for the firm.[3]

When Chris heard about this idea, he lit up like a blowtorch: "Now that's a training program! They invest in you, and if you don't look like you fit, they buy you out. Learning doesn't mean anything if it never gets tested in the heat of the battle." Chris saw learning as a lifelong activity. He also believed in the need for a test to determine if what's taught is learned and what's learned, mattered to the business.

The Learning Organization

After years of success in business, a friend persuaded Chris to seek a Master of Business Administration degree. When presented with the idea, Chris immediately agreed. Lifelong learners don't think of the degree as a credential, they think of it as a structured way to learn what they may not know. He considered constant learning to be essential because so much changes so fast. He often quoted a fact that the half-life of a college degree is five years, meaning that half of what you learned in college was outdated or obsolete within five years. This was a reality and choosing to ignore was shortsighted. Not only did Chris believe learning should be ongoing, it should be voluntary and self-motivated.

Chris fully embraced Peter Senge's concept of the learning organization. "As the world becomes more interconnected and business becomes more complex and dynamic, work must become more 'learningful.'"[4] From birth, we set out on a learning journey and unless you choose, it never ends. "How, or even if, you decide to take part, what you learn determines your course in life," Chris said.

Senge said learning organizations exist because people are all learners. The problem is some of us just stop learning, become satisfied with the status quo. This zaps us of our ability to grow and learn with others. The following passage resonated with Chris: "Most of us at one time or another have been part of a great team, a group of people who functioned together in an extraordinary way—who trusted one another, who complemented one anothers's strengths and compensated for one another's limitations, who had common goals that were larger than individual goals, and who produced extraordinary results."[5]

Building an organization that values learning requires a process or set of practices and beliefs about how human beings in organizations learn. Joseph E. Stiglitz and Bruce C. Greenwald wrote: "Some learning is a result of explicit allocation of resources to research and development, but much learning is a by-product of production and investment."[6] The authors distinguish the formal approach to learning, R&D, and the informal approach found in routine business practice. Chris knew it was not practical for Apex to have an R&D operation; but there was much to be learned by examining day-to-day business practices on an ongoing basis.

IT'S OBVIOUS ONCE YOU KNOW THE ANSWER

Agnes gave Chris a hug (as she always does when he arrives) and poured his coffee. Before he could speak, she had something to say.

AGNES: *In our recent conversations, you've been stewing over your decision about confronting your people with the troubling truth that you could be about to lose half your business. But for all the right reasons. By refusing to sell something that was really quick, but really wrong, is really bad. Is that about, right?*

CHRIS: *That pretty well sums it up, yep.*

AGNES: *You have pretty much made up your mind.*

CHRIS: *Yes, they have to know that we can't play that way.*

AGNES: *Do they know that? Better yet, do you know what they think?*

CHRIS: *He paused and thought about what she said). I think I see where you're going with that. If I am serious about seeing the business through their eyes, shouldn't I ask them what they think?*

AGNES: *You are such a smart boy. Agnes smiled proudly. We have a little fear telling people the truth when it's not all that good. Do you recall bringing home your 5th grade report card?*

CHRIS: *How could I forget.*

AGNES: *You came home real quiet. You didn't even want a snack. I knew then something was wrong.*

CHRIS: *It was the worst report ever. I had two Ds!*

AGNES: *You finally brought it up after dinner. You told Doc you had some news that wasn't too good.*

CHRIS: *I look back and realize you both knew and yet you didn't say a thing.*

AGNES: *True. You had a lot going on that semester and Doc and I could both see it took a toll on you.*

CHRIS: *You could have just told me and spared me the grief.*

AGNES: *Naw, it was better to let you learn for yourself how we felt.*

CHRIS: *It's pretty simple stuff, isn't it?*

AGNES: *Everything obvious once you know the answer.*

Chris couldn't help but grin a little as Agnes had just unknowingly blurted out the title of a book he was reading by Duncan Watts.

CHRIS: *I've been reading this book about how we are so good at solving scientific problems and so inept at solving people problems. You remind me of the mistakes I make when I refuse to let go of the controls and invite others into the issue. I often act out of fear that the other person will not take it well.*

AGNES: *Thank Doc, so many lessons of life came from dealing with animals. He never lost sight that he wasn't healing animals as much as he was the people who own them and rely on their animals to make a go of it.*

Chris was convinced that he would return to the office and challenge his people to determine a course of action on the dilemma he faced with Apex' largest customer.

Learning to Learn

Early in this book, we established that human beings learn in different ways. This is premised on each individual's unique, inherent strengths and interests. Further, we recognize the way we learn often flows from our interaction and observation of one another. Unlike the air we breathe or the water we drink, knowledge may be ubiquitous, but isn't symmetric. In other words, we don't individually know what we all know, nor do we learn in the same manner.

Therein lies the magic. "Knowledge is created by individuals, typically working within organizations, and then transmitted to others within the organization. It's then conveyed from one organization and individual to another. But the extent, ease, and rapidity of transmission of the new knowledge is itself one of the central features of a learning society: for the new knowledge spurs new thinking; it's the catalyst as well as the input out of which new ideas and creativity emerge."[7]

In 1977, American aeronautical engineer Paul MacCready won the Kremer prize for his work to develop a human-powered airplane with his Gossamer Condor. In his attempt, he identified a major insight into designing the plane was a learning to learn. Previous attempts involved large investments based on well-conceived theories. Yet, "when the vehicle crashed there was no opportunity to make refinements. Learning from this fatal flaw, MacCready focused on how to build a plane that could be rebuilt in hours. This enabled him to *learn*, to correct mistakes at reasonably low costs, and in short order...."[8] MacCready credited the *learning to learn* concept enabled him to construct the Gossamer Condor.

When Things Go Wrong

You will recall in Chapter 5 we took a look at the explosion that occurred in the first planned Apollo mission. The leadership at mission control—Gene Kranz and his team—studied the factors leading to the disaster in the singular effort to learn from it and never let it happen again. Figure 8.1 is a reminder of that day and how that the team committed to being *tough* and *competent*; learning that made a difference in what might have been NASA's worst nightmare instead was its finest moment.

The race to the moon was filled with memorable milestones, but one of the most lasting images was the well-publicized Apollo 13 mission, which actually occurred *after* man walked on the moon. Due to a minor part that malfunctioned on Apollo 13, an uneventful mission became a legendary adaptive challenge for NASA that fulfilled the notion that a disaster can become the best test for members of the team rise to the occasion. When it launched, Apollo 13 was a

Learning From Tragedy

Source: NASA.gov

FIGURE 8.1 The lesson from Apollo 1 explosion served the resolve that made Apollo 13 a success

routine technical challenge and a lackluster event in comparison to Apollo 11 which safely deposited Neil Armstrong on the moon garnering the attention of the world.

However, Apollo 13 turned into an adaptive challenge that tested the limits of learning. Lead flight director Gene Kranz worked with a highly talented and committed team that innovated on-the-fly to save three astronauts and successfully tackle one of the most difficult adaptive challenges in history. When we take a timed exam, the time limitation intensifies the need to think clearly and quickly.

The pressure, if we allow it, can become paralyzing.

In his book "Failure is not an Option" Kranz described the mindset communicated to the team in the moment: "I want nothing held back, no margins, no reserves. If you don't have an answer, they need your best judgment and they need it now. Whatever happens we will not second guess you. Everything goes in the pot."[9] Kranz took charge. He gave specific direction on how to behave exhibiting classic leader behavior in mobilizing adaptive work.

Kranz demonstrated each of these steps. Further, he communicated clearly and without equivocation: "My message to everyone is: rely on your own judgment, update your data as you go along. If you are not the right person, step aside and send me someone who is. When you leave this room you will pass no uncertainty to our people. They must become believers if we are to succeed."[10]

By preparing people for bad news, he actually empowered them to create the good news. Acting in the heat of the moment brings extra stress on the situation and acting like Kranz, puts the leader in a position to act with great calm and conviction.

A famous and memorable exchange from the Apollo 13 movie went like this:

FLIGHT DIRECTOR: *I know what the problems are, this could be the worst* disaster NASA has ever experienced.

KRANZ: *With all due respect sir, I think this is going to be our finest hour.*

The story ended with the three astronauts—Jim Lovell, Fred Haise, and Jack Swigert—*safely splashing down in the warm South Pacific.*

The Apollo 13 incident unfolded without a script. It was up to the team to write it in real time as it emerged in a cloud of great uncertainty. At times like this, it is too late to prepare the team. The preparation is complete. Now, leaders and followers must exercise their adaptive capacity to engage in problem-solving work in the midst of pressures and resulting disequilibrium. Figure 8.2 enumerates valuable practices to develop for such occasions.

It Begins with Orientation

Chris believed the most important day for a new employee is their first. "Why do we so often make this special day an afterthought for the new hire? We carefully

Adaptive Cultures Engage in Five Practices
❶ Name the elephants on the room,
❷ Share responsibility for the organization's future,
❸ Exercise independent judgment
❹ Develop leadership capacity, and
❺ Institutionalize reflection and continuous improvement.

SOURCE: Heifetz, R., Grashow, A., & Linsky, M. (2009).
The practice of adaptive leadership: Tools and tactics for changing your organization and the world. **Boston, MA.: Harvard Business Press., (p.165).**

FIGURE 8.2 These practices are instilled when the team forms

screen and hire to get the right people on board, and then when they show up, we treat them like the delivery guy. Heck, maybe we treat the delivery guy better!" Chris let out a hearty laugh at the thought.

When new people came to work on their first day at Apex, they received the royal treatment. Welcomed by a senior officer. Given personalized business cards. And entered into an extensive weeklong program aimed at truly *orienting* them to Apex. Chris learned that how people are treated on their first day was a predictor of their initial long-term buy-in to the firm.

This was reciprocal. Firms that gave attention to new hires subsequently felt fully committed to their long-term success. While we hire for fit, the assessment of fit with the firm continues once the selected employee arrives. By taking this seriously, and having a carefully designed welcoming program, Apex walked the talk and created discipline in the hiring and onboarding process. People became invested in Apex, because Apex invested in them.

Hire People Who Want to Learn... for All the Right Reasons

The idea that learning is something people really get enthused about is ill-conceived. You can blame the education system, if you like. But as we learned from Sir Kenneth Robinson in Chapter 3, education systems are products of the past not visionary views of future needs.

Noted management scholar Henry Mintzberg wrote famously about management what could be applied to any field of study related to people: "The trouble with 'management' education is that it is business education, and leaves a distorted impression of management. Management is a practice that has to blend a good deal of craft (experience) with a certain amount of art (insight) and some science (analysis)."[11]

In short, Mintzberg warned that MBA educations may mistakenly produce an individual with the potential to be out of balance, and therefore, be too calculating, fancy herself as an artist, or wish to be seen as a hero. He concluded, "We need balanced, dedicated people who practice a style of managing that can be called 'engaging'"[12] From Chris' perspective, MBAs were to do exactly as Mintzberg advised.

These two views from education pundits present two risks in attempting to educate people: crushing creativity or creating unbalanced managers. The real challenge of creating is how to create a learning environment that will enfranchise individuals to embrace the wisdom of leading people... to move them to act in potent and powerful ways. In a word: engagement.

Get the Right People

All along the pages in this book we explore the angles that cause people to buy-in, that is, engage to produce leadership as defined at the beginning. Growth is a component. Learning is a component. But the real driver is core motivation. Why do you want to learn? Why do you want to be around people who want to learn?

Carole Dweck distinguished the difference between leaders with a growth mindset as people who "don't highlight the pecking order with themselves at the top, don't claim credit for other people's contributions, and they don't undermine others to feel powerful."[13] Rather, "they surround themselves with the most able people they can find, they look squarely at their own mistakes and deficiencies, and they ask frankly what skills they and the company will need in the future."[14]

If a leader can identify people with a growth mindset and arrange those people proximate to one another through work, projects, customers, and of course, social aspects; a true learning organization may take shape. It's symbiotic. As it turns out, a good learning environment is one "where there are good role models (teachers) for learning and creativity, and where the style of teaching meets the diverse needs of learners ... [in that it] resembles a journey of discovery in which the learner plays the main character and is encouraged to be creative and socially and authentically connected to the learning community."[15]

Author and thought leader Leo Bottary wrote: "As teachers and business leaders, the more collaborative we are with one another, the more likely it is that we will create healthy learning and collaborative environments for students and employees alike. It starts with asking questions and listening for understanding."[16] Chris aimed to create authentic learning cocoons where many diverse voices balance the discussion and render an outcome where the whole is far greater than the sum of the parts.

Learning Breeds Preparedness

Chris trusted his gut. He admitted the motivation to do so depended on an assessment of risk and reward, with emphasis on reward. He regularly reflected on the "threat" box of the SWOT Analysis: *Loss of a major account would be devastating.* He often thought people become afraid of what they don't understand or cannot know. This SWOT entry may become fraught with unknowable facts.

In the face of such ambiguity, Chris remembered the well-worn Boy Scout motto: "Be prepared." Who could forget that old saw: "failing to prepare is preparing to fail." His gut told him hope for the best but prepare for the worst. Chris set the tone for people in the organization to constantly prepare for the unexpected by learning as much as one can every step of the way. He inspired them by taking a personal interest in their development. Seldom does a firm fail to recognize and develop technical skills like how to use business tools such as Excel or learning the power of business writing. But it's far less likely to embrace soft skills that may have the greatest impact.

ONE-ON-ONES

Chris and his senior team met regularly with employees one-on-one to deepen their relationships and determine development needs. Here's a conversation between Chris and a new college graduate named Mikayla. This sort of exchange helped to emphasize to leaders and followers the value of personal development. The subject of their development building skills didn't have to be directly focused on their work; it could be aimed at most people's favorite subject: their self.

MIKAYLA: *I'm so happy to meet with you. I don't think many companies do this, let just anyone talk to the president.*

CHRIS: *Just as when we hired you, it's just as important for us to have a good fit with you as it is for you to have a good fit with us. Tell me about your experience here so far.*

MIKAYLA: *I'm just happy to be here. I have such a passion for this job.*

CHRIS: *Wait, you have a passion for preparing statistical reports for mortgage bankers to make a lending decision? Tell me, Mikayla, how long have you had this peculiar obsession?* He had a big smile on his face and just a touch of friendly sarcasm.

MIKAYLA: *Well, I mean, I'm happy to be working in a good job right out of college.*

Chris brought a pad of paper and a pencil and gave it to her.

CHRIS: *Let's take a closer look at your comment. I believe you do have a passion for working here. And I'm happy you feel that way. This little exercise is*

---

a way for you to hone-in on your real passions. Write the word passions *on the left and* goals *on the right.* Take some quiet time in the next few days and complete these two lists. *For now, take some notes to help you learn how to complete this exercise.* Mikayla began taking notes as Chris continued.

Make your passions big and bold, shatter the mold. This is for your eyes only, so don't hold back. This is your dream list. We all think we're only supposed to have a single passion. That's not true. We usually have many. So be honest and open with yourself. They don't all have to be work-related, that would be crazy as most of your time is not spent at work.

Now, on the far-right side, list your goals. In this case, goals are those items, that, if accomplished, will help you live your passion. Think of your goals as something might lead you to living your passion. Make your goals specific and be ambitious. There's no clock on this exercise. It'll take a bit to assess your desires and spell out goals. They may be fuzzy at first, and as you let your seventh sense work, clarity will arrive.

Then, identify the actions and obstacles. Put the short-term items on the left and the long-term on the right. You're making decisions; you're crystalizing your thoughts. This is where you put your presence of mind to work. You'll learn more about that when you attend the Innovation and Rejuvenation seminars. Those learning experiences cover a very important aspect of this exercise, the seventh sense.

Finally, use the space in center to identify the steppingstones to get you from left to right. This space is a constant reminder of your need to be mindful of your journey. Your presence of mind will spring loose the inspiration that's truly unique to you. What do you think?

MIKAYLA: *I think no one has ever asked me to do this or show me how. Do you do this for everybody?*

CHRIS: *Yes, we meet with all newly hired employees before their first 90 days is completed. The nature of the conversation may be different based on them individually and their unique interests and concerns, as well as their place in life. Let's meet in three months to see how you're progressing.*

This session introduced a dimension of human connection that's quite simple, but very effectively accomplished at Apex. What sets the place apart—and creates a deeper level of engagement—is the focus on personal growth directed from the very top. As you can see, it's not about creating a personal five-year plan, as a matter of fact, it's "not a plan—it's a chance to aim high… [but] you rely on your seventh sense to stop you from aiming impossibly high and wasting a lot of time, energy, and a passion."[17] When people can sense that the firm has *their* personal development in mind—and not just for selfish reasons—they typically lean in and form a bond.

The Seventh Sense

As we will learn in Chapter 11, your sixth sense gives you the old idea, and while you may retrieve it quickly, it doesn't necessarily address the new unfamiliar situation you face. "The seventh sense is the mechanism of the human mind that produces new ideas. It's the epiphany, the flash of insight, the Eureka moment—in the form of an idea you never had before. And in its highest form, it's an idea that no one else had before either."[18]

We know new ideas can change the world. However, before that happens, the idea changes one person. That's why we call it an epiphany. Yet, as much as you like, it's not likely you will coax a flash of light out of the dark recesses of the mind.

Chris related the process of generating new ideas in a meeting one of the work groups held on process. After an hour of brainstorming, a flight of ideas filled the room, but nothing rose above the others as a direction to pursue. After a long pause, Chris stood up and said: "An old adman friend of mine had a favorite line on how he claimed how he get his ideas: 'Three martinis and a bolt of lightning', he'd say. We'd all laugh and then realize booze really had nothing to do with it." There are other ways to set our creativity in motion.

What Chris related was a process that prepares the mind to tap into the seventh sense developed by William Duggan and incorporated into his classes at Columbia Business School. Chris related the four steps to reaching the 7th sense (a) examples from history, (b) presence of mind, (c) flashes of light, and (d) resolution.

- The first step, examples from history, provides the content for an epiphany to take place. Understanding historical examples of achievement primes the mind, prepares it to give you a new idea. It can't give you an idea for someone else, only you.
- The second element—presence of mind—allows you to expect the unexpected. "Presence of mind is the ability to clear away all your previous thoughts about the situation you face."[19] We get bogged down by our embedded thoughts and mental models of our reality. "Presence of mind lets you move through all kinds of random thoughts that seem to make no sense at the time. Your mind unhooks from your current goal and searches for a new one."[20]
- The first two prepare you for the third element—the flash of light itself. The timing may vary, but the experience is real and can be jarring. This is the proverbial "bolt of lightning." Some say, when the flash of light comes, it

seems anti-climactic because once you can apprehend it, it's so obvious. However, once you try to explain it, it doesn't seem so obvious. Personally, all too often when I explain my Eureka to someone, they stare at me. They're speechless. It's easy to accept this reaction and dismiss it as just another random thought. "However, the contrast between the old ideas and the new is black and white."[21]

- The fourth element is resolution. "That means resolve, determination, persistence. You don't just say, 'I see what to do.' You say, 'I see what to do and I want to do it.' The idea lights a fire in your mind and in your heart, and this final crucial step makes you follow through and make your idea come true."[22]

Chris practiced the process regularly by filling his mind with salient details of experiences and past happenings; allowing them to bubble up and produce an insight. Perhaps the most challenging part of the process is recognizing the insight when it arrives. To practice this process, he often taught it to others.

Chris and his management team had a process for interviewing every newly hired employee. They then met monthly among themselves to review their interviews. Every interview mattered because every new employee mattered to the strengthening of the firm. Here's a sample of personal strategy map presented in Mikayla's interview.

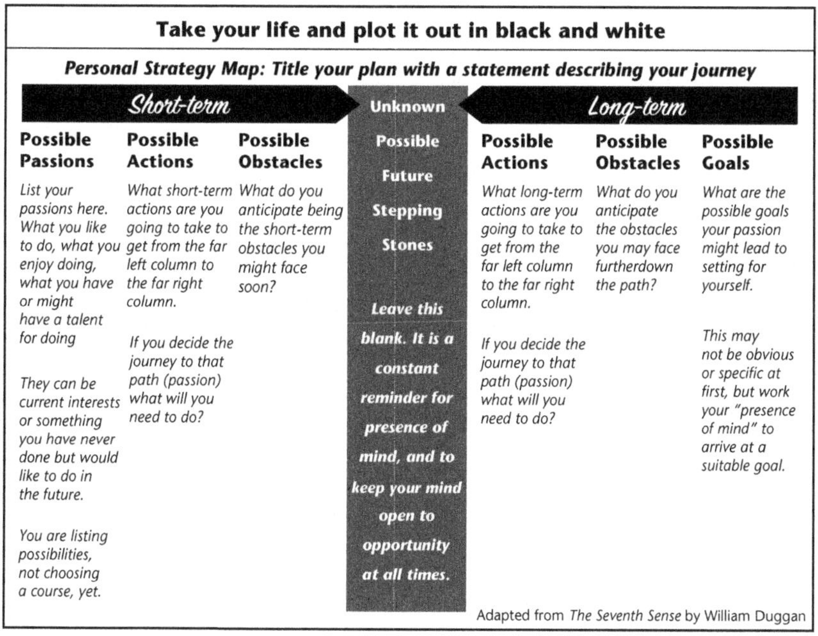

Take your life and plot it out in black and white

Personal Strategy Map: Title your plan with a statement describing your journey

Short-term			Unknown	*Long-term*		
Possible Passions	**Possible Actions**	**Possible Obstacles**	**Possible Future**	**Possible Actions**	**Possible Obstacles**	**Possible Goals**
List your passions here. What you like to do, what you enjoy doing, what you have or might have a talent for doing	What short-term actions are you going to take to get from the far left column to the far right column.	What do you anticipate being the short-term obstacles you might face soon?	Stepping Stones	What long-term actions are you going to take to get from the far left column to the far right column.	What do you anticipate the obstacles further down the path?	What are the possible goals your passion might lead to setting for yourself.
They can be current interests or something you have never done but would like to do in the future.	If you decide the journey to that path (passion) what will you need to do?		Leave this blank. It is a constant reminder for presence of mind, and to keep your mind open to opportunity at all times.	If you decide the journey to that path (passion) what will you need to do?		This may not be obvious or specific at first, but work your "presence of mind" to arrive at a suitable goal.
You are listing possibilities, not choosing a course, yet.						

Adapted from *The Seventh Sense* by William Duggan

FIGURE 8.3 Adapted (with permission) from The Seventh Sense by William Duggan

Figure 8.3 serves as a road map for laying out "multiple possible goals, some of them contradictory, and possible paths to get part of the way to each one, without deciding anything. This leaves room for your seventh sense."[23]

By the way, the training at Apex, if you can call it that, is unlike you'll see in traditional environments. It recognizes that soft skills[24] are the intangible, the X-factor, if you will, that raises people to the next level of performance. Teaching/learning soft skills is a circular, not linear process. And, it is iterative, that is, it's repetitive and re-visits emerging ideas as a matter of development.

This features such learning sessions as developing your presence of mind, as a means to get in touch with your seventh sense—the source of truly creative, new ideas—because that's the magic that allows you to combine experiences, ideas, concepts into new flashes of insight. The seventh sense is a general skill, it is possible to improve your ability to have new ideas of any kind. This is a powerful personal skill and when a leader takes the time to help a person out on the quest of thriving in life, it's highly likely they'll earn an important place in it, and the individual skill will add to the organization's creative capacity.

Learning is Influence

David Levin and Mike Feinberg devised a program more than 20 years ago to develop the learning skills and self-motivation needed by a young student to prepare learning in college and success in life. They developed The Knowledge is Power Program, or KIPP, aimed at lower-income youth. KIPP has grown to 255 open-enrollment college prep schools in low-income communities across the country. KIPP features five differentiators that help a student complete college at a rate four times higher than that of students in similar backgrounds without the preparation. They are:

- High Expectations. KIPP is built on a culture of support and achievement through personalized learning based on the student's needs, skills, and interests;
- Focus on Character. Students need both a strong academic foundation and well-developed character strengths to succeed in college and the world beyond;
- Highly Effective Teachers & Leaders. KIPP empowers educators to lead school teams and invest in training to help them grow as professionals.
- Safe, Structured & Nurturing Environments. KIPP schools know these three elements serve to cause students to thrive and maximize their learning; and
- KIPP through College. Once students leave the walls of a KIPP school for college, they're accompanied by counselors who support and help them navigate social, academic, and financial challenges.[25]

KIPP is one of the innovative learning interventions featured in the book "Influencer: The new science of leading change" (2nd ed.). The authors place special attention on three actions common to all influencers featured in their book: (a) focus and measure, (b) behaviors that drive results, and (c) engagement in six sources of influence. KIPP was cited as a shining example of employing the six sources, which are:

- Personal motivation;
- Personal ability;
- Social motivation;
- Social ability;
- Structural motivation; and
- Structural ability.

Though there has been no connection with KIPP, it is not surprising that Chris has demonstrated these six behaviors his entire career. He believes a source of motivation is doing things right. He thought of how he seldom felt the connection between success/happiness and the pointlessness of many of his classes in school. "I couldn't make a connection between what they wanted us to learn and what I felt good about doing." Unlike his brother who earned a Ph.D. from Cornell, Chris's natural ability didn't come to life until he got out of college.

When he compared his grades to his brother's, Chris said, "they screamed: You're not a student!" (at least not like his brother!). Chris' social connections likely kept him in school. He had street smarts, and the other kids could see it, and this reaction motivated Chris. That's probably why he could make fun out of the hot and brutal detasseling job!

Besides his natural social ability, his parents provided structure for Chris and his siblings to stay the course. Chris said he even felt a little validation when his brother earned a generous scholarship to that prestigious Ivy League school! Chris could see without all three elements—personal, social, and structural—at work, he would've never have done as well in college as he did.

Teachers Among Us

Apex managers cultivated and recognized much needed skillsets among the ranks—a fact that energized them. All they needed to do was ask. When Chris encouraged the human resource people to put together an effective training program, everyone was enthused when one of the case expeditors in a previous life was a highly qualified training expert.

In their search for this very specific skillset, one of the HR interviewers remembered Gary, then working as an expeditor. Gary was a highly experienced instructional designer who couldn't find a position in his field at the time. Chris said, "We're looking all over the landscape for this rare ability that we needed badly, and he's sitting 10 feet from the HR department. Go figure!"

This fortuitous finding fit with a mindset that vigorous discussion across the company would turn up the most beneficial findings. Remember, after Chris' interview with all the managers shortly after buying Apex, he discovered some great people. They knew a lot about the operation, but worked in positions most truly loathed. However, all that changed when Chris put them in the right places.

TAKEAWAYS

- Learning today is varied and dynamic. Perhaps the biggest impact is when leaders connect learning to greater possibilities for individuals.
- Effective learning occurs in training when the event is embedded in the social fabric of the firm and the approach becomes multifaceted.
- A learning organization is one that recognizes the fleeting nature of knowledge. A learning organization can produce greater understanding and creative new ways to deal with problems and opportunities while strengthening the DNA of the firm.
- When members of an organization stop learning, that is, believe college was the end of the learning road, growth and vitality cease.
- Learning to learn recognizes that human beings live in different ways and is aided by interaction and observation of one another.
- Some of the most effective learning in an organization may occur in trial-and-error when mistakes occur; the organization is allowed to repair and resume.
- If you want employees to fulfill all expectations, welcome them into the firm and commit to their growth and learning.
- Formal education has a detrimental effect on learning when it crushes creativity and coaxes extremes rather than balance, resulting in a failure to engage.
- If a firm wants maximum results from learning, pay attention to re-cruiting the right people and cause them to interact with real problems in an affirming manner.
- Preparedness is a hallmark of an aware organization positioned to deal with uncertainty and ambiguity.
- Training moves past skills into developing soft skills like how people tap into their seventh sense, or how they identify and solve problems.
- The seventh sense is a means for people to tap into the unexpressed thoughts that often have significant impact on the success of the business.

- Teaching and learning soft skills is a circular, not linear proves, further, it's iterative taking into consideration the way novel ideas emerge.
- For people to learn, they need an environment where learners feel safe, and permits new ways of doing.
- Three keys are necessary to leading through learning: focus and measure, focus on behaviors that drive results, and engage in personal, social, and structural aspects of ability and the leader's ability to motivate.
- Most organizations fail to recognize the wisdom and knowledge within the four walls, that when tapped, may set of a wildfire of learning.

Notes

1 Christoffersen, T. (June 1, 2017). Our common core: Deliver WOW through service. *Culture* [company magazine]. Retrieved on November 10, 2020 from https://www.zappos.com/about/stories/core-values-one.
2 Ibid.
3 Christoffersen, T. (June 5, 2019). 20 years, 20 milestones: How Zappos grew out of just shoes. *Culture* [company magazine]. Retrieved on November 10, 2020 from https://www.zappos.com/about/stories/zappos-20th-birthday.
4 Senge, P. M. (2006). *The fifth discipline: The art and practice of the learning organization* (Rev. ed.). New York: Currency Doubleday., (p. 4).
5 Ibid, (p. 4).
6 Stiglitz, J. E., & Greenwald, B. C. (2015). *Creating a learning society: A new approach to growth, development, and social progress.* [Reader's Edition]. New York, NY: Columbia University Press., (p. 50).
7 Ibid, (p. 46).
8 Ibid, (p. 49).
9 Kranz, G. (2000). *Failure is not an option.* New York, NY: Berkley Publishing Group., (p. 321).
10 Ibid, (p. 321).
11 Mintzberg, H. (2004) *Managers Not MBAs: A hard look at the soft practice of managing and marketing development.* San Francisco, CA: Berrett-Koehler., (p. 1).
12 Ibid, (p. 1)
13 Dweck, C. S. (2006/2016). *Mindset: The new psychology of success.* New York, NY: Random House., (p. 110.) Dweck reflected on Jim Collins *Good to Great* study that identified leaders who inspired a firm to thrive were self-effacing, inquisitive, confronted reality, and refused to accept failure but, rather, maintained the faith that they would succeed in the end.
14 Ibid., (p. 110).
15 Hess, E. D. (2014). *Learn or die: Using science to build a leading-edge learning organization.* New York, NY: Columbia University Press., (p. 46).
16 Bottary, L. (2019). *What anyone can do: How surrounding yourself with the right people will drive change, opportunity, and personal growth.* Abingdon, UK: Bibliomotion, Inc., (p. 58).
17 Ibid, (p. 102).
18 Duggan W. (2015). *The seventh sense: How flashes of insight change your life.* New York, NY: Columbia Business School. (p. 4).

19 Duggan, (p. 16).
20 Ibid, (p. 17).
21 Ibid, (p. 18).
22 Ibid, (p. 18).
23 Ibid, (p. 102).
24 There are many interpretations of soft skills, but here are seven soft skills that cover the landscape of firm whose people are motivated and engaged: emotional intelligence, team player attitude, growth mindset, openness to feedback, adaptability, active listening, and work ethic. You will find them explained in greater detail at the Hubspot website. See blog.hubspot.com/marketing/soft-skills.
25 The information here is drawn directly from the Knowledge is Power Program retrieved November 1, 2020 from www.kipp.org/

PART IV
The Tools for Crafting Leadership That Thrives

In this section, you'll read about tools for thinking and acting to accomplish buy-in through communication, innovation, and operations. As with the entire text, the chapters that follow serve as a reader for leaders to survey long-held wisdom and new-found theories to constructively think about the dynamics of the workplace today.

In Chapters 9 and 10, you'll read about how strategy and execution work to bring strategy to life and goals to fruition. In Chapter 11, we'll investigate the ins and outs of common sense and how leaders can further understand the way people think and how it influences actions. In Chapter 12, we expose the world of innovation and how it may contribute to or detract from organizational resolve. In Chapter 13, we'll shine a light on how leaders' efforts to establish shared values, well-conceived and actively managed operating practices can establish accountability among leaders and responsibility among followers that invite active involvement in the well-being of the organization.

These tools serve to enlighten leaders and followers in the vital business of creating value that will get and keep customers, the lifeblood of the firm.

9

COMMUNICATION STRATEGY

In their book Strategic Public Relations Management, Erica Weintraub Austin and Bruce E. Pinkleton put goal, objective and strategy in a coherent light: "If the goal represents the direction we plan to go and the objective represents destinations at which we plan to arrive, then strategies represent how we plan to get there."[1] Strategy is the how. Think of the metaphor of a weight-loss program. We know the goal: lose weight. We've identified various objectives that, if accomplished will move us closer to our goal, while providing key measures to evaluate our success. We use strategy(ies) to develop informed creation of the tactical activities to be used to measure progress against the goal.

In the next two chapters, the role of communication in generating buy-in is explored from two perspectives: strategy and execution. Strategy is the "how" and execution is the "what" of communication. Further, you'll begin to feel the distinction made between messaging (one-way-sending) and communication (two-way-receiving) that completes the loop inherent in creating effective communication.

Figure 9.1 depicts the strategy for personal health. It is a topic all can relate to in some fashion, so it is worthy to explore as a means to inform us how the steps to complete this strategy inform the way Apex completed its strategic business plan. So, we'll use it as a proxy to understand the strategic process.

Personal health may encompass many factors, but here it focuses on body weight because a visual scan suggests that could be the major contributor to health problems. Brief research points to using the Body Mass Index (BMI) as a quantification of healthy weight. Calculating the BMI using height and weight measures indicates the subject of this inquiry has a BMI of 29, at least 5 points too

FIGURE 9.1 Strategy is born of clear thinking

high to be considered normal weight, reaching into the overweight category. That is in this example, a KPI or key performance indicator.

The first three components of strategic development address Mission, Problem, and Goal. From there it breaks down the goal into specific objectives, which are: eat less, exercise more. From this emerges a two-part strategy, how to accomplish the objectives. After further consultation, a diet of 1,200 calories is set to reduce input. Second, to burn calories an exercise regimen of walking 10,000 steps a day is established to burn an additional 2,500 calories per week. Dietary statistics show a weight loss will result if that daily count is maintained. If this strategy can be successfully implemented, the goal should be accomplished over time. Makes sense, right?

Human Factor

All strategy is hypothetical. That is, management generates a scheme they believe will get them to their destination. But, until it's executed, it has no effect on the organization's performance. All strategy is executed by people. As demonstrated repeatedly in this book, people are more likely to buy-in if they genuinely feel what they do will make a difference. It's the human factor.

This process is called strategic planning. It originates at the business level (the front lines), then flows through the organization. That's not to say, members of the firm are merely recipients of the marching orders. The assumptions, observations, and assessments that executives use to inform themselves should bubble up in the organization to inform the strategic plan. The SWOT analysis, and corporate goals, objectives, strategies, and eventual tactics flow from the strategic plan. In other words, the process yields a communication strategic plan developed around communication issues such as:

- What is the purpose of communication?
- Who are the audiences?
- What channels will be used to reach the various audiences?
- Who are the communicators?
- What are the messages?
- What resources are available to execute the plan?
- What obstacles must be overcome for successful execution?
- What strategies (theories) will be used to create understanding and buy-in?

This list will serve to create a framework where—through vigorous discussion with members of the firm—an action plan will be born. The quality of analysis is seldom the source of failure. As David Maister wisely advises: "The necessary outcome of strategic planning is not *analytical insight* but *resolve.*"[2] This is truly a matter of winning the hearts and minds of those individuals expected to execute the plan. Maister has a realistic view of the workplace that informs the underlying driver of buy-in: deep commitment to the personal adaptation necessary to create compelling resolve in all members of the organization. Resolve is another way of saying buy-in.

Testing Resolve

Maister offers three CEO actions that move resolve front and center by re-inforcing a single strategic idea, in this case client service:

1. Once a quarter, the CEO sends an email to all active clients (without consulting the lead people serving those clients), asking them to click on one of three buttons in the email: *green* if they're satisfied with the way their work is being handled, *amber* if they have some concerns and *red* if they're un-happy. The CEO reviews and evaluates all replies and publishes the group average scores for all to see;

2. At compensation-setting time, the relevant senior management group con-ducts a phone or face-to-face interview with every client served by each partner in the last year (or a scientifically chosen random sample if the number of clients is too high to be practical). These assessments carry a 40 to 60% weighting in determining pay; and

3. The organization adopts and publicizes an unconditional satisfaction guarantee, allowing disappointed clients to pay only what they thought the work was worth.[3]

These three examples get at the heart of strategy, how well it's executed to make an impact on behavior. Moreover, they signal the high degree of importance the CEO places on execution. Radical, you say? Only in that these tests are proactive efforts to stress test the execution. Much better to assess that early and make adjustments than to find out too late when failure of execution results in failure of the business.

Conducting an Orderly Inquiry

With an understanding of the strategic plan in mind, let's look at the way we approach an orderly investigation of our communication challenge. One of the biggest mistakes that people make in developing communication strategy is to lead with the question, *what do I want to say?* For the record, that's the last question on the agenda.

Helio Fred Garcia wrote: "Strategy is a process of ordered thinking: of thinking in the right order... the essential questions that make sense of the situation, establish goals, identify audiences and attitudes and describe the course of action to influence those attitudes."[4] He suggests this sequence:

- What do we have? What is the challenge or opportunity we're hoping to address?
- What do we want? What's our goal? Communication is merely the continuation of business by another means. We shouldn't communicate unless we know what we're trying to accomplish.
- Who matters? What stakeholders matter to us? What do we know about them? What are the barriers to their receptivity to us, and how do we overcome those barriers?
- What do we need them to think, feel, know, or do in order to accomplish our goal?
- What do they need to see us do, hear us say, or hear others say about us to think, feel, know, and do what we want them to do?
- How do we make that happen?[5]

Big Ideas Actively Engaged

Chris brings in experts from the community to speak to the troops during town hall meetings every quarter. One speaker was a college professor Chris heard speaking on organizational performance. Central to the professor's message was personal accountability. Chris asked the professor to address that issue at a

Town Hall meeting. The professor began with an effective way to engage the audience. He didn't talk about organizational performance, he addressed personal performance.

He told those assembled about his course. "We encourage each member to take the time to engage personally with individual exercises that will expose them to the leadership concepts in a very real way. Their assignments are geared to imagining their ideal self and contrasting that with their real self. The idea is to identify the gaps to be closed in order to become self-aware and motivated to become their best self." He provided a process that helped them identify their real self and the ideal self. He asked people to talk to friends and family to understand their perceptions on when they're at their best.

Students walk away from that exercise with a deeper understanding of how they're perceived by others. Often, that sharpens their opinions about self. Then, the professor led those assembled through visioning exercises by writing a brief statement about their personal vision; then pairing them up for one-on-one peer coaching. The outcome is most students know themselves better and can see how they can contribute to the overall performance of the organization or team or fraternity of which they're a member.

These talks, and this one was no different, gave employees something to discuss with one another. Chris encouraged that outcome by breaking the large group into smaller circles where true communication—sending and receiving—could take place. Then, he had each group summarize their findings. The takeaway that day was a greater recognition of how each individual contributes or detracts from the performance of the team.

As he did in this situation, Chris learned that the trite phrase "Go big or go home" lands well with people. To win their hearts and minds, think big, then let them reach inside and find a way to deliver on the challenge.

Some may argue these sorts of activities have nothing to do with strategic communication. In fact, as we established, strategy is a waste of time if it cannot be executed well. Such interpersonal drills heightened the awareness of people to know themselves and what they do well and where they need to close the gaps.

A Word From The Master

Management guru Peter Drucker places great value on the exercises described in the previous passage. He writes: "Throughout history, people had little need to know their strengths. A person was born into a position and a line of work: The peasant's son would also be a peasant; the artisan's daughter, an artisan's wife; and so on. But now people have choices. We need to know our strengths in order to know where we belong."[6] Drucker's observations call for the need of much greater self-understanding. To be a truly effective contributor—whether leader or follower—knowing our strengths will help inform our optimal place and our maximum contribution.

"The only way to discover your strengths is through feedback analysis. Whenever you make a key decision or take a key action, write down what you expect will happen, Nine or 12 months later, compare the actual results with your expectations."[7] Drucker revealed every time he has done this, he found an insight about himself, like how he relates to technically-minded people—engineers, accounts, market researchers—but doesn't connect well with generalists. This self-reflection process is not new. John Calvin and Ignatius of Loyola each incorporated this into practices of their followers.

Learn Strategy, Value Execution

"A good strategy process is one of the best devices to teach people about execution."[8] Perhaps, the best way to appreciate driving a car is to work on it from time to time. Not all of us have that aptitude, however. Chris often said, "I don't have to understand the workings of the internal combustion engine, to be a good driver!" True, but Chris had his own experience with cars.

As a kid, the first car he drove belonged to an uncle who had died and left a 1950 Ford in the backyard shed. Chris tinkered with changing the spark plugs, flushing the fluids, getting a new battery, and shoeing it with a new set of rubber all around. Voilà Transportation. Just that brief interaction with the mechanics of a car gave Chris a closer look at how it worked. It made him more aware. When he felt a rough ride, or heard a funny sound, his mind kicked in thinking what may have been the cause.

In strategic planning, if you have good knowledge of business, it's easy get deep in the weeds. In doing so, one can appreciate when things don't go as planned. Curiosity helps form good questions. "How is the plan put together? How is it synchronized? They discover insights, and develop their judgments and intuition. They learn from mistakes: 'Why when we made our assumptions, did we not see the changes that overtook us?'"[9]

Chris found the process energizing. He also found it terrifying, like when he pondered that lingering "threat" posted on the SWOT: *Loss of major account would be devastating.* Perhaps, that's why the idea dominated one of his Mom visits.

THE GIFT OF PRESENCE

CHRIS: *Remember Rev. Fairway and his Sunday morning sermons? He would get so worked up and it always seemed to be something people were concerned about.*

AGNES: *He had a gift for reading people's minds. What I remember is that when he was preaching, he was looking into my eyes! I felt his presence, I'm sure everyone felt that.*

CHRIS: *Yeah, he had a gift. I think some of the magic was that he knew what we needed to hear at that specific moment. He was speaking to us about what we needed to hear right then. Like after the big tornado, when everybody felt like they were literally forsaken. Many lost everything.*

AGNES·   *I'll never forget that. He reminded us that we all have a free will, and we could put it to use anyway we wanted. It could be productive, or it could be destructive. I walked away from that with a little bit of hope that I was in control, not a victim.*

CHRIS: *Amazing how that feeling can change your entire attitude.*

AGNES: *When others acknowledge our pain, it validates us and justifies our concern.*

Chris drove back to the office thinking he needed to be a preacher sometimes in his job. He also remembered how much more effective communication is when it strokes the audience with the right message at the exact right time. The only question was how, how did that preacher know what everyone wanted and needed to hear? Not just during the obvious things like tornadoes, but through everyday life. Then, Chris remembered no one spent more time listening than Rev. Fairway. In that way, he was a great communicator. Chris recalled the pastor saying, "You ought to communicate the way the maker created you. You have two ears, and one mouth, use them proportionately."

Committing it to Paper

The primary benefit of a strategic communication plan is to guide implementation of your communications. While communicating may seem intuitive, sometimes we fall in love with a tactic or a vehicle and fall short in accomplishing our objectives intended to accomplish our overall goal. Chris loved old school communications, like town hall meetings, one-on-ones, and well-written messages. Plus, he was good at them, which may explain why he liked those types of communication. But, as he said, "Sometimes, you speak more loudly when you let everyone know your concerns." When sending messages, repetition was the name of the game.

Chris was a believer in Jim Schaffer's view of organizational communication: "To bring about clarity and build shared meaning communication must be managed as a business process, just as planning, engineering, manufacturing and distribution must be managed as a business process."[10]

The difference with communication is it serves as a boundary spanning function. In other words, communication connects the organization and its entities (including those named above) with the constituencies that affect its success. The others are silos, business divisions that operate independently and avoid sharing information. Enterprise-wide communication is the conduit that connects silos, unifying their efforts with other parts of the company.

By spanning boundaries, both inside the firm and out, a clear picture of reality emerges for all. Those external entities include customers, suppliers, community leaders, competitors, regulators, inspectors, politicians, and even family friends of employees. From a credibility point-of-view, there's no group with greater impact on "publics" than your employees. Let's unpack this concept to shed light on the strategic nature of communication.

All Eyes on Chris

"Whether I want to believe it or not, when I walk in the room, all eyes are on me ... always. They're on me even when I don't walk in the room when everyone was expecting me to walk in the room!" Chris said with a grin. He's right, you know. He's not being self-centered or arrogant. Shaffer writes: "People watch everything for meaning and in the process they discover some of the tiniest things that scream out messages about a leader's preferences, priorities, and moods."[11]

Chris had a boss who used to say, "We need to connect the dots for people. What we do at the top of the house needs to be decoded for everyone in the place." Employees call headquarters "Puzzle Palace" because they can't make sense of what's happening. Figure 9.2 shows developing a communication strategy must first recognize the components of engagement—the road to buy-

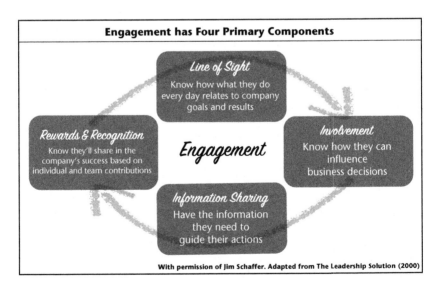

FIGURE 9.2 With permission of Jim Schaffer. Adapted from The Leadership Solution (2000)

in—is contingent on four primary components: (a) line of sight, (b) involvement, (c) information sharing, and (d) rewards and recognition.[12]

Clarity is a job motivator. When they have an unobstructed *line of* sight at the workplace, clarity prevails. People who know what is expected of them can act appropriately and with much less stress. Further, when people know how they make an impact they're validated by their efforts and this confirms their sense of purpose on the job. Simply put, it's the means to *connect the dots* to make sense out of the puzzle.

Involvement is nurtured when development of the strategic plan receives measurable input from all members of the team. This means that their ideas about improving business results are "generated, captured, prioritized, and implemented."[13] There's discernible value in involving everyone from the start. Chris once set up idea kiosks with whiteboards and markers placed throughout Apex office space so employees could offer ideas and observations about their workplace issues. Each day, Chris and his senior managers read comments, and in some cases, asked follow-up questions on-the-spot. People could see that management reviewed their input and took their ideas seriously. The whiteboards could be seen by all so they could add comments or support ideas they liked.

The Currency of the Workplace

There's an unwritten rule in most human settings that information is power. Some people trade on this information like it's a black market of secrets and unmentionables, gossip! Chris believed secrets could do far more harm than good. Realistically, not all information in a firm should be open for public inspection. Certain facts demand limited exposure to insure privacy and security. However, if the company expected people to keep focus on the business it's wise to share information freely. However, this isn't easy to accomplish.

Fear is the greatest roadblock. Senior managers fear what might happen if sensitive information is made public to competitors, unions, even the government! This last one is actually true in that public companies have an obligation to protect the release of "material" information. That notwithstanding, Chris relentlessly sought to provide his people the information they needed to guide their actions.

Finally, and maybe the most obvious, *rewards and recognition*, address the most important person in the workplace, ME, the individual employee. When the leader takes this person seriously, she recognizes and validates them on a personal level.

Chris self-insured his company. That is, rather than buying insurance from a third party, Apex covered itself. While this may sound risky, it provides an "all-in-it-together" mindset. Chris was relentless about the safety and security of employees and their families.

Chris routinely encouraged human resources to provide clinics, seminars, and programs to address employee health risks, like smoking cessation, yoga for stress reduction, walking clubs, recreational bowling, basketball, golf, and softball, to name a few. Chris reached out to sick and injured employees and their loved ones. He insisted on clean air and safe working conditions and insisted people take care of themselves.

This attitude carried over into how Chris used bonuses and incentives. One unique incentive was his "Catch someone doing something good" on-the-spot cash award. When a manager recognized such behavior, they could award $100 on observance. Along this idea that incentive must be closely related to desired behavior, Chris required each supervisor, manager, and vp to perform quarterly coaching sessions in addition to annual reviews.

He believed without more frequent contact annual reviews were too far removed from the "do" and the "pay." Requiring managers to perform these mini evaluations made them pay close attention to the daily activities of their direct reports. Moreover, the accumulation of the timely reports made the annual review much richer and meaningful.

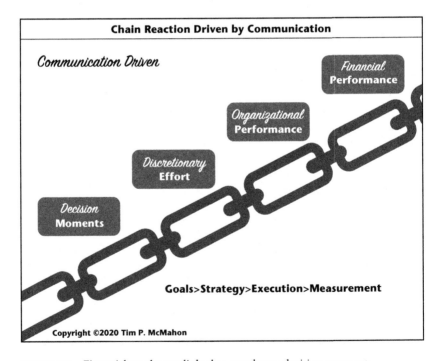

FIGURE 9.3 Financial results are linked to employee decision moments

The Chain Reaction of Financial Results

Chris frequently reminded people the chain of performance as depicted in Figure 9.3. It begins with the overarching goal: get and keep customers. Do that, mind your expenses, and the firm will likely make money. Whether you sell goods or services, getting and keeping customers is dependent on two items: do you know exactly what they want from your firm; are you delivering it! How well people carry out their duties plays an important role in whether your firm thrives or merely survives. This is delivered through a chain reaction of financial results.

To reach favorable financial performance, members are entrusted with managing decision moments throughout the day. Each employee may or may not exercise the discretionary efforts that will positively affect overall organizational performance, which leads to financial performance. If this is a negative experience, why? Three decades ago, the president of Scandinavian Airlines (SAS), cracked the code on this challenge. Jan Carlzon wrote: "Loyalty to vision, not the details of execution, is a must—or else. People shine only if demands are sky high … Part and parcel is rigorous, honest measurement."[14]

Moments of Truth

Carlzon was adamant that the biggest challenge to energizing employees was supplying the energy itself. While igniting employees had significant positive impact on business, it's difficult to sustain. "We must be willing to welcome change rather than fight it, to encourage risk-taking rather than snuff it out, to empower rather than demotivate our first-line people, and to focus outwardly on the fast-changing market rather than inwardly on Byzantine bureaucratic maneuvers."[15]

Carlzon inspired top managers to look more deeply at the customer experience. While the goal of SAS was efficiency, the initiative provided significant benefit to the customer experience. No doubt, this dedication to the frontline provider permeated such legendary customer-leading firms like Southwest Airlines, Nordstrom's, and Trader Joe's. Creating a norm-breaking culture that gives employees the freedom to accommodate customers by removing the unintended roadblocks to their experience can have delightful effect on the employee as well as the customer.

Carlzon acknowledged this wouldn't be accomplished through an employee training program, although that's an effective way to create acceptance and understanding. He advocated that these moments of truth be identified, measured, and accounted for to demonstrate commitment and thereby engender commitment to sustaining the effort.

The Meaning of Customer-Centric

Peter Fader argues that being customer friendly isn't enough, a firm must be customer-centric. He distinguishes firms based on whether they're customer-centric or product-centric. The aim of each is the same: to make the company as profitable as possible. Fader asserts that "customer centricity is a strategy that aligns a company's development and delivery of its products and services with the current and future needs of a select set of customers in order to maximize their long-term financial value to the firm."[16]

Fader warns that adopting a customer-centric perspective requires a firm to adopt radical new means to assume a long-term view toward creation and delivery; that means changing its "organizational design, performance metrics, and employee and distributor structures."[17] Perhaps the most difficult concept for firms to adopt is the notion not all customers are the same. Customer-centric means being focused on the specific customer the firm chooses to serve. Not all customers are alike.

Chris encouraged Apex people to dig deeper into their customer's profile. Like Fader, he believed once you identified specifically how a customer made progress against her situation, the better prepared Apex could serve them like no other competitor. Fader points out, "Once you have identified your right customers the next steps are obvious. You find out what they want, what they need, and what they will demand going forward."[18]

This demands the firm adopt a long-term strategic view. Communication takes on a similar perspective. When a firm focuses on its customers, develops the data tools to deeply understand customer, it can begin to predict the value the customer represents to the firm over time. Customer Lifetime Value or CLTV[19] is a calculation used to identify this number. CLTV represents the present value of the future cash flows or the value of business attributed to the customer during his or her entire relationship with the company.

To determine the CLTV of your customers, the firm must run the calculations for each. While the calculation inputs may be imperfect, the exercise enables managers to identify factors that will contribute to maximizing the value of each customer and each is unique. This attitude knowing how much a customer contributes to the company must be embedded in the collective mindset of management. It is a strategic imperative.

Three Sources of Communication

Every leader knows communication matters, but seldom do they act to improve it. Ineffective communication creates confusion and uninformed people; thus, reducing a firm's ability to function and crippling its ability to compete. If you spend any time in an organization, you'll soon begin to understand that substantive communication emanates from three sources:

- formal communication media;
- systems; and
- leadership

What may come as a surprise is the degree of effectiveness of these three components. People must understand what's expected of them, how they contribute to the mission, and how that benefits them. It is up to the leader to *connect the dots,* as has been mentioned. Too often, leaders believe communication is restricted to formal items like texts, e-mails, and phone messages. Often these items—the conventional tools such as presentations, training classes, posters, and even impromptu discussions—get all the attention. Yet, employees in a firm recognize the messaging power of systems and leadership as much more authentic and meaningful. We'll examine these to understand the nature and effectiveness of each.

The formal media that firms employ are intentional and visible. However, the credibility of which is subject to a simple rule: do what you say you'll do. In the next chapter, we'll explain this aspect of communication in detail.

When we think of the systems at work in our lives, the terms that come to life are processes, policies, procedures, and programs. Further, we may think of it also includes the physical layout of the spaces we occupy, the organization structure, pay policies, promotion and succession plans, and the measurement and evaluation tools by which we measure progress. As the business grows, the need for these systems play a bigger role in how we perceive ourselves and our tasks.

When Chris took over Apex, he looked for the way these systems communicated to everyone. He soon discovered—through his own personal experience—that payday for salaried workers was the first of the month. That was arbitrary policy. Chris' first check was due on first, too, which during that month fell on a Monday. Chris thought, what if my rent was due on the last day of the month? Or my car payment? Or credit card bill?

Chris knew this might be a bit of a squeeze for people who didn't have enough paycheck at the end of the month. It was only a day, and all probably worked out for the best most of the time, but what harm was there in delivering the pay on the final day of the month, instead of the next day? If nothing, it reduced any anxiety employees had about their cash flow to pay bills on time.

He arranged to change the deposit date of salaried employees to the last day of the month. People went out of their way to thank Chris for the change of policy. Such an action seems inconsequential in communication of appreciation for the work that people perform for the firm, but to many, this signaled someone at the top cared for them, and that sends a big message.

The Big Five

The firm's many systems must be aligned in order to communicate clearly and consistently. Schaffer wrote: "What they say needs to drive behavior toward winning, every system communicates. However, five big systems have emerged to communicate the loudest,"[20] and they are:

- Structure
- Measurement and rewards
- Policies and procedures
- Resource allocation
- Working environment

Structure

From the organizational chart to the location and use of the lunchroom to the sizes and appointments of the offices and cubes speaks loudly to people. In a meritocracy, which is the governing structure of Apex, the layout of the office facilitated the flow of work with the intent to shorten the distance between the most highly interactive areas. Each functional area was nearly identical. Never considered lavish, the environment is best described as comfortable and functional. Chris was a stickler about taking care of the space and often commented if someone was either disrupting or hogging the resources available to all.

Making his usual rounds, Chris noticed employee had installed a SiriusXM feed on his computer. He stopped and asked, "Is that music coming from your computer?"

The employee, thinking it was too loud, quickly responded, "Sorry, I'll turn it down."

Chris bounced back, "Don't turn it down, get it off your computer, or should I say, *our* computer."

Looking puzzled, the employee was struggling for words, then Chris continued in a calm explanatory tone. "If music makes you more productive and happier, by all means, listen away. My concern is you're soaking up bandwidth that we desperately need to conduct business. If you want a little musical accompaniment, bring a radio or something that doesn't draw down on our wi-fi!" Chris finished up the conversation by saying, "music must be working for you, your production numbers look great!"

The employee smiled and agreed happily. During her next quarterly review, Chris stepped in with a gift of a SiriusXM receiver so she could take the signal off the satellite! This incident reflects a level of candidness and honesty that is uncommon in the workplace between the top dog and the rest of the pups in the kennel. But the metaphor of a pack mentality is apt and may be explained by a framed quote that hung prominently in Chris' office. It was the Law for the Wolves from Rudyard Kipling's Second Jungle Book:

> Now this is the law of the jungle, as old and as true as the sky,
>
> And the Wolf that shall keep it may prosper, but the wolf that shall break it must die.
>
> As the creeper that girdles the tree trunk, the law runneth forward and back;
>
> For the strength of the pack is the wolf, and the strength of the wolf is the pack.

Measurement and Rewards

The famous old phrase, *what gets measured, gets done,* sounds good but besides being misattributed to many, it's dismissed by many management experts. The real message is that we live in a data-rich environment and it behooves management to use data to help inform and convince people what matters to their performance. When people don't know what's needed to win, they lack the clarity in performing their job. Alternately, if you can measure and reward folks on specific behaviors and outcomes, you provide context to evaluate performance and coach for results.

Policies and Procedures

The role of policy is to reduce confusion about the way to do business. The role of procedures is to spell out how to accomplish the work. Chris discovered a major bottleneck between two departments that served as a critical link in the information report eventually sent to the customer. A cursory tracing of work-flow suggested this was significant and demanded further investigation and understanding. He thought, if people could see the flow, they might be better prepared to make smoother and less subject to bottlenecks.

So he brought in a process management professor from the college to conduct a day long "sticky note" session with all parties involved to identify the kinks and iron out the process, so it flowed smoothly. Tracking pre- and post- Chris' managers could inform their people of a 25% reduction in errors, and a 90% improvement in throughput. Chris adopted the new process as a best practice and reflected changes made in the firm's policies and procedures.

Resource Allocation

One of the most important functions of senior managers is to manage resources, specifically, to focus the limited wherewithal of the firm on the overall goal: get and keep customers. When the controller's arbitrary freeze on travel resulted in a flurry of canceled customer meetings, Chris got involved. He called together the salespeople to gather routine intelligence mostly gathered from the firm's Customer Relationship Management (CRM) database. Analysis of the numbers showed a 35% decrease in customer contact. The idea was to manage these touchpoints, not eliminate them.

Further, the data could demonstrate a break in the pipeline of new business opportunities. Using data, a major issue regarding the firm's key goal of getting and keeping customers was underwater due to a seemingly prudent effort by the controller to reign in expenses. This example should by no means suggest that the controller was trying to undermine the business. Yet his actions had unintended consequences felt by the sales force. Chris highlighted the *unforced error*, as he called it. Chris opened the meeting by saying, "It's tough enough facing the competition let alone when it is ourselves! Okay, so we about shot ourselves in the foot. But thanks to the quick actions of our teams coming together, we caught the bullet before it did any damage!"

Working Environment

Chris lives by the formula ESI = CSI, meaning employee satisfaction index runs parallel to the customer satisfaction index. Chris recalls making a call on a customer when upon entering the executive lobby he saw this message on the wall in gold-plated letters: *Profit Tops Everything!*

Looking around the place with its expensive furniture, museum curated artwork, and lavish appointments, Chris couldn't help but think: Was there some mistake in that sign? Shouldn't it have read: *Profit stops here?* While it is good to remind employees of the importance of profitability, it is not a great message to send to your customer. If you are obsessed with profits and the fine life, you're not obsessed with me, any customer might conclude.

The point is that when there's discernible difference between the vision and values of the firm and the way it presents itself to the public, it's a breeding ground for skepticism and cynicism to grow. Working environments are communication tools, too. When the organization proclaims to be flat, it had better show a sense of equity in its workplace.

Systems speak loudly, sometimes too loudly with the wrong message. The converse is true, too. Figure 9.4 shows how the progression of information leads to decisions that inform actions; when this occurs congruently with both employees and customers a coherent relationship may form.

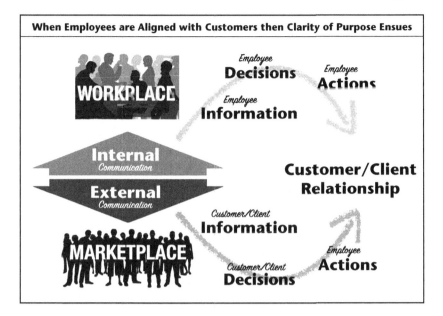

FIGURE 9.4 A balanced approach to messaging. Adapted from The Leadership Solution (2000) McGraw-Hill, New York

Leadership, the Big Communicator

Nearly 40 years ago, James Kouzes and Barry Posner began asking a single question to identify leader best practices: They asked thousands of executives: What did you do when you were at your personal best as a leader? Today, their survey continues to generate more than 400,000 responses annually. Their seminal work yields five leader behaviors that inspire extraordinary outcomes in organizations. They call them the Five Practices of Exemplary Leadership:

- Model the way;
- Inspire a shared vision;
- Challenge the process;
- Enable others to act; and
- Encourage the heart.

The authors point to several takeaways from these practices that punctuate the vital role that leadership plays in communicating. Perhaps the most potent messaging a leader can exhibit is personal behavior. "Exemplary leaders know that if they want to gain commitment and achieve the highest standards, they must be models of the behavior they expect of others."[21]

The Vision Appears in Our Dreams

By now, we've explored the role of a vision in aligning and motivating followers. "You can't command commitment; you must inspire it. You have to *enlist others in a common vision by appealing to shared aspirations.*"[22] For this to come alive, the leader must have a schedule of messaging—in both words and action—with which they embrace daily.

There's no more dangerous area for an employee to enter than that of challenging the process, as Kouzes and Posner call it. If an organization is going to benefit from the eyes and ears on the front line, it's incumbent upon leaders to set the pace. "Not one person (respondent in the survey) achieved a personal best by keeping things the same. Regardless of the specifics, they all involved overcoming adversity and embracing opportunities to grow, innovate, and improve."

A popular ditty goes: "Teamwork makes the dream work." Leaders should pay attention to this advice because it's a marker of leader communication that matters. "Leaders foster collaboration by building trust and facilitating relationships."[23] To move people to act, the leader must *enable* others to act.

Often the reason change efforts fail is they run out of energy. Just like the Energizer bunny needs a regenerating jolt of juice to keep banging that drum, so too, workers in an organization need emotional fuel. "Leaders recognize contributions by showing appreciation for individual excellence. It can be one to one or with many people. It can come from dramatic gestures or simple actions. It can come from informal channels, just as well as through formal hierarchy."[24]

Suffice to say, leaders hold the keys to the kingdom in the manner by which they serve as models of behavior. Leadership author John Maxwell advises leaders must go first in three key areas: (a) believe in yourself, (b) set expectations, and (c) keep commitments. As Maxwell puts it: "You must be willing to pay the price of example if you want others to follow your lead."[25]

Communication is a broad topic and to provide a cohesive take on how it works to create buy-in, we will: (a) establish the framework for a communication strategy, (b) identify internal and external tools and tactics, and (c) review traditional and digital platforms for creating meaningful and lasting engagement.

Dimensions of Communication

Finally, we wrap up the strategy of communication by summarizing five aspects of traditional personal communication: (a) listening, (b) writing, (c) speaking, (d) amplifying, and (e) evaluating.

By *listening* we mean that too little attention is placed on one-half of the message (sending) and too little on the more important half (receiving). Many resources are devoted to speaking and relatively few on listening. The emphasis should be reversed. Stephen Covey's sage advice is that we would do well to first seek to understand before we expect to be understood.[26]

Writing is an ever-present concern of business executives, often complaining new students aren't properly prepared in the art of writing. We do well to remember that writing well requires ongoing practice. Writer and critic William Zinsser wrote: "thinking clearly is a conscious act that writers must force on themselves, as if they were working on any other project that requires logic."[27]

Speaking is what most of us associate with the principal means of communication. In reality, speaking is one element, but it thrives when it's informed by the others. Hal Holbrook, famous for his six decades portraying Mark Twain, said he had more than 20 hours of material for a two-hour show. He was constantly adding to the cache of his portrayal. He is "editing and changing it to fit the times."[28] Speaking well requires knowing and understanding the audience and having the range of content and technique to reach them in a meaningful way.

Amplifying means spreading the message to wider circles of constituents through traditional and digital media. Like a garden, communication requires constant tending and weeding. Communication is by definition resident in people; it's subject to change, manipulation, and yes, hijacking. Therefore, we do well to live with it, make it a part of our daily routine, and above all, use all five aspects of the practice listed above.

TAKE-AWAYS

- Communication is both sending (messaging) and receiving (listening) to complete the loop. Without recognition of the feedback, communication is incomplete.
- Strategic planning includes mission, problem/opportunity, goal/objective setting, strategy, tactics, and evaluation. While this is a linear portrayal; of the process, in reality strategic planning is an iterative exercise.
- In every planning exercise, the thinking and scheming matters greatly, but it's in the human execution that intentions become reality and goals or achieved or abandon.
- Strategic planning always gets its impetus from the top, where the strategic plan for the firm is developed. However, it must lean on the input from the entire organization if success is expected.
- Communication strategy relies not on analytical insight but resolve. Communication must address the challenge of winning the hearts and minds of the members of the firm for execution to take place.
- Communication strategy is dependent on conducting an orderly inquiry to determine the key questions that must be answered to inform the plan.
- Big ideas will land more effectively than safe ideas, and people who know themselves are in a better position to deliver on big expectations.

Knowing our strengths and how we perform best is rudimentary to the organization performing at its best.

- Strategy is dependent on valid assumptions (what we believe to be true about the firm and its environment) and this is dependent on engagement of all members of the firm.

- The strategic communication plan guides execution of the overall corporate strategy because it spans the boundaries of the departments, functions, and even external publics such as community, politicians, and regulators.

- Like it or not, the CEO is the one who sets the pace. All eyes are focused on what's said and what's done by the CEO. It can validate or deny all formal communication methods.

- Engagement is essential and involvement, that's genuinely valuing the input of all, is key to generating involvement and eventual commitment to the plan. Moreover, it is the duty of leaders to actively tend to four primary components of engagement: (a) line of sight, (b) involvement, (c) information sharing, and (d) rewards & recognition.

- The life of the organization is dependent on making money, it's a requisite. Getting is dependent on the actions by individuals driven by communication (goals > strategy > execution > measurement). We call this the chain reaction of financial results: (a) decision moments, (b) discretionary effort, (c) organizational performance, and (d) financial performance.

- The objective of a firm is to get and keep customers. Firms accomplish this by building expertise and commitment. This is inherent in delivering on the expectations of customers. We articulate this in the statement *helping them make progress on their situation.*

- Empowering individuals through an understanding of how the firm delivers value is the essential step in freeing frontline workers to act on behalf of the customer.

- This effort must surpass the hollow promise of doing whatever it takes. Rather, leaders must provide the precise and critical identity of the customer the firm seeks to serve. However, it's difficult for top management to see the specific value proposition at the depth at which it truly matters to customers, so they must dialogue with frontline workers who are directly in touch with customers.

- Using tools like the Customer Lifetime Value (CLV) calculations delivers in concrete terms the specific components of each customer's lifetime value. Then, it's necessary to devise the detailed plan valued by each customer.

- Three sources of communication in a firm include: formal communication media, systems, and leadership. The most effective of all is leadership.

Notes

1 Weintraub Austin, E. & Pinkleton, B. E. (2015). *Strategic public relations management (3rd ed.).* New York, NY: Routledge – Taylor & Francis Group., (p. 41).
2 Maister, D. (2008). *Strategy and the fat smoker.* Boston, MA: Spangle Press., (p. 6).
3 Ibid, (pp. 6–7).
4 Garcia, H. G. (2012). *The power of communication: Skills to build trust, inspire loyalty, and lead effectively.* Upper Saddle River, NJ: Pearson Education., (pp. 81–82).
5 Ibid, (p. 82).
6 Drucker. P. (2017). *Managing oneself and what makes an effective executive.* Boston, MA: Harvard Business Review Press., (p. 8).
7 Ibid, (p. 8).
8 Bossidy, L., & Charan, R. (2004). *Execution.* New York, NY: Crown Business., (p. 186).
9 Ibid, (p. 186).
10 Schaffer, J. (2000). *The leadership solution.* New York, NY: McGraw-Hill., (p. 49).
11 Ibid, (p. 55).
12 Ibid, (p. 30).
13 Ibid, (p. 32).
14 Carlzon, J. (1987). *Moments of truth: New strategies for today's customer-driven economy.* New York, NY: Ballinger Publishing Co., (p. xi).
15 Ibid, (p. xii).
16 Fader, P. (2012). *Customer centricity: Focus on the right customers for strategic advantage.* Philadelphia, PA: The Wharton Digital Press., (p. 39).
17 Ibid, (p. 39).
18 Ibid, (p. 43).
19 Definition of "Customer Lifetime Value" (n.d.). Retrieved from https://economictimes.indiatimes.com/definition/customer-lifetime-value.
20 Schaffer, (p. 68).
21 Kouzes, J. M. & Posner, B. Z. (2017). *The leadership challenge* (6th ed.). Hoboken, N.J.: Wiley & Sons, Inc., (p. 12).
22 Ibid, (p. 13).
23 Ibid, (p. 16).
24 Ibid, (p. 17).
25 Maxwell, J. C. (February 12, 2019). Are you a "Go First" leader? John C. Maxwell blog. Retrieved November 26, 2020 from www.johnmaxwell.com/blog/are-you-a-go-first -leader/.
26 Covey, S. R. (2013). *The 7 habits of highly effective people: Powerful lessons in personal change.* New York, NY: Rosetta Books.
27 Zinsser, W. (2006). *On writing well.* New York, NY: HarperCollins., (p. 9).
28 Lauer-Williams, K. (October 11, 2004) Channeling Mark Twain: Hal Holbrook performs one-man show In Easton. *The Morning Call.* Retrieved November 26, 2020 from www.mcall.com/entertainment/art-theater/mc-hal-holbrook-easton-state-theatre-20141011=stpry.html.

10

COMMUNICATION EXECUTION

"Office Space" is the 2005 cult movie that spoofs the American workplace. In one scene the big cheese Bill Lumbergh (played by actor Gary Cole) hovers in for a landing on the corner of the cube of the movie's main character Peter Gibbons (played by Ron Livingston) to remind him that he has failed to put a cover sheet on his TPS report.

LUMBERGH: *(In a snarky voice) Did you see the memo about this?*
GIBBONS: *Yeah, Yeah, yeah, I have it right here… I just a forgot. It's not shipping out 'til tomorrow, so there's no problem.*
LUMBERGH: *Yeaaaa. If you could just go ahead and make sure you do that from now on that would be great. And, a, I'll go ahead and make sure you get another copy of that memo. O-Kayyy (talking over Peter's response while walking away) Bye-bye, Peter…*

The dialogue (if there was one) is an example of the way the boss communicates at the fictitious Initech. This black comedy connects with workers today, more than two decades after its release. If you really want to discover the sad reality of the scene, go to YouTube and read the comments, a string of endless affirmations from workers everywhere who relate the scene to their personal experiences in the workplace. The scene's been the source for a string of internet memes over the years. This is a parody that loudly bashes management's anemic attempts at communication.
It's funny because it really happens, all the time.

What's Ahead?

In Chapter 9, we established a foundation for execution by explaining strategy, the "how" of communication. This chapter deals with execution, the "what" of communication and execution. Strategy is the "how" and execution is the "what" of communication. More change has occurred in the tools and channels of communication this decade than ever in our history. This revolutionary change has amended the rules about communicating effectively.

This chapter begins with timeless observations and theories about how to create and practice the art of communicating to move people to action. Then, you'll see a brief update of the contemporary tools and platforms used by leading practitioners in the world of digital communication. Before this, take a look at Figure 10.1 as it sets the tone for how the organization must come together to confront reality and shape its challenges.

The simple illustration borrows a phrase used frequently in business: close the loop. In business, this means to make sure everyone is in the communication loop. That develops clarity for all. In systems thinking, the loop is closed in order for the system to remain stable. We use systems thinking to help members of an organization see how events, patterns, and structure affect an organization. This diagram presents communication as a closed loop that serves to coalesce shared understanding and add stability to the system. An open system has no feedback, and thus, will likely lose stability, spin out, if you will, because it loses balance. Think of a two-way radio transmission where sender and receiver exchange roles as they converse.

Speaker A speaks and ends the message with "Over" meaning "I am done, you can talk." Then Speaker B states: "Roger that." Though it's not used as much today, Speaker B would add, "Wilco" concise and clear affirmation

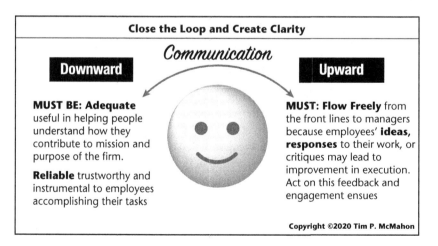

FIGURE 10.1 Go with the flow with this simple advice about effective communication

meaning "will comply" and may have followed that up with "Out" meaning I'm done. This pattern of ending transmissions left no doubt in the mind of the receiver of the communication and eliminated potential confusion or misunderstanding. We've used such practices even in the simplest of communications to deliver clear and actionable messages thereby closing the loop.

Chris' pet peeve in communication regularly occurs in the retail environment. "I order a meal through the drive-up window. I drive around to the window to pay for it. The person there takes my money and I head to the pick-up window where my order is poked out and without a word the window closes. No, 'here you go' or 'thank you'... they don't even look you in the eye! Sometimes, I am not sure I have my entire order!" It doesn't matter the transaction is completed. Not everyone agrees with Chris, suggesting, "you got your food and are free to go, what more do you want?"

Chris would say, "it may sound trivial, but closure. I want closure."

Clarity Creates Shared Meaning

The unfortunate fact about communication is that too many leaders picture a big megaphone. They think of effective communication is about amplification. Their priority is that their voice is heard above the clutter. Perfect communication is measured if the message is received. If only they knew, if you want someone to hear what you have to say, listen more and use your words sparingly. In other words, seek to close the loop. Two-way communication is essential.

Professor James Grunig expanded on the idea that "with the two-way symmetrical model practitioners use research and dialogue to bring about symbiotic changes in ideas, attitudes, and behaviors of both the organization and publics."[1] In this model, advocacy is balanced with inquiry to form skills of honest investigation.[2] Imagine this happening if the relationship fails to acknowledge a response from the receiver.

Disciplined Communication Defined

Chris learned the secret of the less popular side of communication (listening) shortly after he was married. His wife enrolled the two of them in Parent Effectiveness Training.[3] Program developers discovered that kids don't rebel against parents, they rebel against the destructive methods parents use to attempt to force them to comply, often referred to as discipline. We know coercion has limited effectiveness. It fails at the goal of gaining compliance through true communication.

One of the core principles of effective parenting is effective listening, or active listening as it's termed. Active listening is the act of listening in a way that keeps you engaged with your conversation partner in a positive manner. When the other person is speaking, the listener must be attentive, hold back judgment.

When the time is right, the listener then paraphrases and reflects what was understood to be heard. Simple concept but difficult to master as it flies in the face of the way we communicate, with a megaphone, not an earphone.

ACTIVE LISTENING?

Chris was listening to a talk show on his way to his mother's when it dawned on him just how much talk radio had changed. He was reminiscing about the early days traveling from customer to customer with the radio as his companion, when he arrived at his mom's place.

CHRIS: *I just was thinking how much radio has changed.*

AGNES: *If it weren't for cars, I am not sure we'd have any radios these days.*

CHRIS: (Chris chuckled). *True. But I remember when we'd listen to talk radio when I was a kid and it seemed like it was either chit-chat about community stuff or some serious bickering.*

AGNES: *Oh, boy. I remember that. We used to laugh when they'd fight it out over everything from health care to child rearing.*

CHRIS: *And now, it's all political, or better, factional. And it's mostly about people tuning in to hear what they already believe.*

AGNES: *They call it the echo chamber.* (As an octogenarian, Agnes was truly up-to-date and enlightened). *All that stuff on the radio but also in the social stuff, too.*

CHRIS: *I am not sure it's better this way. I think a good argument helps me think a little more deeply about issues to find the truth.*

AGNES: *No one wants the truth these days, unless it's **their** truth!*

They both laughed and chatted about the usual stuff, family, the weather, obituaries ... all the stuff that interests a 80-plus year old and her son. Then Chris kissed her good-bye and went back to work.

Are You Actively Listening or Scrambling for a Response?

Have you ever caught yourself in conversation when you realized you were searching for the proper response and not listening to the message being sent? It happens, a lot. Most of us have a need to fill the quiet space. So, we are always running a response mechanism in the background that's formulating a reply. While many deny it, multi-tasking is simply not possible in certain situations. Yes, it's possible to sing and play the piano at the same time; but reading about one thing and writing about another simultaneously are not. Those two tasks compete for the same information processor in our brains. When people say they are multitasking, it is more likely, they are switching back and forth on tasks. It happens so quickly they believe they're reading and writing simultaneously.

The problem is that with any discreet action, the other action is unattended. In the case of listening, it's not optimal to listen in spurts. If you ever listened to a distant crackling radio signal you can relate to the challenge. "In Burm … many …. oxen were ex … for human life." What was that message? Was it, "In Burma today, many oxen were exchanged for human lives"? Or was it "In Birmingham, after many workers who were exposed to a toxin were examined and assured it would not affect human life." While that represents a true communication breakdown, that is, actual words were missing, so there's only partial delivery of the message. What about messages that receivers process without full attention, or while misinterpreting what they hear because they were distracted or filtering it through their biases? There are many ways communication falls short. Think about your own conversations with your spouse or co-worker.

HE: *Are we going to that dinner party at Millers on Saturday?*
SHE: *I thought we were. Why wouldn't we?*
HE: (thinking on the background while listening to the previous statement, I noted a sense of dissatisfaction so, I quickly attempt to stub the conversation or at least divert it because I don't like where it is going). *No, yeah, of course we're going.*
SHE: (hearing me stumble makes an assumption what I am really saying is that I don't want to go and don't like those people). *They're nice. It's always fun.*
HE: (Nice? Is she crazy? They drink a lot and get out of control fast. But I hold back to avoid conflict). *Sounds good. Let's go.*

While it may have sounded like two people in agreement with plans for Saturday, that's not the case as you know since I filled you in with all the back channel going on in the brain of each participant. What you witnessed in the recesses is bound to be brought forward at some point because at least one party has an unaddressed concern. The concern over the couple that makes everyone uncomfortable is the source of a much bigger conflict that may rise up later.

Through active listening, the discussion may have adopted a more productive course. Consider this:

HE: Are we going to the Miller's on Saturday?
SHE: Yes, it sounded like fun. Sounds like you are hesitant.
HE: Yes, I am.
SHE: What makes you feel that way?
HE: Last time, they started with the booze and got a little out of hand. It was embarrassing and I have to do business with that guy.
SHE: I do recall. I did not know you had business with Jim. Did it cause problems with him?

HE: Kind of, it just made us uncomfortable, I think. I don't know for sure, much
       was left unsaid.
SHE: So, you don't want the drama because it leads to problems later on?
HE: Yes.

The second conversation didn't resolve the conflict, but it opened up a view to a
deeper problem than simply an uncomfortable exchange on an otherwise pleasant
Saturday night. The little talk was honest and respectful and because SHE was
willing to hear HE without jumping to unfounded conclusions and vice-versa,
they could unpack the real reason for the conflict. Too often, the shorthand nature
of our exchanges leaves much to the imagination and we complicate our ability to
reduce conflict and move toward a shared view where compromise may result.

Not in the Written Word?

The impediment to effective communication may lie in our failure to listen, or it
may be we aren't saying what we really want to say. William Zinsser advises
when writing we must remember, "readers read with their eyes. But in fact, they
hear what they're reading far more than you realize. Therefore, such matters as
rhythm and alliteration are vital to every sentence."[4]

Simply put, Zinsser asks writers to select words that fit with one another like a
hand in glove, so it not only sounds right but feels right. Zinsser illustrates the
value of developing a writing style, the specific way your writing reads. Listen to
the advice of E. B. White: "All writing is communication: creative writing is
communication through revelation—it is the Self escaping into the open."[5]

White illustrates his point with this challenge: try to improve upon Thomas
Payne's timeless line from his pamphlet "Common Sense:" "These are times that
try men's souls." The words are not flashy: "Yet in that arrangement, they have
shown great durability; the sentence is living on in its third century."[6] The
message: words matter and how you arrange them demonstrates your style and
the power of your thoughts. So, when you hear Chris say, "Win one, then pop
off!" or "When in doubt, better head out" just know that the way he writes, or
puts together a sentence, hits home in both message and style and followers oblige
with their commitment.

Measuring Our Progress in Meaningful Terms

No one disputes the importance of communication. However, there's a gap
between what should happen and what actually takes hold in the organization.
To close the gap, we must first agree on the purpose of communication. Helio
Fred Garcia wrote: "The goal of communication is not to communicate, but to
accomplish some tangible business goal."[7] This statement resonates with the
heads of organizations—not placated by awards or fancy brochures. They want,

like everyone, to make progress against their situation; their situation is the business goal for which they're held accountable.

While communication practitioners are smitten with the cool features and fancy functions of the latest bright, shiny object, what truly matters is how communication causes the organization to thrive—that's what we must identify, do and measure to mark success. This requires moving past the face of numbers and metrics as they're merely a scorecard. In a sense, metrics are abstractions. By definition that means considering something removed from its concrete nature. In modern communication, metaphors and storytelling carry the day, they always have. Chris remembered his accounting professor's lesson as if it was yesterday.

The class was studying financial reports, specifically, the balance sheet and the profit and loss (P&L) statement. The balance sheet is a report of assets, liabilities, and shareholder equity at a specific point in time, like the end of the period or quarter. The P&L is also a snapshot in time, but it accounts for revenues, costs, and expenses. Chris recalls the professor tried to deliver a deeper message that these documents are a *reflection* of the performance of a firm, not its actual performance. Her caution was to move past the numbers to the real human performance they represent. Chris picks it up from there.

"So, Dr. Pandya told a story. Not just any story but one originally told by Plato in his work, the 'Republic' specifically a tale called the 'Allegory of the Cave.' Plato describes how Socrates talks about these people who lived in a cave and chained to the wall for their whole lives. All they could see were shadows projected on the wall from objects passing in front of a fire behind them. But to them these shadows are not reflections, they are real. They see them with their own eyes!"

She continued, therefore, they seek to remain chained to the wall because they know no better life. It's kind of silly, isn't it? So why do so many people think they can read a balance sheet and a P&L and be informed about the business and how to make it thrive. Just like the prisoners in the cave, they see a *reflection* of reality, not reality, and therefore become self-deluded.

Chris waited to see how people reacted to the story. One young woman piped up and said, "But, in the allegory of the cave, one of the prisoners breaks free and ventures out of the cave to the sunlight; but he is blinded by the light until his eyes adjust. Then he truly sees the reality around him."

Chris is delighted to hear the second part of story unfold through the employee. "So, once he saw the truth, so to speak, how did that change his thinking?" Chris asked.

She responded, "He wanted to tell the others and let them know they were not seeing the full story. But, when he returned, he discovered his own vision in the cave was impaired as it was too dark in there. He was blind just as when he left the cave for the first time. Therefore, his news fell on deaf ears or should I say blind eyes."

Chris said, "That's exactly the way the professor told it. The prisoners interpreted the man's blindness as a result of leaving the cave and resolved they're a lot better off chained to the wall. Ignorance is bliss. Therefore, it's much safer sticking with what you know. That's the problem when we rely on reports to inform us about business decisions. They aren't real, they're a reflection of real. If you want to solve business problems, get out and experience the business under the light of day. The reports will serve as a means to inquire, but they're not the final story." This was an example of a typical kind of meeting Chris would have from time-to-time to help people see for themselves. It gave his people a perspective outside of the day-to-day, in which we often lose sight of the bigger picture.

Why Narratives Work

You will see Chris' story—actually, it's a narrative—follows a formula that scientist turned filmmaker Randy Olson developed to join the cerebral (informational, literal, analytical, scientific) world of academia with the visceral (feeling, non-literal, intuitive, artistic) of Hollywood. In doing so, Olson cracked the code of creating powerful narrative. Olson credits Trey Parker as introducing him to the formula Chris just depicted in several ways through his narrative about the "Allegory of the Cave" and its message about seeing the reality of business.

Parker and Matt Stone developed a structure used repeatedly in the wildly successful "South Park" series on Comedy Central. He writes: "Parker's brain had become buff with narrative muscle. With that strength he was able to distill much of the whole story development process down to his simple rule of replacing *and*'s with *but*'s and *therefore*'s."[8]

Look through the story above and see its structure. Olson observes that when practiced repeatedly, one develops narrative intuition: "The ability not just to know the basic rules of narrative but to have absorbed and assimilated them so thoroughly you can actually sense them."[9] Mastering this structure enables one to produce clear and concise storytelling, and more importantly, recognize when it's missing in a story and how to fix it.

Narrative, Not Numbers

New York Times columnist Nicholas Kristof points to the challenge of communicating in a manner that your message will be received and welcomed by the recipient. Though counterintuitive, he warns not to be gobsmacked by the allure of big numbers. "As we all vaguely know, one death is a tragedy, a million deaths is a statistic,"[10] advised Kristof. To reach people, to move them; don't threaten, but enthrall them with their unique ability to make a life, or a significant number of lives in a village, better by their compassionate actions.

In the mind, massive is swallowed up by indifference but seeing the possibility of healing a single suffering soul is empowering. If you want a storytelling lesson to take to the bank, that's it! Put another way, Kristof wrote: "The challenge is to acknowledge both the desperate needs and also the very real progress in ... the prospect of improvement in real people's lives if the help goes forward."[11] Make people feel good if they act rather than guilty if they don't.

Along these lines, capturing the hearts and minds is far better accomplished with emotion that travels deep into the mind past the place where facts and statistics can reach. When the pandemic settled into the United States, we faced no shortage of numbers, measures, and markers. The news exposed us to daily, even hourly, projections of infection rates, available hospital beds, and the ultimate: lives claimed by the virus. Yet, despite the flood of daily digits, a significant number of Americans failed to capture the deadliness of the situation. Why?

As real as the numbers are, they're conveyed in our minds as abstractions. That is, until they reach our emotions. We believe college students are unaffected by COVID-19 until we view a video from a student who we see cursing himself for not listening to the warnings and vowing to take the precautions to stay out of the reach of the coronavirus. Images of a healthy young man brought to a sickly state with tubes and monitors invading his body suddenly jars us loose from the abstraction created by meaningless numbers. It hits home when he verbalizes the pain and suffering and worse, the long-lasting effects of the virus. Connecting deeply matters because until it hits home, we won't likely commit to solving the problem.

In his book, "Leaders Eat Last," Simon Sinek articulated the challenge presented by abstractions identified in the previous paragraphs. He wrote: "The moment we are able to make tangible that which had previously been a study or a chart, the moment a statistic or a poll becomes a real living person, the moment abstract concepts are understood to have human consequences, is the moment our ability to solve problems and innovate becomes remarkable."[12]

The Digital Difference

The shift from analog to digital began in the late 1970s. Who could forget that cacophony bangs and sizzles when you heard your first dial-up Internet connection? Clunky online service providers like Compuserve were the slick new digital pioneers changing our lives. Back in the day, search relied on exceedingly slow and limited web crawlers like Gopher. WHO is, one of the first such tools, was query and response protocol, limited to finding registered users of the nascent World Wide Web.

Once developers came through with protocols that created interoperability, and when start-ups like Global Crossing and Level 3 began plying Earth with fiber networks, did the future become clear. It was then that the innovators discovered ways to attract and connect millions of users seeking the new world of social media. From Mark Zuckerberg's campus-based Facebook to Marc Andreessen's Netscape, the unlimited power of the digital age erupted.

The Triumvirate of Unlimited Influence

Social media expert Eric Schwartzman identified three characteristics of digital/ social media that powers its popularity: It's searchable, shareable, and scalable.[13] "In traditional, old school media, the task focused on finding new prospective customers. Today, the challenge is to entice them to find you. This new digital world makes this possible because it's searchable (you can be discovered through search) and shareable (when individuals advance you or your firm with others on Pinterest, Instagram, Twitter, etc.), and when this exchange is scalable (it can be widely cast)."[14]

As marketing expert, Phil Kotler wrote: "In the digital economy, customers are socially connected with one another in horizontal webs of communities. Today, *communities* are the new *segments*. Unlike segments, communities are naturally formed by customers within boundaries that they define themselves. Customer communities are immune to spamming an irrelevant advertising. In fact, they'll reject a company's attempt to force its way into these webs of relationship."[15]

Employees are part of the labyrinth of connections that permeate the Internet. Moreover, it is wise to think of people not as homogeneous groups based on demographics and psychographics but rather, as individuals who connect with others because they share a desire to make progress as well and band together in a mutual effort. It is a progression from being aware to taking action to sharing your experience with others in a similar way.

Kotler, et al. point to three tools that a firm must employ to move the customer from aware to act to advocacy, that is, promoting your brand. They are: (a) mobile applications that facilitate the customer experience, (b) Customer Relationship Management (CRM) to engage customers in conversation to understand and inform them on the capabilities and benefits of the brand, and (c) gamification—introducing elements of game playing like point scoring, rules of play. These tools ultimately involve employees and provide a way for them to engage customers.

Think of It as a Voting Machine

Using social/digital media depends on knowing how it works. Think of it as a virtual voting machine and each time a "netizen" clicks, she has voted in some manner. Sometimes it's just a vote for search, sometimes for an idea or product, and sometimes it's a vote for sending a message. Whatever the case, some web player is taking notice and racking up a tally that might be used to inform, engage, or interpret. The currency of these votes appears as a like, a retweet, a review, or a purchase. To profit from the web, we must find our way into the conversation through content that creates currency.

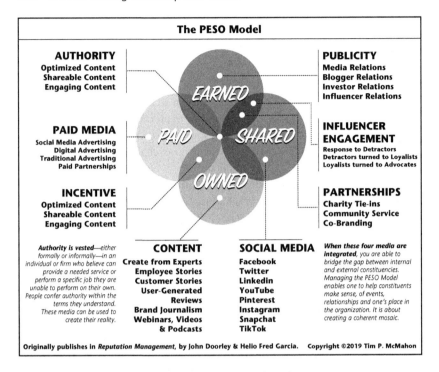

FIGURE 10.2 The dynamics of messaging in social media

The PESO Model in Figure 10.2 was originally developed by Gini Dietrich.[16] PESO identified media by its origin, that is, how the content finds its way to the web. It may be *paid* for and placed as an ad; or may be *earned* as a preferred end to a search, or it's *shared* by someone with one or many within their network, or it's simply resident on a web site *owned* by a firm or person. The "it" is what's called *content* and it appears in form of words, music, videos, recipes, photographs, memes, or anything that can be uploaded in some suitable manner.

This makes the web a democracy of sorts because all of us with a social media account can build our skills at attracting followers and rival the audience of a major media outlet. All it takes is an salacious tweet or intriguing post shaped to get attention. It's called clickbait because it has an arresting headline that causes people to click to see it, like: "This gadget won over all the Sharks!" On the receiving end, people can choose to shape their content, or self-select (with a little help from algorithms) the kind of news, information, offers, and propositions they desire. The prize on the Internet is you!

Advertisers are ready to pay. They participate in ongoing auctions conducted by platforms such as Google and Facebook that track your every move. Through this surveillance, advertisers can identify you and your online behaviors. With this, they develop models. Then, they plug your online profile in and produce a profile of you an advertiser will readily buy. This process is aimed at delivering prime prospects with the resources and interest to consume online. And, as they say, if you don't know what the product is, it's probably you.

All you need to do is be a buyer, and because they know what you want, you're primed to buy when the advertiser reaches out to you with an appeal. And there is a vigilant hunt on for you, the customer, and the shortest route to your purchase. This all works because the platforms gather massive amounts of data about you and your internet behavior, which you happily supply because they make living your life more efficient and productive. Robust development of hardware, software, connectivity, and protocols make search, share and scale all possible from the confines of your mobile phone.

As discussed briefly earlier in this chapter, well before the convergence of technology, James Grunig[17] identified that two-way, symmetric communication was the superior model to assess and engage audiences, and construct decisions made by an organization to be mutually beneficial between itself and its publics. Grunig's work made it possible to see two components of communication: one-way/two-way and symmetric/asymmetric. Grunig settled on the two-way, symmetric model as the best choice to produce effective public relations. With a look at how it's implemented in Figure 10.3, it becomes clear that model could be equally effective executed in an organization.

With shared understanding, accomplished through ongoing dialogue, members of the firm have a voice in thinking and decision-making, which expands understanding and alignment possibilities. As you will note, when

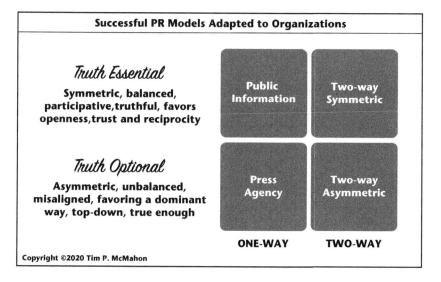

FIGURE 10.3   When "truth" is the way to sway

communication is two-way and accommodates dialogue, truth is the product most likely to emerge.

Making the Technology Work for You

Like it or not, that's 21st century marketing. How can this machinery be used to create buy-in? Think of yourself as an advertiser interested in getting your people to buy-in to the challenges facing your firm. Then, turn the technology on to tap into the profiles of your people. Dozens of emerging workplace platforms include Salesforce.com, Slack, Microsoft Teams, Zoom, and new entries to this list are added daily. Most are proprietary business communication tools that provide chat and videoconferencing, storage, and application integration to make employee usage seamless and natural.

The key benefits for leaders seeking buy-in are:

- Keep members of the organization informed;
- Make the tools people need within reach by everyone;
- Monitor productive ideas generated through employee interchange;
- Make customer behaviors and preference accessible to sales and service people;
- Automate essential reports and progress against initiatives;
- Visual mapping to create greater visibility of workplace processes and productivity; and
- Instant tracking and auditing of the flow of ideas, expenses, profitability, and retention of clients/customers.

With the rise of social media, your employees go to the same sources for daily information. Why not leverage the traditional employee engagement activities through technology? Some advantages of email newsletters for corporate communications:

- Company newsletters help syndicate every other channel of internal communications, including videos, podcasts, and company public relations;
- Regularly scheduled newsletters offer insight into the company's performance as a whole;
- Mobile proliferation of email means that employees are more likely to be checking their email, with 55% of emails being opened on a mobile device and 40% of workers admitting to checking their work email at least five times a day outside of the work day;
- Company newsletters allow employees to hear company news prior to external audiences;
- Internal-only tools keep your email contacts on your own IT servers, without the security risks of going through a third party; and
- Newsletters are the best way to communicate change to employees.

Leveraging Digital

Firms can choose from plenty of opportunities to leverage digital technology for getting and keeping customers. Veteran social media guru Eric Schwartzman offers these options:

- Digital marketing analytics to determine what's working and what's not;
- Marketing automation to build funnels for brand introduction and engagement;
- Paid media performance to determine how well your site doing;
- Search engine optimization to leverage search to driveway leads to your site—both desktop and mobile;
- Personalizing email to more fully engage your contacts;
- Automating content aimed at reaching prospects and customer in a variety of different formats (e.g., blogging, videos, white papers, offers, etc.);
- Content testing to determine the most effective means, times, and messages; and
- Podcasting to create dynamic connections between your clients/customers and your people.

Schwartzman's latest list of top performers in these areas are:

- Digital Analytics: Google Analytics, Google Search Console, Hot Jar;
- Marketing Automation: Salesforce, HubSpot, Zoho;
- Performance Evaluation: Screaming Frog, Lighthouse, GT Metrics;
- Search Engine Optimization: SEMrush, Ahrefs, Moz;
- Email Marketing: Convert Kit, MailChimp, OptinMonster, Zoho Campaigns;
- Content Marketing: Ink for All;
- Copywriting: RelatedWords.com, RhymeZone, IdiomSearch;
- Podcasting: Blubrry, Levelator, Audacity, Chargeable;
- Social Media Marketing: Hootsuite, AgoraPulse;
- Public Relations: Cision, Meltwater, iPR Software; and
- Video Syndication: eCam, Streamyard, Restream.

Consider this guide depicted in Figure 10.4 that decodes the algorithm pointing to what gets attention in popular social media platforms.

Along with the principal drivers of the algorithm, see the unique content strength of each platform. All social media employ content possibilities, but each also the area in which it excels.

Algorithm criteria and principal content for popular digital platforms							
Instagram	Facebook	YouTube	Linkedin	Twitter	Snapchat	Pinterest	TikTok
Interest	Likes	Uploads	Native content	Timing	Interest	Interest	Interest
Recency	Reactions	Subscribers	Relevance	User cared	Recency	Recency	Recency
Relationship	Shares	View volume	Relationship	Engagement	Relationship	Relationship	Relationship
Photos	Interplay	Videos	Career	Micro-blog	Vanishing	Lifestyle tips	Short videos
Copyright ©2019 Tim P. McMahon							

FIGURE 10.4   The algorithm priorities and distinguishing features of popular platforms

Moving to Scale through Technology

The Arthur W. Page Society is a group of professional corporate communicators who push the envelope in cutting edge thinking. In 2019 it issued a detailed report on CommTech, "the application of data and analytics to create communications campaigns that engage a broad range of stakeholders as unique individuals based on their behaviors, beliefs and interests to drive desired actions and outcomes."[18] The report suggests the following shifts from present state to future state:

- From siloed teams to agile teams with diverse skills;
- From analyzing a campaign after it has finished to automating those insights to optimize your campaign creative in real time;
- From targeting generalized audiences to using intelligence/research tools to define and identify audiences with the objective of delivering customized content based on users' specific interests and behaviors (e.g. digital activity, social activity, preference indicators);
- From delivering all content to all audiences to delivering dedicated messages based on interactions with content or channels;
- From media clips to direct attribution of media coverage to business outcomes and connect thought leadership to audience building/engagement:
- Shaping reputation to combining instinct with data; and
- From rigid strategies to strategies that are built around constant evaluations so that you can change course.

The Page Society report fits hand-in-glove with the theme of this book in that it calls upon leaders to embrace the changing world and prepare their companies for integrating organization adaptive attitudes and practices. The goal is to create favorable outcomes, such as:

- The organizational ability to craft multiple journeys and experiences based off of audience with an eye toward improving interaction and results;
- The ability to show how communication improves bottom-line and increases organizational share of voice;
- Connecting communication efforts to employee/customer actions; and
- Obtaining better results and efficiency from campaigns and communication activities.

The field of CommTech is fast emerging as a soon-to-be necessary organizational capability. Go to the Arthur W. Page website (https:/page.org), a not-for-profit organization that generates significant thought leadership for business leaders.

Ethics and Healthy Practices

Digital media has introduced a powerful tool to bring people together around ideas. This can be beneficial when we experience the effectiveness of social media to muster collective will and bring massive awareness to such serious problems as hunger, evil-doers, and collective commitment. Yet, like everything, it also has a dark side that can exert overly compelling force on individuals who become trapped under its magic. In the documentary, "The Social Dilemma," one timeless thought stands out offering fair warning to those who embrace social media. It comes from American 20th Century futurist Buckminster Fuller: "Whether it is to be Utopia or Oblivion will be a touch-and-go relay race right up to the final moment …"[19]

The Fuller quote originally was contained in his work "Critical Path" where he wrote:

> If you read the entire Critical Path book carefully, including its some times [sic] long but essentially detailed considerations, and pay realistically close attention to these considerations, you will be able to throw your weight into the balancing of humanity's fate. While you could be "the straw that breaks the camel's back," compressively you can also be the "straw"—straw of intellect, initiative, unselfishness, comprehensive integrity, competence, and love—whose ephemerally effective tension saves us.
>
> The invisibly tensive straws that can save us *are* those of individual human integrities—in daring to steer the individual's course only by truth, strange as the realized truth may often seem—wherever and whenever the truths are evidenced to the individual—wherever they may lead, unfamiliar as the way may be.[20]

Fuller and Kuromiya frame humanity in a race between "a better-informed, hopefully inspired young world versus a running-scared, misinformedly [sic] brain-conditioned, older world."[21]

TAKE-AWAYS

- This chapter on communication focuses on the "what" of communication, that is, the tactical tools and channels of communication. This includes both traditional, time-honored practices and state-of-the-art digital/social communications that evolve at an ever-increasing pace.
- Fundamental to communication is the act of closing the loop. This considers the top-down and bottom-up nature of communication meeting in a fashion consistent with creating a state of stability; committed to moving people to action.
- Communication also demands people seek to understand before being understood and relies on listening and speaking in a spirit to gain shared meaning and understanding. By listening, that means active listening with the primary emphasis on understanding.
- Too often our ability to listen is jeopardized by our emphasis on preparing a response or answer when we should be devoting our attention to hearing the statement or question.
- For personal communication, leaders and followers must work on their writing skills, too. Making our thoughts clear and well-received requires well-practiced skills of writing.
- The ancients such as Plato provide time-tested lessons in classical stories such as the Allegory of the Cave. Learning how to structure and present a narrative will build and master a skill for winning the hearts and minds of followers.
- Perhaps one of the worst possible deterrents to communication lies in the abstractions and an ineffective attention on the rational rather than the emotional, where people are more effectively moved to action.
- With the evolutionary development of the digital world, we're becoming increasingly skilled at leveraging its three distinct characteristics: it's searchable, shareable, and scalable.
- The outgrowth of communities has surfaced organically and are fertile grounds to develop understanding and commitment at scale because it coalesces the many and diverse thoughts of people.
- The PESO model represents four paths to engagement on the web: paid, earned, shared, and owned. This demands that leaders understand how these elements work and can be used to disseminate content and sway the masses.
- The two-way symmetric model of communication developed by James Grunig has proven successful in its application to the field of public relations and offers great promise when applied to organizational communication.
- Leaders would do well to adopt CommTech, the application of data and

analytics to create communications campaigns that engage a broad range of stakeholders as unique individuals based on their behaviors, beliefs, and interests to drive desired actions and outcomes.

* In all communication, we can use powerful tools for influencing others. With this power comes the responsibility to accommodate and exercise ethical practices.

Notes

1 Grunig, J.E. (2001). Two-way symmetrical public relations: Past, present, and future. In R. Heath (Ed.), *Handbook of public relations* (pp. 11–30). Thousand Oaks, CA: Sage.

2 Senge, P. M. (2006). *The fifth discipline: The art and practice of the learning organization* (Rev. ed.). New York: Currency Doubleday, (pp. 183–186).

3 Parent Effectiveness Training was the seminar created and inspired by the book of the same name written by Dr. Thomas Gordon and published by Random House. It is essentially a treatise on communicating to resolve conflict; it applies not just to the parent-child relationship, but all interpersonal relationships.

4 Zinsser, W. (2006). *On writing well.* New York, NY: HarperCollins, (p. 35).

5 Strunk, Jr., W. & White, E. B. (2000). *The elements of style* (4th ed.). New York, NY: Longman, (p. 67).

6 Ibid, (p. 67).

7 Garcia, H. G. (2012). *The power of communication: Skills to build trust, inspire loyalty, and lead effectively.* Upper Saddle River, NJ: Pearson Education.

8 Olson, R. (2015). *Houston, we have a narrative: Why science needs a story.* Chicago, IL, and London, UK: The University of Chicago Press, (p. 19).

9 Ibid, (p. 19).

10 Kristof, N. (November 30, 2009). Nicholas Kristof's advice for saving the world. *Outside Online.* Retrieved December 20, 2020 from https://www.outsideonline.com/1909636/nicholas-kristofs-advice-saving-world.

11 Ibid.

12 Sinek, S. (2014/2017). *Leaders eat last: Why some teams pull together and others don't.* New York, NY: Penguin Books, (p. 138).

13 Schwartzman, E. (2013). Social Media Bootcamp. Slide retrieved November 26, 2020 from www.linkedin.com/profile/view?id=3016595&locale=en_US&trk-tyah

14 McMahon, T. P. (2020). Integrated communication. In Doorley, J. & Garcia, H. F. (2020). *Reputation Management* (4th ed.). New York, NY: Routledge, (p. 265).

15 Kotler, P., Kartajay, H., & Setiawan, I. (2017). *Marketing 4.0: Moving from traditional to digital.* Hoboken, NJ: Wiley, (p. 47).

16 Dietrich, G. (2014). *Spin sucks: Communication and reputation management in the digital age.* Indianapolis, IN: Que Publications.

17 Grunig, J.E. (2001). Two-way symmetrical public relations: Past, present, and future. In R. Heath (Ed.), *Handbook of public relations* (pp. 11–30). Thousand Oaks, CA: Sage, (p. 12).

18 Arthur W. Page Society. (2019). The CEO as pacesetter: What it means, why it matters, how to get there. Quick Start Guide, (p. 1). Retrieved November 10, 2020 from https://knowledge.page.org/report/the-cco-as-pacesetter/.

19 Orlowski, J. (Producer). 2929, September, The Social Dilemma. [TV documentary, drama]. Netflix Television.

20 Fuller, B. & Kuromiya, K. (1981). *The critical path.* New York, NY: St, Martin's Press, (p. 58).

21 Ibid, (p. 57).

11

UNCOMMON SENSE

The Uncommon Truth About Common Sense

In his historic appeal—when he made the case for release from the rule of Great Britain—Thomas Paine used simple, common language to convey the message in a pamphlet that swept through the Colonies. Paine anonymously attributed and titled his pamphlet, "Common Sense." Paine avoided elegant phrases and aimed his appeal at equality—two thoughts the new settlers found compelling in their new government.

His words were of the common man for the common man; and, they made sense, that is, his argument was shrewd and practical. While it worked for Paine, why does common sense fail so often? It does, you know, the decisions we make using common sense and other tools of thinking and problem-solving often fail to deliver the solution or even the right answer.

In this chapter, we'll look into a variety of related topics to help us understand how we think, reason, intuit, transmit, infer, discern, distinguish, decipher, investigate, frame, diagnose, prescribe and assess the people, information and objects around us to inform our decisions and behavior. We'll discover influencers, detractors, and inscrutable traps that serve up a potentially problematic dilemma for leaders: in a world of uncertainty that requires ever-present adjustment to their thinking and decisions, how does one lead? While this chapter is but a cursory review, it provides a template for deeper investigation of the concepts presented.

Common Sense: Not Always Common, Not Always Sensible

Common sense "is the loosely organized set of facts, observations, experiences, insights, and pieces of received wisdom that each of us accumulates over a lifetime, in the course of encountering, dealing with, and learning from, everyday situations."[1] If we want to rely on our common sense, it's beneficial to remain open to the unexamined, and to refrain from being rigid in forming opinions. Common sense is a bit of a magical process fed by the sub-conscious mind.

Sociologist Carl C. Taylor determined two features define common sense that set it apart from other knowledge: (a) it's overwhelmingly practical, meaning it's more focused on delivering an answer than in explaining from where it came; and (b) it's applied discretely, that is, each situation is considered on its own terms.[2] In any given situation, *you just know*. AI engineers have repeatedly failed to create a computer-generated proxy for common sense, there's just too many rules, even for a complex algorithm.

Duncan Watts suggests "the kinds of predictions that common sense tell us we ought to be able to make are in fact impossible—for two reasons. First, common sense tells us that only one future will actually play out, and so, it is natural to want to make specific predictions about it.... and [s]econd, common sense also demands that we ignore the many uninteresting, unimportant predictions that we could be making all the time and focus on those outcomes that actually matter." Let's take that apart and understand what he means.

But first, it will be enlightening to drop in on a recent visit Chris had with his Mom.

IT'S COMMON SENSE, BUT NOT COMMON PRACTICE

Mom had prepared a treat that morning. When Chris arrived, her cinnamon rolls were just coming out of the oven. Chris loved the aroma that filled the room. It reminded him of his childhood.

CHRIS: *I feel like we're back in the old house.*

AGNES: *The nose knows no bounds. It has a great memory!*

CHRIS: *I have never tasted a cinnamon roll like yours anywhere. What's your secret?*

AGNES: *No secret. This is the way I have always made them.*

CHRIS: Some time I will have to watch you.

AGNES: *You stick to business I'll make you the cinnamon rolls.*

CHRIS: *I've been trying to figure out why it seems like so many people have trouble with using their common sense. Maybe they don't have any.*

AGNES: *You're saying what every mother thinks. I remember telling you to use your noggin' many times.*

CHRIS: *So, why do we not use our common sense?*
AGNES: *I think sometimes we just forget. As a kid I had to tell you several times before you'd understand certain things. But, when you did you stored it for your common sense to use.*
CHRIS: *Like stuff we should do but we don't. Doc always told me, keep the gas tank full.*
AGNES: *That's just common sense. You never know when you need gas and won't have time to get it.*
CHRIS: *Doc must have told me that more times than he can remember.*
AGNES: *But you're happy you took the time when you did, eh?*
CHRIS: *Reminders help. You used to leave notes in my lunch and sure enough had you not I might have forgotten to stop on the way home from school to get milk or whatever it was we needed. It's also useful to trust your gut when it might be too much bother to think through a complicated decision.*
AGNES: *Just remember common sense is not common practice.*
CHRIS: *Amen to that. It is not common sense to have two of these cinnamon rolls.*
AGNES: *But you seem to make a practice of taking one with you right out the door!*
CHRIS: *It's for a friend.*
AGNES: *Hope it makes it to him!*

Comfort in Common Sense Until...

Common sense is innate, it's natural. Humans are quite comfortable using it to make decisions. Moreover, our brains contribute to its use. Kahneman taught us System 1 thinking is our default mode and it "never pauses to wonder whether the evidence at hand is flawed or inadequate, or if there is better evidence elsewhere,"[3] so it moves swiftly. It is intuitive, it flows like a stream of water fills the cracks and crevices of the riverbed. Kahneman described it with the acronym: WYSIATI, **what you see is all there is**. But that's not the whole story.

There's great benefit for us to accept common sense, but only if we're actually processing the deeper facts surrounding the decision when necessary. Remember, in our brains System 1 gets its directions from the amygdala operating in nanoseconds distributing assignments to System 1 that are acted upon without question. It works to resolve recognized problems or questions swiftly and with a high degree of effectiveness. Unless it doesn't. Like when the product of System 1 is recognized as unsettling. Think: accident—an unseen or unplanned event.

You are driving along on a beautiful day with not much traffic around. You encounter a stale yellow light and your System 1 response—weighing the input at that moment says to speed up a bit and drive through the intersection, albeit a little bit after the signal turned red. All is well, normally, but in this case a bicyclist thinking he caught a timely green light enters the intersection at exactly the same time. The result: an accident with dire consequences. You, no doubt, feel the misery of the event. Yet, once you gather your composure, do you blame your System 1 for sending such a foolish command? Maybe. But more likely you find a way to release yourself from your errant decision. This is quite expected and predictable. When things don't go as planned "[w]e 'normalize' irrational data either by organizing it to fit a made up narrative or by ignoring it altogether."[4]

Making Sense Out of Nonsensical

A defining feature of intuitive judgment is its insensitivity to the quality of the evidence on which the judgment is based.[5] In the end, human beings demand to make sense out of things. The brain seeks order. It searches for rationality to soothe anxieties it might have about things we cannot readily explain. So, we "are creative confabulators hardwired to invent stories that impose coherence on the world."[6] Sounds like a job for our popular friend, confirmation bias.

When we have an inkling something is not right, we seek to *right* it, and no better way than to reach out to the echo chamber that will remove our anxiety with a rush of support rooted in our beliefs and values. See Figure 11.1 for a simple explanation of how confirmation bias surfaces. Poof! Instant peace-of-mind. However, large systems like companies, countries, and cultures present greater complexity than we might encounter in our individual choices. In a large, complex system, the natural flow of thoughts, ideas, and actions will include opposing opinions and belief systems that may pose formidable pushback from dissenters. For leaders, these protestations are not to be trifled with, they are real.

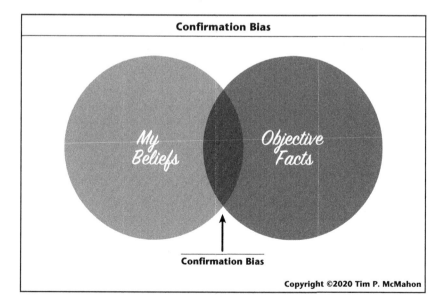

Confirmation Bias

My Beliefs

Objective Facts

Confirmation Bias

Copyright ©2020 Tim P. McMahon

FIGURE 11.1 We filter to support our beliefs … A sort of self-preservation

Misguided Is in the Eye of the Beholder

In studying common sense, Duncan Watts has learned people can be quirky about common sense. For example, when people are presented disconfirming evidence that flies in the face of the wisdom of their decision, they say, "but it doesn't undermine my own confidence in the particular beliefs I happen to hold." It's as if the failure of the reasoning is the failure of "other people's reasoning, not their own."[7] In other words, being misguided is something others are, not me. Example: How is it we all believe we're more honest than the average guy? That's statistically impossible.

Failures of common sense are typically chalked up as *things we didn't know at the time*. Yet, such things are frequently obvious in retrospect. Think of a freeze in Florida. You immediately realize your planned vacation is ruined, but you didn't think it would impact the price of orange juice; at least, not until you saw the increase at the grocery store, then it's obvious. Now, the second time you hear of a freeze in Florida, your commonsense kicks in and instructs you to stock up on OJ.

As Watts suggests, "Knowing this, however, I can at least consider the possibility that I might be deluding myself, and so try to pay attention to when I make mistakes as well as when others do. Possibly I can begin to accept that not every altercation is necessarily the other guy's fault, even if I'm still inclined to think it is."[8] Watts sees an opportunity to learn from experience, "to determine what I should do differently as well as what others should be doing differently."[9]

We think just becoming aware of this trap, we could avoid it and determine how to act differently and how others can as well. The quandary lies in our inability to challenge the assumptions we make that guide our judgment. If we truly want to improve our common sense, we must work on our ability to question our beliefs. That's neither sexy nor motivating! But it is real.

Have we assumed correctly? In strategic planning, we know that assumptions matter greatly as they shape what we believe to be obvious. Scott Berkun suggests "rejecting something because it's obvious (or more likely, **just familiar to you** and your personal knowledge) denies you of the opportunity to experience those things."[10] He suggest to ask questions, like:

- Is the writer making good points?
- Are the stories compelling?
- Is there an angle offered that's helpful?
- Can I use what I'm learning?
- Do I know a person that would benefit from this?
- If there is a better single reference for this obvious thing, name it.

If any of these questions apply, being obvious is probably quite valuable. Dissenters who have an accepted viewpoint that is based on utility and not novelty should be considered credible. If it is purely based on flavor of the day or a novel approach, well then, those protests may be dismissed as unsubstantial. Art blogger Nina Paley said, "Don't be original; be obvious. When you state the obvious, you actually *seem* original…."[11]

It's Obvious: Knowing and Doing Are the Same Thing

Chapter 3 of this book is titled: Knowing is doing. So, the statement must be obvious, right? The author stated it! However, the chapter title is a ditty intended to get the reader's attention. Knowing and doing are not the same thing—though it is very difficult to *do* without the *know*. So, why do we behave like they are the same?

In a narrative ripped from the headlines, check out Figure 11.2 which is a frame grab of a government official setting expectations that proved to be disconnected from reality. When Coronavirus vaccines became available in early December 2020, *Fox Business News* reported, "Health and Human Services Secretary Alex Azar said vaccinations could begin for 'the most vulnerable' next week, and he expects 20 million people to be vaccinated before the end of the year."[12] Hallelujah! The end is near!

In the same story, more detail was provided: "General Gus Perna, who is in charge of vaccine distribution, did say there may only be 2.9 million shots in the arms of Americans in the first week. Vaccines would then be distributed on a rolling basis."[13] His comments provided context and added credibility to Azar's

FIGURE 11.2   Good intentions, dwindling outcomes

statement because it was obvious it would take some time to get up to full speed.[14] However, on December 30, *CBS News* reported: "The Trump administration had pledged 20 million doses of the vaccine by year's end, but so far, not even 3 million shots have been given and just over 11 million doses have been shipped."[15] Yet 10 days after the first full week of vaccinations, it was widely reported that approximately 2.1 million Americans had been vaccinated, falling short of Perna's estimate of 2.9 million after the first week. It is noteworthy to recognize that Gen. Perna took full responsibility for the miss and sincerely apologized, as reported in the *Wall Street Journal* (December 23, 2020).

Conclusion: To Know Is Not to Do

There is little doubt that Azar and Perna sincerely wanted to be right in their predictions. But it wasn't in the cards. Berkun suggests that "our instincts often conflict with our wisdom. In the workplace or family, those in power might not have the common sense. Making it harder for those who do have it to take action based on it."[16]

Perhaps it was irrational exuberance, or simply listening to advisors who were wide-eyed optimists, but Perna and Azar fell to their own kind of confirmation bias. Berkun writes: "A wise person would look for data that both supports and rejects a theory as often there's both, a discovery that forces thinking about how to improve an opinion (instead of merely defending an old one)."[17] Incidentally, the president-elect's coronavirus team was skeptical of the predictions of the Trump administration vaccination predictions. On December 4, 2020, Joe Biden cited the biggest challenge lies in the last stage of distribution: "There is no detailed plan that we've seen anyway as to how you get the vaccine out of a container into an injection syringe into somebody's arm."

All of the common sense in the world does not automatically translate to common practice. As Berkun summarizes: "Common sense is not common practice. Knowing is not the same as doing. It can take months of effort to train yourself new habits for your behavior, work that no amount of knowledge can replace. Sometimes all we can hope to do is improve our humility, as avoiding mistakes and failures completely is beyond us."[18]

Hidden Rules Demand a Decoder Ring

The famous social psychologist Stanley Milgram conducted the controversial obedience studies a half century ago when he tested how much pain a participant in an experiment might inflict on another if told by an authority figure in a white lab coat (a symbol of authority) to increase an electrical shock. In Figure 11.3, a cartoon depicts the surprisingly atrocious behavior observed in the experiment. Milgram discovered people dialed up disturbingly high levels of electrical charge, significantly beyond expectations.

FIGURE 11.3 Milgram's famous test of human limits

"The finding that otherwise respectable citizens could, under relatively unexceptional circumstances, perform what seemed like morally incomprehensible acts was deeply disturbing to many people—and the phrase 'obedience to authority' has carried a negative consequence ever since."[19] What emerged as a secondary finding from the study is that while following the direction of authority is essential for an orderly society, compliance flows from "a set of hidden rules that we don't even realize exist until we break them."

There are so many rules we must follow it is impossible to record them all. But, once we spend some time in a new environment at work or school or even family, we eventually learn them and are able to live a reasonably trouble-free life. Actually, the only way we know there is a rule is after we have broken it. Example: The next time you walk into an elevator with people inside, continue to face one of the riders rather than turning to face the doors. Sure, punishment will not be great, but it will soon be apparent to you that is unacceptable behavior. Imagine you were the person on the elevator who experienced the face-to-face treatment. We all know, there is even an unwritten rule that governs this pedestrian act.

When we think about such a circumstance—the role of following unwritten rules—we realize that sometimes they are more important than written rules. Moreover, we gain an ability for successfully negotiating this complex structure. What enables us to do this? Common sense. It tells us when to obey written rules, when to defer to unwritten rules and how to tell the difference. But, common sense resists easy interpretation.

Anthropologist Clifford Geertz lent a cultural perspective to the term describing it as an "ancient triangle of received practices, accepted beliefs, habitual judgments, and untaught emotions."[20] As much as we associate common sense with subtleties, we are keenly aware it operates in the background of professional settings such as physicians, lawyers, and first responders. This knowledge accumulates over years of practice and personal experience, just as intuition.

Common sense is not formal knowledge, it is developed in the scope of a specific situation. Consequently, common sense varies over time as the specifics of certain situation. So, as rigid as it might be in governing some situations, it is quite inadequate in others. Watts wrote: "How can we be confident that what we believe is right when someone else feels equally strongly that it's wrong—especially when we can't articulate why we think we're right in the first place?"[21]

Social influence plays a part as a tiebreaker, if you will. We rely on the cumulative experiences of others to inform us with respect to the battle between our common-sense evaluations and the chance that they might be wrong. As it turns out, significant influence can grow from a slight initial advantage.

Before There Was Social Media, There Was Social Influence

Social influence is another powerful force that shapes our assumptions and decision-making. Our view of social influence here begins a principle called cumulative advantage, best understood as *the rich get richer, and the poor get poorer.* Cumulative Disadvantage/Advantage theory (CDA) "assumes that advantages and disadvantages are socially structured, and individuals are exposed to them. This can be systems operating at the micro, meso, and macro level but located at the social structure, which means that dis/advantages are not a product of merit or individual performance."[22]

In a web-based experiment reported by Watts, Salganik, and Dodds,[23] 14,000 teenagers participated in a real-life experiment in which they voluntarily joined a site called Music Lab where they were asked to listen to, rate, and download songs by unknown artists. Some participants saw only the names of the songs while others saw how many times the songs were downloaded by previous participants.

The study used a control group and social experiment group divided into eight separate "worlds." Participants could see only downloads of people in their own world. Rankings weren't manipulated, and each started out with zero downloads. The worlds were kept separate and each evolved independently of the others.

The researchers posited if people knew their preference regardless of others' opinions, differences shouldn't exist between the social influence groups and the control group. All songs should receive approximately the same number of downloads. That did not occur. The results found that "when people had information about what other people downloaded, they were indeed influenced by it in the way that cumulative advantage theory would predict."[24]

That is, in the eight social worlds, all popular songs were more popular and unpopular songs were less popular than in the independent group. Further, the hit songs were different in different worlds. Conclusion: in human decision making, social influence reduced equality and predictability and swayed the top and bottom ends of preference. One song was 26th out of 48 in quality yet was ranked No.1 in one social world and 40th in another.

Suffice to say, this experiment strongly suggests social influence can be manipulated.

Is Common Sense Rational?

We think common sense is rational. Yet, as demonstrated in the Music Lab experiment, we have learned it can be influenced in a manner that our leanings are intensified by not so rational stimuli but that we don't consciously calculate. Psychologists have demonstrated that our behavior is subject to stimulus we're not necessarily cognizant of at the very time is working to influence our behavior.

> "[T]here are so many examples—priming, framing, anchoring, availability, motivated reasoning, and loss aversion, to name a few—that it's hard to see how they all fit together. As we saw in the Music Lab case, experiments emphasize one potentially relevant factor at a time in order to isolate its effects. However, in real life, many such factors may be present to varying extents in any given situation; thus, it's critical to understand how they interact with one another."[25]

Consider these tools at work:

- Priming: exposure to a stimulus influences the response. For example, the word "blueprint" is recognized much faster when it's preceded by "architect";
- Framing: can influence the way people perceive reality. For example, opening and closing an eye can mean a wink or a blink;
- Anchoring: reliance on the first information received to interpret what follows. For example, if you see a dog that costs $1,000 and then see a dog that costs $100, you'll likely see the second dog as cheap;
- Availability: In this context, it is a heuristic, or mental shortcut, that rely on options available in a person's mind when evaluating a topic, concept, or decision as in, it's morning coffee will be served;
- Motivated reasoning: This is an emotional appeal used to reduce ambiguity, or cognitive dissonance, to produce a desired response. For example, a police

officer telling a suspect, "if you tell the truth and cooperate, we can go easy on you"; and

• Loss aversion: This relates to a person's preference to avoid loss or pain vis-à-vis acquiring similar gain. For example, it's better not to lose a dollar than to gain a dollar.

Leaders will find these devices as a means to influence and gain buy-in, to challenge objections. They can be effective for leaders who want to create commitment.

Constructing Rationality

Chris never played parlor tricks in an attempt to move people in one direction or another. However, he naturally spoke in a persuasive manner, using the kinds of devices identified above effortlessly and intuitively to make his point. He believed in the concept of enlightened self-interest, that is, if you work to satisfy the interests of others you ultimately satisfy your own. This idea is supported by the notion that people are inclined to make rational choices. Consider the concept of homo economicus, which assumes people know what's best for them premised on what delivers maximum utility for the consumer and profit as a producer. In common terms, we often say, "What's in it for me?"

This economic concept is challenged by concepts of behavioral economics, which examine cognitive biases and bounded rationality. This recognizes the restrictions that the limits on time and information exert on a person's ability to act rationally. Approaching rational from a psychological perspective, consider this: there're only two very different kinds of ways people analyze and solve problems. One is "seeing-that," which is pattern matching; and the other is "reasoning-why" or what's considered intuitive thinking.

Pattern matching is the ability any animal has to perceive patterns, and connect them to behaviors, and possibly new behaviors. Reasoning-why is "the process 'by which we describe how we think we reached a judgment, or how we think another person could reach that judgment. Reasoning-why can occur only for creatures that have language and a need to explain themselves to other creatures."[26] When we try to determine if an idea is right or wrong, we're using moral reasoning, we "reconstruct the actual reasons why *we ourselves* came to a judgment; we reason to find the best possible reasons why *somebody else ought to join us* in our judgment."[27]

Chris recognized that cognition and emotion weren't separate; actually, he considered them inseparable. Cognition was simply information processing, but "emotions occur in steps, the first of which is to appraise something that just happened based on whether it advanced or hindered your goals."[28] If we separate emotions from cognition—as if they weren't interdependent—we couldn't engage the inherent early warning, such as, the *fight or flight,* that make us aware of potential threat. Chris didn't contrast rational with emotional; he contrasted it with intuition.

Making Sense of the Senses

In any discussion about intuition—the sixth sense—we must consider the role of the other five senses. We recognize the smell of diesel fuel, for example, because we have smelled it before. Our olfactory sense—the sense of smell—has many purposes, including warning us of danger. When you smell natural gas, for example, it alerts you to the potential of an explosion or poisoning. Human beings are reliant on such cues, and industrial psychologists know that. The fact is natural gas is odorless. A chemical called mercaptan is added to make us aware of its presence. Since gas can be dangerous, distributors are compelled to give you fair warning. Leaders do well when they consider this idea in appealing to the senses of their people. How will they behave when they get a mere scent of what's about to happen?

Our interest in the senses lies in the potential to acquire new ideas or explain existing phenomena so that we can inform and inspire others to adopt behavior that will benefit our mutual concerns. The way our senses work is straightforward. When our senses detect an odor or sound or any of the other inputs that we receive through our eyes, ears, nose, throat, and skin, our brain makes sense of its meaning. This is accomplished through memory. If you smell something and can identify it, that's because your nose has smelled it before. If you can't then you probably haven't experienced that scent.

"Our ability to acquire new ideas from experience and to retain these ideas into memory... [explains]... we are who we are in good measure because of what we have learned and remember."[29] Once our long-term memory apprehends the event, it can match it to others like it and render very quick intuitive responses.

Malcolm Gladwell wrote: "We really only trust conscious decision making. But there are moments, particularly in times of stress, when haste doesn't make waste, when our snap judgments and first impressions can offer a much better means of making sense of the world... [simply put] decisions made very quickly can be every bit as good as decisions made cautiously and deliberately."[30] Further, tools can be used to speed up and improve our decision-making skills.

Heuristics and Gut Feelings

Heuristics are the shortcuts to make decisions such as trial-and-error, educated guess, or rule of thumb we use to reduce cognitive load.[31] We use heuristics when we're trying to solve problems and when uncertainty prevails. Tversky and Kahneman developed three heuristics to help us make judgments: availability, representativeness, and anchoring and adjustment.

Availability refers to what might be readily available in our mind to explain the likelihood of an event occurring. For example, dying from a plane crash. While you're more likely to perish in a household mishap, when planes crash, they gather an inordinate amount of attention, so we assume it's more likely; and that's because it's a more psychologically available explanation.

Representativeness comes into play when an individual object is highly represented, or highly similar to a prototype of that category. For example, making the snap judgment that an evergreen tree is indeed a tree based on the prototype used for comparison being representative of what is considered a tree—a trunk growing form the ground with green coverage on its branches.

Anchoring and adjustment are a heuristic used in many situations where people must estimate a number by starting from a readily available number and moving up or down to determine a number that makes sense.

While heuristics can differ from answers given by logic and probability, decisions based on heuristics can be good enough to satisfy a need.[32] Psychologist Gerd Gigerenzer credibly argues that heuristics are effective tools for leaders to "do things right... [or] at least learn to.... [use]...heuristics, rules of thumb, and other shortcuts [that] often leads to better decisions than the models of 'rational' decision-making developed by mathematicians and statisticians."[33]

Gigerenzer predicts that if we "teach young people the mathematics of uncertainty, statistical thinking, rather than just the mathematics of certainty—trigonometry, geometry, all beautiful things that most of us never need—then we can have a new society which is more able to deal with risk and uncertainty."[34]

Gigerenzer places great value in gut feelings, explaining they're tools for an uncertain world. "They're not caprice. They're not a sixth sense or God's voice. They're based on lots of experience, an unconscious form of intelligence. I've worked with large companies and asked decision makers how often they base an important professional decision on that gut feeling. In the companies I've worked with, large international companies, about 50% of all decisions are at the end a gut decision."[35]

Forecasting Predicts the Potential of Possibilities—Good and Bad

"Forecasting is a technique that uses historical data as inputs to make informed estimates that are predictive in determining the direction of future trends. Businesses utilize forecasting to determine how to allocate their budgets.... This is typically based on the projected demand for the goods and services offered."[36] The biggest issue with forecasting is that it looks backward to see the future.

Paul Saffo wrote: It is a "common but fundamentally erroneous perception that forecasters make predictions. We don't, of course: Prediction is possible only in a world in which events are preordained and no amount of action in the present can influence future outcomes. That world is the stuff of myth and superstition "[37] So, forecasting is about revealing a full range of possibilities—both good and bad.

Helmuth von Moltke (the Elder) was a Prussian field marshal who served as chief of staff for 30 years in that historically prominent German state. His main thesis was that military strategy should be viewed as a system of options since war planning was predictable only until the first encounter with the enemy's strength.[38] He advocated it was necessary to improvise to prevail in battle when circumstances were seldom predictable.

Chris would often say, "All plans firm until changed." This brief directive echoed lessons learned from war. Although Chris never served, he studied the military and believed truly effective field generals knew that battle is shrouded in uncertainty, often called the *fog of war*.[39] As a leader, decisions ultimately rely on intuition and judgment, and as discussed here, common sense. In a world of uncertainty, effective forecasting considers the context that informs your intuition. By broadening our understanding, we expose possibilities. Moreover, unexamined assumptions are revealed and in these two bookends, decision-making space is narrowed and facilitates the efficacy of intuition.

Decision-Making at the Speed of Life

Recognition-primed decision (RPD) is a model to help explain how leaders make decisions in high-stakes situations. The RPD model was developed when researcher Gary Klein studied fire commander's responses to fighting fires. He eventually discovered the "commanders' secret was their experience let them see a situation, even a nonroutine one, as an example of a prototype, so they knew the typical course of action right away."[40]

Their decision stemmed from their experience. Having seen situations many times before permitted them to identify a prototype—an original model on which something is patterned. After careful observation of decision makers in action, they determined that deliberation about options happened quickly, in about a minute. Second, while several options were considered, they were not compared. In other words, "he thought of the options one at a time, evaluated in each turn, rejected it, and turned to the next most typical rescue technique."[41] By evaluating each option on its own merits, or as Nobel Prize winner Herbert Simon called it, satisficing, that is, it's selecting the first option that works. The study eventually determined that seasoned veterans were more likely to use the first viable option, as opposed to comparing options to assess the best choice. Best is the enemy of good!

The RPD model involves recognizing a situation as familiar, then setting priorities to satisfy goals, assessing which cues are important to minimize overload of information, to determine what to expect next so as to recognize and prepare for surprises. Klein wrote: "The recognition of goals, cues, expectancies, and actions is part of what it means to recognize a situation. That is, decision makers do not start off with the goals or expectancies and figure out the nature of the situation,"[42]

RPD applies to trauma nurses, fire fighters, game players, and market traders. It functions well in conditions in which time is limited, information is partial, and goals are ill-defined. There are limitations, mostly from unfamiliar situations, but the idea of singular, not comparative, evaluation dominated recorded quantitative actions more than 80% of occasions.

RPD analysis identifies a critical difference between experts and rookies when presented with recurring situations. Experienced people arrive at a decision more quickly because the situation has the earmarks of a previously encountered situation. Without the prior experience, it is lacking the decision-maker must cycle through different possibilities and lack a reliable intuitive course of action. Additionally, newbies tend to make more use of trial and error facilitated by their imagination, and presumably waste more time getting to action.

TAKE-AWAYS

- Common sense appeals to our desires to simplify. Yet, if we want to rely on our common sense it's wise to remain open-minded and resist embracing a rigid mindset.
- Common sense works well on a personal level, but when applied to complex organizations it often fails, and we tend to excuse the error by justifying we didn't know that at the time. In other words, certain common sense is only obvious *after* we know the answer. Consequently, our common sense is a work-in-progress and we might be best served learning from its failings.
- Leaders possess many tools to move people such as priming, framing, and anchoring. However, rather than using these devices to trick people, it's far better to employ enlightened self-interest where the leader's interests are served by serving the followers interests.
- Cognition and emotion aren't as separate as we might believe. They're intertwined and work in harness to unearth people's true motivation. So, rational is not held in contrast with emotional (either-or) but, rather it's held in contrast with intuition.
- Intuition refers to our ability to know or understand something without reasoning or proof. We rely on our senses to gather the data used to determine a response. While it is common to think of separating rational and emotion; it's far better to contrast rational with intuition.

- Our interest in the senses lies in the potential to acquire new ideas or to explain phenomena so that we can inform and inspire other to adopt behavior that will benefit our mutual concerns.
- Heuristics are the short-cuts we take to make decisions. Three commonly used heuristics are availability, representativeness, and anchoring. While heuristics can differ from answers given by logic and probability, decisions based on heuristics can be good enough to satisfy a need. Gut feelings, similar to intuition, is based on years of experience, an unconscious form of intelligence.
- Forecasting is a technique that uses historical data to look at the future. The challenge is to predict future demand. Prediction is dependent on that which is preordained. The problem with even the best renditions from this model is that plans are met with competitive response. This requires establishing well-examined assumptions and well-honed judgment.
- Recognition-primed decision-making works well in circumstances where a quick, effective decision must be made in light of a complex situation. It works because the challenges are similar; the decision-makers have experienced the situation many times before.

Notes

1 Watts, D. J. (2011). *Everything is obvious once you know the answer*. New York, NY: Crown Books, (p. 8).
2 Taylor, C. C. (1947). Sociology and common sense. *American Sociological Review, 12*(1), 1–9, (p. 1).
3 Tetlock, P. E., & Gardner. D. ((2015). *Superforecasting: The art and science of prediction*. New York, NY: Crown Publishers, (p. 34).
4 Atlas, J. (May 12, 2012). The amygdala made me do it. *New York Times*. Retrieved December 20, 2020 from https://www.nytimes.com/2012/05/13/opinion/sunday/the-amygdala-made-me-do-it.html.
5 Ibid, (pp. 34–35).
6 Tetlock & Gardner, (p. 35).
7 Watts, (p. xv).
8 Ibid, (p. xvi).
9 Ibid, (p. xvi).
10 Berkun, S. (May 14, 2012). *Why common sense is not common practice*. Retrieved from scottberkun.com/2012/why-common-sense-is-not-common-practice/
11 Quote taken from the blog of Scott Berkun. Retrieved December 30, 2020 from scottberkun.com/2010/why-its-okay-to-be-obvious/
12 Phillips, M. (December 9, 2020). *Azar says vaccinations could begin next week, 20M people inoculated by end of year*. Fox Business. Retrieved December 15, 2020 from https://www.foxbusiness.com/politics/azar-says-vaccinations-could-begin-next-week-20m-by-end-of-year.
13 Ibid.

14 According to the *Wall Street Journal,* the first U.S. Covid-19 vaccinations outside of clinical trials began Monday, December 14, 2020. So, the first full week of vaccinations would have been completed on December 20, 2020.
15 Oliver, M. (December 30, 2020). *Vaccine rollout slower than expected as Americans wait for doses.* CBS News. Retrieved on December 30, 2020 from https://www.cbsnews.com/news/covid-vaccine-rollout-slower-than-expected/.
16 Berkun.
17 Ibid.
18 Ibid.
19 Watts, D. J. (2011). *Everything is obvious once you know the answer.* New York, NY: Crown Books, (p. 4).
20 Geertz, C. (1975). Common sense as a cultural system. *The Antioch Review, 33*(1), 5–26, (p. 12).
21 Watts, (pp. 15–16).
22 Melo, Guedes, & Mendes.
23 For more detailed reporting of the experiment, see Salganik and Watts (2009).
24 Watts, (pp. 76–77).
25 Ibid, (pp. 42–43).
26 Haidt, J., (pp. 50–51).
27 Ibid, (p. 52).
28 Ibid, (p. 53).
29 Duggan W. (2015). *The seventh sense: How flashes of insight change your life.* New York, NY: Columbia Business School, (p. 2).
30 Gladwell, M. (2007). *Blink: The power of thinking without thinking.* New York, NY: Little, Brown and Company, (pp. 22–23).
31 Cognitive load refers to our working memory. There are three: (a) intrinsic (associated with a specific topic), extraneous (the way information is presented to a learner), and germane (the work to storing the information). Retrieved November 20, 2020, from en.wikipedia.ord/wiki/Cognitive_load.
32 Gigerenzer, G. (January 1, 2008). Why heuristics work. *Perspectives on Psychological Science, (3)*1, 20–39.
33 Ibid, (p. 4).
34 Ibid, (p. 5).
35 Fox, J. (June 20, 2014). Instinct dan beat analytical thinking. *Harvard Business Review.* [Reprint HOOVFV], (p. 4).
36 Investopedia. Retrieved July 18, 2020 from https://www.investopedia.com/terms/f/forecsasting.asp.
37 Saffo, P. (July–August 2007). Six rules for effective forecasting. *Harvard Business Review.* Retrieved July 18, 2020 from https://hbsp.harvard.edu/download?url=%2Fcatalog%2Fsample%2FR0707K-PDF-ENG%2Fcontent&metadata=eyJlcnJvck1lc3NhZ2UiOiJ Zb3UgbXVzdCBiZSByZWdpc3RlcmVkIGFzIGEgUHJlbWl1bSBSZHVjYXRvciBvBv-biB0aGlzIHdlYiBzaXRlIIHRvIHNlZSBFZHVjYXRvciBDb3BpZXMgYW5kIEZyZ-WUgVHJpYWxzLiBOb3QgcmVnaXN0ZXJlZD8gQXBwbHkgbm93LiBBBY2Nlc3M-gzZXhwaXJlZD8gUmVVhdXRob3JpemUgbm93LiJ9
38 Dupuy, T. (1984). *A genius for war: The German army and general staff 1807–1945.* London, UK: Hero Books, Ltd.
39 "A phrase now much used to describe the complexity of military conflicts (*The Fog of War* was the title of Errol Morris's 2004 award-winning documentary about Robert S. McNamara, US Secretary of State during the Vietnam War). Fog of war is often attributed to [Carl von] Clausewitz, but is in fact a paraphrase of what he said: 'War is the realm of uncertainty; three quarters of the factors on which action in war is based are

wrapped in a fog of greater or lesser uncertainty.'" Retrieved July 16, 2020 from https://www.oxfordreference.com/view/10.1093/oi/authority.20110803095826962.

40 Klein, G. (1998/2018) *Sources of power: How people make decisions.* Cambridge, MA: MIT Press, [Kindle edition], (loc. 522).

41 Ibid, (loc. 571).

42 Ibid, (loc. 679),

12

INNOVATION

Clayton Christensen identified the innovator's dilemma. Christensen also discovered the depth of the decision a firm faces between serving their customer's needs or adopting new innovations and technologies, which will answer their future needs. He identified two kinds of innovation: sustaining and disruptive. "A sustaining innovation targets demanding, high-end customers with better performance than what was previously available."[1] Such innovations are frequently incremental, so established firms typically win these sorts of contests with competitors. This is not the case with disruptive innovations that aren't as good as current offerings, but "are simpler, more convenient, and less expensive products that appeal to new or less demanding customers."[2]

Ironically, for established firms, it's the adoption of disruptive technologies, not sustaining, that lead to failure. "Generally, disruptive technologies underperform established products in mainstream markets. But they have other features that a select few (and generally new) customers value."[3] Christensen's findings warn that generating and implementing new ideas and ways of operating are quite complex and replete with unintended consequences.

Innovation is Elusive

While there's substantial hue and cry over the imperative for firms to constantly innovate, it's fraught with danger. Perhaps, that's why so many firms find innovation as difficult to accomplish as any organizational effort they encounter. Vijay Govindarajan and Chris Trimble recognized "a simple answer: organizations aren't designed for innovation. Quite the contrary, they're designed for ongoing operations."[4]

They argue that firms start out fresh and settle into a rhythm and pattern of activities that aims at serving their customer better than their rivals. Looking at it from an investment perspective, "early investors want innovation, excitement, and growth. Later, investors want profits. They want reliable profits."[5] Think of two engines: performance and innovation. Performance is premised on achieving productivity and efficiency. "They get a little bit better, a little bit faster, and a little bit cheaper, every day, every month and every year. They're disciplined and accountable at every level."[6]

Tug-of-War

Unfortunately, when the performance engines become strong, innovation becomes a more difficult task. Innovation demands resources and investment, which negatively impacts performance. The first rule of innovation is that "innovation and ongoing operations are always and inevitably in conflict."[7] For a firm to perform, it seeks consistency—it seeks to be repeatable and predictable.

Past performance serves as a baseline measure. Naturally, expectations are built upon previous performance. Leaders can be held accountable to a performance standard with respect to profit improvement. Accountants keep track and turn out reports measuring the firm's performance on revenues and profits. Since performance plans work on data, managers seek to pump sales and reduce costs as the most reliable way to improve the numbers. A better choice than developing innovations is to acquire them. Besides adding to the score, they reduce competition.

Innovation, on the other hand, works on assumptions. Assumptions require members to learn and investors to take risks on new and unproven ideas and discoveries. If that weren't enough, innovative efforts will more likely fail than produce immediate sales and profits. The struggle between operations and innovation is a tug-of-war that favors incremental improvement in the status quo. When a leader is attempting to attract buy-in, conflict is not a favorable backdrop.

The Innovative Approach to Innovation

Chris consistently struggled with how Apex should deal with the innovation. Apex didn't need to be a cutting-edge business. Most innovative efforts focused on how available technology might be employed to improve productivity, efficiency, and intelligence collection. Chris' innovation strategy focused on leveraging the existing business model. A good way to look at it is the Innovative Landscape Map developed by Harvard researchers Abernathy, Clark, Christensen, Henderson, and Tushman.

Using the map, companies plot their strategic position based on technical capabilities and business model. Four categories emerge: (a) Disruptive, new business model and existing technology; (b) Architectural, new business model and new technical competencies; (c) Routine, existing business model and existing technology; and (d) Radical, existing business model and new technical competencies.

Chris considered Routine to be the best choice for Apex. "Routine innovation builds on a company's existing technological competencies and fits with it existing business model—and hence its customer base."[8] It is important to note that though it is not radical, it is indeed innovation in that it provides "a clear understanding and articulation of specific objectives related to helping the company achieve a sustainable competitive advantage."[9] What type of investments in innovation must Apex make? Those that advance the customer's progress.

Apex recognized its business model and use of technology produced loyal relationships with its customers. Apex was focused on its client's customers. Its technology and business competencies worked in harmony to produce continuous improvement in errors and productivity. Turnaround time for work orders was consistently dropping as its people learned how to leverage existing technology to improve quality and speed of service.

Chris and the senior management team invested in developing new vertical products to serve the information gathering and reporting needs of other business sectors. When venturing out, Apex was presented new situations and opportunities to leverage its exemplary customer service. While not always successful in displacing existing competitors, the firm did learn from failure without disrupting its core business.

Chris relentlessly focused on refining assumptions held about the business. He saw it as a way to improve the firm's strategic planning. Chris took guidance from an article about evolving the business model.

Learning from Doing

Gary Hamel and Liisa Välikangas wrote: "Strategic resilience is not about responding to a one-time crisis. It's not about rebounding from a setback. It's about continuously anticipating and adjusting to deep, secular trends that can permanently impair the earning power of a core business."[10] This appealed to Chris because he saw business as an ever-evolving environment to accommodate its future. Learning is part and parcel of its ability to build institutional knowledge. Learning also establishes a trusted way of doing business that marked the organization's culture. The learning, as discussed in Chapters 7 and 8, was a means of embracing real change, in other words, renewal.

TIME FOR A RE-CHARGE

Chris arrived at Mom's place with a big grin on his face. As soon as Chris sat down, he reached into his jacket pocket and pulled out a bulging envelope.

CHRIS: *There you go. Those are your tickets to Disneyland! You always wanted to take us kids there, well, now we're taking you there.*

AGNES: *Sounds great, did you get me ears, too?*

CHRIS: *Oh yeah, the whole package.*

AGNES: *This will be fun. Haven't been with the family much lately and this will give us all a chance to catch up...*

CHRIS: *And have some yuks!*

AGNES: *You always seem to know when we all need a little something to look forward to...*

CHRIS: *Just trying to keep myself amused. Can't be all bidness.* (Chris always used the made-up word, bidness, instead of the formal word, business. It took the edge off of being all business)

AGNES: *You know, life can get a little long sometimes and we all need something to look forward to... it puts a little bounce in our step.*

Chris and his wife were famous for entertaining. One time they bought a bowling party at a silent auction and invited 30 of their best friends to a beer and bowling bash. Every year, they hosted a lobster boil at the end of summer inviting the entire neighborhood to take part.

Chris loved to have fun. Planning trips and events made the day go by so fast along with a big smile on your face.

Inspiring Innovation

In a book about buy-in, romancing innovation may be used to power through the status quo. It is evident that buy-in can be complicated and at odds with routine operations in the firm. Yet, innovation may also serve to create breakthrough initiatives if employees can be deputized to reach within and adopt an innovative approach to their routines.

Peter Skarzynski and Rowan Gibson offer four perspective on how firms innovate. In their study of a variety of organizations, the pair advise: "innovation came not from some inherent, individual brilliance but from looking at the world from a *fresh perspective*—if you will, through a different set of lenses ... that enabled the innovators to look through the familiar and spot the unforeseen. In fact, four essential perspectives—four "perceptual lenses"—seem to dominate most successful innovation stories...."[11] The authors found in case after case, insights arose from four areas:

- Challenging orthodoxies;
- Harnessing discontinuities;
- Leveraging competencies and strategic assets; and
- Understanding unarticulated needs.

Chris saw these as areas where people needed to be attuned and perceptive. He saw these lenses as a sharp view of the values and practices of Apex, much like the idea depicted in Figure 12.1 with heavy bombs being dropped. He encouraged people to stay true to operating practices, but to always question the dogmatic or taken-for-granted assumptions about what causes success. He believed that everyone, should look for changes in those patterns that could change the rules. He thought of Apex as a portfolio of skills and assets with unlimited potential rather than departments and functions with limited range, the infamous silo!

Finally, and most importantly, Chris saw that success runs through the customer. He encouraged everyone to observe and query customers to determine the root-cause of their pain and what helped make progress against their circumstance. This last item permitted Chris to see the tremendous pressure that his clients were under to capture customers quickly. The housing market was red-hot putting pressure on the need for a quick approval report.

The "quickie' was a sign of trouble. It was one of the "changing patterns" bombs would change the rules only way Apex would compete. While the customer loved it. inadequate information quickly delivered was still inadequate. This industry innovation introduced a different kind of dilemma—an ethical dilemma.

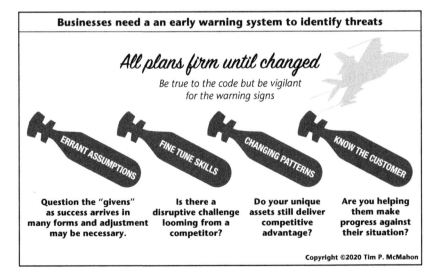

FIGURE 12.1   A firm can respond to external threats only if it knows they exist

Innovation Needs a Home

Innovation is kind of like the story of the three bears, not too much, not too little, but just right. Chris believed a firm should build a home for innovation, but not for innovators. In other words, he believed, like management sage Henry Mintzberg, that analysis of planning and intuition of management was the right combination to address fast developing issues. Mintzberg referenced Herbert Simon's viewpoint: "Every manager needs to be able to respond to situations rapidly, a skill that requires cultivation of intuition and judgment over many years of experience."[12]

Learning from early experiences in the IT business, Chris knew the early stages of a firm were all about innovation. How would the firm develop its unique selling proposition? How would it shape its people and infrastructure resources to deliver the offering succinctly and efficiently? It all begged the question, "How would innovation fit in?"

Henry Mintzberg asserts innovation fits through a combination of analysis and synthesis. As he put it: "One creates direction through synthesis, the other clarifies and orders that direction through analysis. Such a sequence of roles is deeply rooted in our cognitive makeup."[13] This was the way Chris thought of it, as innovation architecture, "a process that produces a deeply and widely shared view of your company's future *throughout* the organization—among the people who have the power to make it happen."[14] As mentioned, Apex adopted a Routine innovation approach: leverage existing technology against the existing business model. This is understood through systems thinking.

Blinded by the Facts in Plain Sight

If industry observers had viewed the mortgage industry from a systems-thinking perspective at the time of the emerging crisis, they may have spotted some problematic patterns, structures, and plenty of warning signs. In fact, some did. The Woodstock Institute published a study in 2004 reporting higher foreclosure rates in neighborhoods with a higher incidence of subprime mortgages during "the first high-risk lending boom, during the 1995–1999 period, that primarily involved refinance loans, with little penetration of the home purchase market."

Subprime lenders in the first boom often made loans with modest loan-to-value ratios. This meant the "loans were substantially smaller than the market value of the property in order to reduce the severity of any losses."[15] That should have been a warning shot. Lender's dodged a bullet in the first go-round. They certainly wouldn't let it happen again, would they?

Given this foreshadowing, the second wave of the subprime mortgage problem should have been spotted by everyone early on. As early as 2004, "three types of exotic mortgages—interest-only, payment-option, and 40-year balloon loans—accounted for just 7 percent of the U.S. mortgage market. However, by

2006, these three types had grown to 29 percent of the market."[16] Also in 2006, the Consumer Federation of America issued a report on the dangers of exotic mortgages.

Shifts that should have Raised a Concern

At the end of 2006, the Center for Responsible Lending forecast that "subprime foreclosures would accumulate to 2.2 million nationwide and that 19% of sub-prime loans would end in foreclosure."[17] Despite virtually no adverse reaction to this prediction at the time, this disconfirming data required an innovative response. Yet, looking back, the report significantly underestimated the depth of the problem while unhealthy loan practices kept rolling along.

The robust growth in home prices—the boom preceding the bust—masked the risk inherent in the subprime borrowers, and thus, the ultimate crash. In a market where the asset on which risk is placed is growing, there's a sense that risk is reduced by the growth. Further, lenders believed the latest wave of borrowers were new home buyers, and the boom scattered in hot spots around the country. Yet, the signs were clear. So why did the entire industry miss the indicators of impending doom?

Tools of Understanding

Virginia Anderson and Lauren Johnson are systems thinkers. As such, they recognize the value of seeing the big picture when it is tempting to focus on the immediate, most visible problems. Often time this creates a tendency to see and deal with symptoms rather than root causes of problems. "When you look at the world systematically, it becomes clear that everything is dynamic, complex, and interdependent. Put another way: Things change all the time, life is messy, and everything is connected."[18] Failing to recognize this leads to unavoidable peril.

Businesses routinely balance short- and long-term effects to optimize resources. It may employ consultants to deal with a particularly thorny problem that demands specialized expertise the firm does not possess. Then, when its people have embraced the deeper level knowledge and expertise to deal with the problem, it may dismiss or reduce the role of the experts as it can more efficiently deal with the issue once it has developed the capacity inside the organization.

Firms use both qualitative data (pictures) and quantitative (numbers) to inform their decision making. However, it is hard, measurable data that becomes the default means to measure organizational performance. The trouble is, while the numbers are good for a dashboard, they seldom reflect the deeper understanding of human behavior.

Systems thinking looks at the whole rather than the parts over time, in a circular rather than linear fashion. In that way, it examines closed interdependencies where x influences y, y influences z, and z loops back to influence x. See Figure 12.2 for a depiction of this phenomena as it occurred in the 2007 subprime mortgage debacle. At the bottom of this causal loop diagram (CLD) is a desire by the federal government for employment and economic growth, a variable.

"We can think of feedback loops as closed circuits of interconnection between variables, as sequences of mutual cause and effect. The links between each variable show how the variables are interconnected, and the signs (s or o) show how the variables affect one another."[19] The "s" leading to the second variable—government pressure to expand home ownership—indicates it's a support link. The third variable—credit standards—is labeled "o" meaning opposite. When government pressure goes up, credit standards go down. Reviewing the rest of the loop, it appears to be a reinforcing loop as it compounds change in one direction.

These patterns and structures are repeatable behaviors, what systems experts call system archetypes. Archetypes are one of the tools of systems thinking. Knowledge of archetypes makes it possible "to recognize them at work within a particular system and enables managers to use them to explain counterintuitive outcomes and identify leverage points for improving system performance."[20]

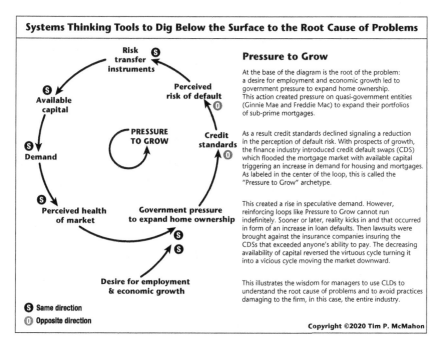

Systems Thinking Tools to Dig Below the Surface to the Root Cause of Problems

Risk transfer instruments ⓢ

Available capital ⓢ

Perceived risk of default ⓞ

PRESSURE TO GROW

Credit standards ⓞ

Demand ⓢ

Perceived health of market ⓢ

Government pressure to expand home ownership ⓢ

Desire for employment & economic growth ⓢ

ⓢ Same direction
ⓞ Opposite direction

Pressure to Grow

At the base of the diagram is the root of the problem: a desire for employment and economic growth led to government pressure to expand home ownership. This action created pressure on quasi-government entities (Ginnie Mae and Freddie Mac) to expand their portfolios of sub-prime mortgages.

As a result credit standards declined signaling a reduction in the perception of default risk. With prospects of growth, the finance industry introduced credit default swaps (CDS) which flooded the mortgage market with available capital triggering an increase in demand for housing and mortgages. As labeled in the center of the loop, this is called the "Pressure to Grow" archetype.

This created a rise in speculative demand. However, reinforcing loops like Pressure to Grow cannot run indefinitely. Sooner or later, reality kicks in and that occurred in form of an increase in loan defaults. Then lawsuits were brought against the insurance companies insuring the CDSs that exceeded anyone's ability to pay. The decreasing availability of capital reversed the virtuous cycle turning it into a vicious cycle moving the market downward.

This illustrates the wisdom for managers to use CLDs to understand the root cause of problems and to avoid practices damaging to the firm, in this case, the entire industry.

Copyright ©2020 Tim P. McMahon

FIGURE 12.2 A causal loop diagram (CLD) depicting the housing market that led to the subprime mortgage crisis.

Figure 12.2 illustrates the *pressure to grow* archetype. All such archetypes eventually turn from virtuous to vicious as other phenomena come into play.

Information providers like Apex may be ensnared in an archetype known as *shifting the burden*. Applying it here, an "underlying problem generates symptoms that demand attention. But the underlying problem is difficult for people to address, either because it is obscure or costly to confront. So, people 'shift the burden' of the problem to other solutions—well-intentioned, easy fixes seem extremely efficient."[21] The problem is that the symptom—loss of business for failing to respond to the client's need for a quick decision—is treated but not the underlying problem—providing reliable data to make an informed decision.

Perhaps because Chris was relatively new to the business, he could see the dangers of the quickie report offered by competitors and accepted due to lowering of *credit standards* as noted in Figure 12.2 at the three o'clock position. However, with the CLD perspective, lenders could only see heated demand for lending (where they make their money) and since home prices were rising fast (mitigating risk), a quickie report is just what they needed to capitalize on the opportunity. Further minimizing the risk, mortgage firms often sold a portfolio of loans to a third party, thereby, reducing their exposure and further justifying use of the quickie report.

Let it be known that someone at each of the big mortgage lenders considered the quickie report to be a key innovation to capitalize on the flush market. They might have described the competitor who thought of it as an innovative thinker. But if the report was anything it was a dumbing down of decision criteria, if you will. True innovations advance the client's progress against their situation. The quickie, as we shall see, merely delays the inevitable setback the client will experience.

The Responsible Role of Ethics

Such developments call into question the firm's ethics. Specifically, when is it time to blow the whistle on yourself? One of the basic ethical guideposts that is easily violated by business practitioners is rationalization. As discussed previously in this text, fixation on goals can blind leaders to their responsibilities. Unwittingly, "the unbalanced pursuit of a goal transforms the goal into a kind of idol.... What started out as the *choice* of the goal on the part of the decision-maker ends up as an enslavement of the decision-maker by the goal."[22] How do we avoid enslavement?

Rationalization is the process of convincing one's self that a decision is fair and defensible, when it really serves one's own interests. Business scholars at the Darden School at the University of Virginia suggest three tests a leader may use to free themselves from their fixation on goals:

- **The Publicity Test.** Could you defend your reasoning if it were made public, or you had to explain it to your mother?

• **Reversibility.** Could you defend your reasoning if you were on the losing end of your decision?

• **Generalizability.** Could you defend using this same reasoning in similar cases?[23]

These tests cause you to clarify what you know, inform the decision-making process, articulate standards of conduct, focus on character and virtue, enumerate consequences, and ultimately, avoid rationalization.

Recalling from Chapter one, Chris offers his own test, "The Mother Standard" for any member of Apex to evaluate ethical behavior:

> We will treat all stakeholders respectfully, fairly, and ethically. We will use the "Mother Standard." If you would feel comfortable explaining to your mother what you are doing, it is almost certainly the right thing to do from a values standpoint. If you would not feel comfortable explaining to your mother what you are doing, then it is almost certainly wrong, and you should reconsider your actions.

Learning Should Enlighten

We learned in Chapter 8 that people sometimes fail to learn. "Schools train us never to admit that we don't know the answer, and most corporations reinforce that lesson by rewarding people who excel in advocating their views, not inquiring into complex issues."[24] Failing to inquire robs us of new understandings that may serve us to better compete or defend an advantage.

Adherence to knowing (when you really don't) creates distance between yourself and the sources of knowledge that may rescue you from your own misinformed devices. But it's hard to do. We are wired to function on clarity, certainty, even when it's not available. This explains why leaders love to give advice. Michael Bungay Stanier wrote: "Even if it's the wrong advice—and it often is—giving it feels more comfortable than the ambiguity of asking a question... . You have the best of intentions to stay curious and ask a few good questions. But in the moment, just as you are moving to that better way of working, the Advice Monster leaps out of the darkness and hijacks the conversation."[25]

Whether you blame schools or your brain circuitry, thinking we know impairs the fundamental purpose of an education: to learn how to think. These are essentially learning disabilities and serve to substitute short-term harmful policies such as use of quickie reports, for innovative solutions that will address the fundamental problem. History is replete with stories of leaders who couldn't see the consequences of their policies even when forewarned. So, why do we fail to think critically?

Critical thinking—which is the use of objective analysis and evaluation of an issue to form a judgment—is available to help people make decisions. However, Gass &

Seiter make the case that there are two enemies of critical thinking: ignorance and stupidity. Ignorance is "a fundamental lack of knowledge ... [and] *stupidity* refers to a person who knows better, but still engages in foolish or risky behavior."[26]

Chris was neither ignorant nor stupid. He was a lifelong learner and when he seized on knowledge that could be put to use, he adopted it wholly.

Chris discovered a book called "Rockefeller Habits" by Verne Harnish. It was a business manual tracing effective practices of one of titans of industry John D. Rockefeller. Later re-titled "Scaling Up," Harnish warned business operators to make people accountable for every aspect of the business. If it's the profit & loss statement, have a single person in charge of each line on the statement. Harnish warns: "Unless you get accountabilities straight, productivity and innovation will slow, and you'll waste a lot of time oscillating between centralizing and decentralizing various shared functions among business units."[27] As you will see, it became the Apex operating manual and there were plenty of copies in the Apex library to go around.

Releasing the Power of Vulnerability

Organizations are made up of many people operating in many contexts. Regarding contexts within the organization, consider these three: trust, logic, and power. In a healthy organization or relationship, people feel free to act in an experimental way, that is, explore and innovate. That's good because this is essential for a firm to build adaptive capacity to thrive.

For this vibrancy to take place, we need a trusting relationship to permit the freedom from retribution for stepping outside the lines, and possibly making a mistake, maybe a costly one. However, the freedom to try and fail is part and parcel of eventual success—the earmark of a resilient and engaged workforce. The opposite of this is people struggling to discover a safe place to stand when bad news is spread through a firm. Let's look at these a little more closely.

The first of these contexts is trust and is witnessed in members of the firm "in their easy exchanges, open communication and often frenetic activity."[28] The second context is logic, "where cause-and-effect relationships are well understood and people in both their management and leadership roles understand what to do and how to do it."[29] Finally, there's the context of power, which deserves a deeper look.

Chris knew the mortgage industry appealed to him because it represented a rock-solid segment of investor. This meant dealing with well-qualified home buyers well within the risk parameters associated with riskier investments like foreign emerging markets or high yield bonds. These last two are labeled junk earnings, reflected by a BBB- rating on a Standard & Poor's scale. Serving clients who served high quality, low risk mortgage borrowers provided a sense of comfort in Apex's growth projections.

However, as discovered, the once-solid mortgage borrower became compromised by an industry too eager to write loans that looked good but maybe felt bad. The quickie report helped to resolve that bad feeling and give lenders a sense of security albeit paper thin. As it turns out, Chris needed to expose this to his people and get them on board with a plan to deal with this potentially crippling development.

The Seventh Sense

As we discovered, your sixth sense gives you the old idea, and while you may retrieve it quickly, it doesn't necessarily address the new situation you face. "The seventh sense is the mechanism of the human mind that produces new ideas. It's the epiphany, the flash of insight, the Eureka moment—in the form of an idea you never had before. And in its highest form, it's an idea that no one else had before either."[30] We know new ideas can change the world. However, before that happens, the idea must infect a single person in a way that changes the course of their dreams. That's why we call it an epiphany. Yet, as much as you like, it's not likely you'll coax a flash of light out of the dark recesses of the mind.

Chris related the process to new recruits in a personal way. So, when he introduced it to teams across Apex, they were grounded in its purpose: to tap into possibilities. It was a tool used when searching for creative ways to solve problems.

In one such session, after an hour of brainstorming, a flight of ideas filled the room, but nothing rose above the others as a direction to pursue. After a long pause, he decided he needed to stoke the creative fires. He stood up and said, "Remember I told you about the old adman who said he got his ideas from 'Three martinis and a bolt of lightning'?, That may be cute but not true. Creative thinking is really about re-combining thoughts and ideas into new thoughts and ideas."

What Chris related was a process devised by William Duggan, a Columbia professor and thought leader, that will prepare the mind to tap into what he called the seventh sense. He identified the process steps and reminded them this is a process to which most were introduced when they joined Apex (See Chapter 8). Chris was a pioneer in creative thinking and, more importantly, in spreading new ideas and possibilities. He often said, "My job is to make learning contagious, and I am an active carrier!" The session continued with renewed energy.

Contagion Unleashed

Why is it Tik-Tok, Uber, the Ice Bucket Challenge and other gimmicks catch on so quickly when similar ideas languish? In a word, contagion. Jonah Berger asserts all the usual explanations simply weren't acceptable explanations. We may believe that quality, price, and advertising are the reasons, but they don't factor into why Olivia is a more popular name than Rosalie or why some YouTube videos get a million or more views and others a couple dozen.[31] Both are free, quality is imperceptibly different, and advertisements for each don't exist. So, why? Berger concluded social transmission is the reason.

When we think of social transmission, we may spark to the current rage of social media. However, Malcolm Gladwell put social transmission into a longer-term context when he related the key role a Boston stable boy had in signaling citizens across the Massachusetts countryside that the British were coming. With that advance warning, the colonists, took up arms and soundly defeated the invading British soldiers at Concord the next day.[32]

While we may not find words to explain it until 200 years later, that epic word-of-mouth epidemic triggered the American Revolution, memorializing a stable boy named Paul Revere. And all because "A piece of extraordinary news traveled a long distance in a very short time, mobilizing an entire region to arms."[33]

The concept of socially connected world is well supported in research originating with Stanley Milgram's work developing Small World Theory in the 1960s. He conducted experiments to determine average length of the path of social networks of people in the United States. The research was a breakthrough discovery because it showed how everyone connected to everyone else through six or fewer connections, later dubbed six degrees of separation.

Subsequently, social influence has played a huge impact on whether products, ideas, and behaviors catch on. "A word-of-mouth (WOM) conversation by a new customer leads to an almost $200 increase in restaurant sales. A five-star review on Amazon.com leads to approximately 20 more books sold than a one-star review. Doctors are more likely to prescribe a new drug if other doctors they know have prescribed it. People are more likely to quit smoking if their friends quit and people get fatter if their friends become obese. In fact, while traditional advertising is still useful, word of mouth from everyday Joes and Janes is at least 10 times more effective."[34]

Figure 12.3 is a movie promotional peace aimed at taking advantage of fear and concern over the pandemic. The movie company, Warner Brothers, tapped into the social zeitgeist generated by the pandemic. Clearly attempting to generate movie contagion riding on the back of the true virus contagion of COVID-19, the images no doubt permeated the social media accounts of the movie's many stars and their fans, as well.

Influence Rides on Credibility

WOM works for two reasons: (a) it's more persuasive than paid advertising that many consider skeptically because ads are funded, therefore, lack credibility; and (b) it's more targeted. WOM travels naturally to the individual most likely to act on the information.[35] We've learned that digital/social media is truly integrated communication. "It's searchable, shareable and scalable. In traditional, old school media, the task focused on finding prospective customers. Today, the challenge is

FIGURE 12.3   Grabbed from the headlines, Contagion (the movie) rides on real world COVID-19

to entice you to find them. This new digital world makes this possible because it's searchable (you can be discovered through search) and shareable (when individuals advance you or your firm with others on Pinterest, Instagram, Twitter, etc.), and this exchange can be widely cast. In this new world, collaboration trumps control; engagement tops trumpeting; and communities outlast audiences."[36] A term that explains something is catching on fast is one in which we've all become too familiar: epidemic.

We've become well aware of epidemics. We recognize how a relentlessly out-of-control pathogen may become given the right set of circumstances to expand into a pandemic (a global version of the epidemic). In "The Tipping Point," Malcolm Gladwell wrote that ideas, trends, and social behaviors spread like viruses do, once they reach a tipping point they expand rapidly. The tipping point is the moment it catches on and spreads broadly; is subject to three rules: (a) the law of the few, (b) the stickiness factor, and (c) the power of context.

The law of the few refers to the three types of people who are gifted with the ability in some aspect of spreading by word-of-mouth. He identified *connectors* (people with large social circles); *mavens* (information specialists who people find credible); and *salesmen* (charismatic people with effective persuasion skills). The stickiness factor states, "there are specific ways of making a contagious message memorable; there's relatively simple changes in the presentation and structuring of information that can make a big difference in how much of an impact it makes."[37]

Think "Keep Calm and Carry On."[38] The phrase has been adapted and replicated in many places as a modern-day answer to the hurried pace of life. Evidence that people are very much influenced by power of context, "says that human beings are a lot more sensitive to their environment than they may seem."[39]

These three rules form a metaphor to inform the leader how to go about spreading the message that will drive desired behavior through a social group. The tools present a framework for who, what, and where to attempt to engage people in the challenges and opportunities that lie before them.

"Epidemics are a function of the people who transmit infectious agents, the infectious agent itself, and the environment in which the infectious agent is operating. And when an epidemic is jolted out of equilibrium, it tips because something has happened; some change has occurred in one (or two or three) of those areas."[40] Recent global experiences with the novel coronavirus pandemic brought these rules up close and personal for every soul on the planet. Who knew the wearing of a mask could become a political statement?

TAKEAWAYS

- Generating and implementing new ideas and ways of operating are quite complex and replete with unintended consequences.
- Organizations are not designed to serve two masters efficiently: innovation and ongoing operations. Each demands a different set of resources resulting in a tug-of-war that often thwarts successful innovation.
- Innovation is just one more aspect of adaptation that firms must effectively deal with in accomplishing integration of successful new innovations.
- To adopt a healthy attitude toward innovation, firms do well to challenge orthodoxies, harness discontinuities, leverage competencies, and understand unarticulated needs.
- Managers must develop the ability to analyze and synthesize because one creates direction and the other clarifies and orders the direction.
- The subprime mortgage crisis of 2007 was predictable. However, the warning signs were ignored. This led to destructive practices that catered to expanding the number of loan approvals when the industry should have been more deeply scrutinizing applications.
- Using Systems Thinking is a means to analyze and synthesize the challenges facing firms. Firms use both qualitative data (pictures) and quantitative (numbers) to inform their decision making. However, hard, measurable data generally becomes the default means to measure

performance. Yet, we've learned there's always a story behind the numbers that reveals a deeper understanding of human behavior.

* For firms to grow and for their members to buy-in to the proposition leaders must marshal trust, logic, and power. For this vibrancy to take place, we must develop a trusting relationship to permit the freedom from retribution for stepping outside the lines, and possibly making a mistake, maybe a costly one.

* Using tools like exploring the seventh sense, is a practice in which members can engage, exploit, and bring to life true innovative and growth-driving movements. However, it takes individuals learning how to unleash creative abilities that lead to developing the adaptive capacity to thrive.

* Contagion is a means to accelerate adoption. But how do we make this happen? Social influence plays a huge impact on whether products, ideas, and behaviors catch on. The challenge is to move the idea into the social conversation through social media. This has a place in the workplace and takes on the characteristics of an all-too-familiar term: epidemics.

Notes

1 Christensen, C. M., & Raynor, M. E. (2003). *The innovator's solution*. Boston, MA: Harvard Business School Publishing, (p. 33).
2 Ibid, (p. 34).
3 Christensen, C. M. (1997). *The innovator's dilemma: When new technologies cause great firms to fail*. Boston, MA: Harvard Business Review Press, (p. 23).
4 Govindarajan, V., & Trimble, C., (2010). *The other side of innovation: Solving the execution challenge*. Boston, MA: Harvard Business Review Press.
5 Ibid, (p. 10).
6 Ibid, (p. 10).
7 Ibid, (p 11).
8 Pisano, G. P. (June 2015). You need an innovation strategy. *Harvard Business Review*. Retrieved December 1, 2020, from hbr.org/2015/06/you-need-an-innovation-strategy.
9 Ibid.
10 Hamel, G., & Välikangas, L. (2003). The quest for resilience. *Harvard Business Review*. [Reprint R0309C]. Retrieved November 15, 2020 from https://hbsp.harvard.edu., (p. 2).
11 Skarzynski, P., & Gibson, R. (2008). *Innovation to the core: A blueprint for transforming the way your company innovates*. Boston, MA: Harvard Business Press, (p. 46).
12 Simon, H. A. (1987). Making management decisions: The role of intuition and emotion. *Academy of Management Executive*, (p. 329).
13 Mintzberg, H. (1994). *The rise and fall of strategic planning*. New York, NY: The Free Press, (p. 336).
14 Skarzynski & Gibson, (p. 156).
15 Immergluck, D. (2011). *Foreclosed: High-risk lending, deregulation, and the undermining of America's mortgage market*. [Kindle version]. Ithaca, NY & London, UK: Cornell University Press, (loc. 620)

16 Ibid, (loc. 100)
17 Schloemer, E., Li, W., Ernst, K., and Keest, K. (2006). *Losing ground: Foreclosures in subprime market and their cost to homeowners.* Durham, NC: Center for Responsible Lending.
18 Anderson, V., and Johnson, L. (1997). *Systems thinking basics: From concepts to causal clops.* Waltham, MA: Pegasus Communications, Inc., p. 19).
19 Ibid, (pp. 54–55).
20 Stephens, A.A., Brian Atwater, J., & Kannan, V.R. (2013). "From tulip bulbs to sub-prime mortgages examining the sub-prime crisis: The case for a systemic approach", *The Learning Organization, 20*(1), 65–84. https://doi.org/10.1108/096964 71311288537, (p. 8).
21 Senge, P. M. (2006). *The fifth discipline: The art and practice of the learning organization* (Rev. ed.). New York: Currency Doubleday, (p. 103).
22 Goodpaster, K. E., (2007). *Conscience and corporate culture.* Hoboken, NJ: Blackwell Publishing, (p. 30).
23 Harris, J. D., Wicks, A. C., & Parmar, B. L. (July 31, 2015). Ethical business decisions: The framework. *UVA ideas to action.* Retrieved November 15, 2020 from ideas.darden.virginia.edu/ethical-business-decisions-the-framework.
24 Senge, (p. 25).
25 Stanier, M. B. (2016). *The coaching habit: Say less, ask more & change the way you lead forever.* Toronto, ON: Box of Crayons, (p. 59).
26 Gass, R. H., & Seiter, J. S., (2019). *Arguing, reasoning, and thinking well.* New York, NY & London, UK: Routledge - Taylor & Francis Group, (p. 63).
27 Harnish, V. (2014). *Mastering the Rockefeller habits: What you must do to increase the value of your growing firm.* Ashburn, VA: Gazelles Inc., (p. 51).
28 Hurst, D.K. (2012). *The new ecology of leadership: Business mastery in a chaotic world.* New York, NY: Columbia Business School Publishing, (p. 47).
29 Ibid, (p. 47).
30 Duggan W. (2015). *The seventh sense: How flashes of insight change your life.* New York, NY: Columbia Business School, (p. 4).
31 In 2010, there were almost 17,000 Olivias born in the United States but only 492 Rosalies. In fact, while the name Rosalie was somewhat popular in the 1920s, it never reached the stratospheric popularity that Olivia recently achieved, (p. 6).
32 Gladwell, M. (2002). *The tipping point: How little things can make a big difference.* New York, NY: Little, Brown and Company, (p. 32).
33 Ibid, (p. 32).
34 Berger, J. (2013). *Contagious: Why Things Catch On.* New York, NY: Simon & Schuster, (p. 7).
35 Ibid, (p. 8).
36 McMahon, T. P. (In Press). Integrated communication. In Doorley, J. & Garcia, H. F. (2020). *Reputation Management* (4th ed.). New York, NY: Routledge, (p. 265).
37 Gladwell, M. (2002). *The tipping point: How little things can make a big difference.* New York, NY: Little, Brown and Company, (p. 25).
38 It is reported "[t]he words are not Winston Churchill's but the famous World War II poster "Keep Calm and Carry On" is now indelibly associated with his spirit and his leadership of the British people. Ironically, the poster itself was never issued during the War and was only 'discovered' just over ten years ago in a bookshop in the northeast of England. Since then the image and phrase have been reproduced, lionized and parodied around the world. Retrieved July 17, 2020, from https://winstonchurchill.org/publications/churchill-bulletin/bulletin-045-mar-2012/keep-calm-and-carry-on-the-real-story-1/
39 Ibid, (p. 29).
40 Ibid, (pp. 18–19).

13

SMOOTH OPERATIONS

When a firm has a handle on its priorities, the flow of information to accommodate decision making, and established a rhythm with specific agendas and individual accountabilities it is prepared to grow and thrive. It moves beyond strategic planning to competent execution. A plan is merely a good intention until enacted and therein lies the challenge. In the famous words of world champion boxer Mike Tyson, "everyone has a plan until you get punched in the mouth." The message is that an organization must be prepared to adapt on the fly as new challenges emerge because they are sure to arise.

Verne Harnish has dedicated his life to developing rigorous, yet simple tools and practices that deliver growth to businesses across the world. He draws the distinction between accountability (the one person who counts), responsibility (all who are able to respond), and authority (the person or team with the final decision-making power) that creates clarity in the organization. Harnish illustrates the distinction between functional accountability and process accountability. This chapter borrows from Harnish and many others to provide guidance on developing smooth operations that create direction and guidance for buy-in and accomplishment of critical challenges that Chris faces in leading Apex.

Timidity Never Won Any Ballgames[1]

Previously we have discussed the idea of dissenters. Opposition and how it surfaces and is dealt with by leaders and followers is the essence of the ability to create buy-in—the theme of this book. In the midst of a change initiative, leaders often become so gung-ho in their push for change that they are prone to see any obstacle as a threat to success. They become unduly wedded to their perspective to the point of being unable to see fruitful alternatives or options. Alternatives flow from dissenters, people who see the same things others see but see it differently.

Public relations veteran Ron Rhody captured the idea of organizational commitment in these words: "Buy-in is that happy state when the people who are important to the success of your initiatives understand what you want to do. They approve of it. They support it. They actively participate in ways that are appropriate to help you reach your goals...."[2] Leaders who fail to grasp this notion are doomed to fail to obtain the commitment that gives an initiative lift.

While the desired change may be worthy, it doesn't matter if you cannot connect it to the well-being of employees and customers; embed it in daily preferences and practices. Yet, leaders regularly display an aloof posture on this critical matter. When leaders are able to set aside their über enthusiasm and entertain the idea that they are in partnership with their people, an energy enters the building that puts the *force* in workforce. It is an energy born of inter-dependence, reliant on the better angels in each of us.

However, when a laser-like focus blinds the leader's peripheral vision, she effectively shuts out the people needed to gain commitment. It is in the wider circle that the buy-in will emerge, that is, when members of the organization have visibility and understanding of the scope of the issue. Moreover, it will take flight when priorities are set, and feedback is ingrained in the daily rhythm of the organization.

When the people in an organization have learned what works for survival, they instinctively resist suggestions they see as antithetical. It is a kind of organizational inoculation warding off a threat to the status quo. Understanding culture and dealing with it as suggested in Chapter 6 is a means to adapt the culture to the mission. However, it is in the daily operating practices that commitment is realized.

The Gauntlet

Do not be confused about how this gets done, that is, how people are led to commitment. As has been discussed in Chapters 9 and 10, it takes shape (or doesn't) through the critical decision moment when members of the firm face the devil in a showdown. Both leaders and followers confront a reckoning and arrive at commitment or find themselves unwilling, unable, or unworthy of the mission. When a firm faces the gauntlet, it will break through when members execute with competence and commitment accomplished through effective business practices.

Throughout this story, we have seen Chris take a strong stance on the way Apex must operate to thrive. He has faced the challenge of shaping a new culture

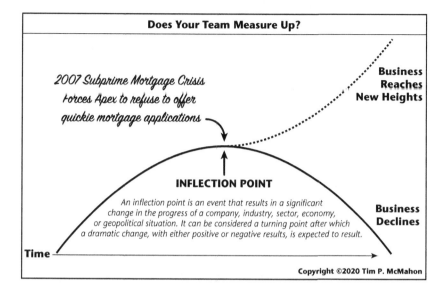

FIGURE 13.1 The inflection point at Apex and the entire mortgage lending industry

based on merit, not seniority; he has confronted the reality of an external threat that is rising to a crisis level; and is soon to confront the challenge that will highly affect the life of the firm and livelihood of its people. Chris is poised to lead Apex through an inflection point, the point in the life of a firm that its direction is altered by a single event.

The trajectory after the inflection point is illustrated in Figure 13.1, dependent on how the firm deals with the event. Historically, firms or industries that have encountered an inflection point, typically jump start a growth spurt or enter a death spiral which results in an unwinding of the firm's activities. Due to the machinations that have re-written the stabilizing rules of the mortgage loan industry, Apex may pay a hefty price, perhaps extinction. But first, a final chapter about the preparedness of Apex.

Barriers to Growth

All firms at some point face an inflection point. The post-event direction will be determined by its ability to thrive. When the rules change, firms who cannot adapt are overpowered. Adaptation is inherent organization skill developed long before it becomes essential. It "requires resilience of people and the capacity of systems to take the best from its traditions, identity, and history into the future."[3] unless a firm can muster the response to capitalize on the triggering events to move the trajectory of the curve in a positive direction. See Figure 13.1.

Every firm with its sights set on growth will face barriers, specifically: leadership, systems, and market dynamics. The first two a firm can control, the third will dictate the response the leader must cause to happen. In a nutshell, preparation for this relies on "the need for the executive team to grow as leaders in their abilities to delegate and predict; the need for systems and structures to handle the complexity that comes with growth; and the need to navigate the increasingly tricky market dynamics that mark arrival in a larger marketplace."[4] You have witnessed Chris' perspective and efforts on many commitment generating ideas and practices in this book. Now, we look at how it is implemented.

The Two Accountabilities

Verne Harnish advises leaders to have the "right people doing the right things right."[5] With regard to people, he urges organizations to have members of the firm complete a one-page personal plan that "looks at four key [life] decisions—Relationships, Achievements, Rituals, and Wealth—which mirror the four key decisions for business: People, Strategy, Execution, and Cash."[6] Chris committed to this idea, believing his own clear outlook on life provided a foundation for contributing to the success of his marriage, his role as father, and his contributions to career and workplace.

Accountability drives performance. There are two kinds: one that holds people accountable to their individual commitments; and the one that holds each leader accountable to one another. This means, as Chris often said, "having the right people in the right paces doing the right things," and "if we can think it, we can do it." Harnish advises that functional leaders must be "people who fit your culture and pass two tests: 1. They don't need to be managed and 2. They regularly wow the team with their insights and output."[7] Regarding process, he places great emphasis on deciding on "two or three KPIs [key performance indicators] that track the health of the process—the most important being the length of time, from start to finish, for a specific *process*."[8]

As we have learned, Chris is adamant about recruiting, engaging, and retaining employees. Following Harnish's guidance, Chris practices his advice:

- Help people play to their strengths;
- Don't demotivate, dehassle;
- Set clear expectations and give employees a clear line of sight;
- Give recognition and show appreciation; and
- Hire fewer people, but pay them more (frontline employees, not top leaders).[9]

Know People Deeply

Chris favored a practice of familiarity. He was always connecting with people in the firm in his daily routine of MBWA. It kept him aware of people at all levels, observing their interactions and assessing who needed to be managed and who regularly WOWed the organization. "Who you gonna believe me or your eyes?" he'd say with a chuckle. But he was serious. Facts are facts but they're nothing without the benefit of personal witness. Chris learned this at a very young age.

Perhaps because his mother encouraged young Chris to hit the streets at a ripe age to sell any number of nifty products door to door, Chris intuitively embraced the need for support in peddling magazine subscriptions or cleaning supplies on a cold-call basis. In his adult life, Chris understood this to mean what Boyatzis & McKee identified as self-renewal and connection with others through *mindfulness, hope*, and *compassion*.[10]

In those formative years, Chris' mom encouraged him when he encountered rejection and guided him with sage advice, not unlike Dale Carnegie's famous message, "If you want to gather honey, don't kick over the beehive."[11] On that note, Carnegie quoted the famous department store magnate John Wanamaker: "I learned thirty years ago that it is foolish to scold. I have enough trouble overcoming my own limitations without fretting over the fact that God has not seen fit to distribute evenly the gift of intelligence."[12] Chris was never scolded by his mother in such entrepreneurial endeavors. Rather, she emphasized reality and offered ways to deal with the cold, hard facts.

Top-Down or Bottom-Up

Chris was not timid about his views on what needed to be done, nor was he adamant that people blindly follow orders. As has been witnessed in this story, he encouraged pushback, and considered it a sincere form of engagement. There are two directions that change may take shape: top-down and bottom-up. While revolutions are directed from the central command, an alternate approach to creating change in organizations is equally effective: evolution. Evolution emanates from the opposite end of the change strategy spectrum, the grass roots.

While this approach is most often associated with incremental instead of radical change, Management author Gareth Jones suggested this strategy is more inclusive of the people ultimately responsible for change: "Managers using a bottom-up strategy prepare the organization for change by involving managers and employees at all levels of discussions about the need for change and the need to identify the problems facing the organization."[13] Because employees are involved in this strategy, it is believed that resistance to change is broken down and employees become open to searching for new solutions.

Jones wrote, "Organizations that are accustomed to change and that have institutionalized mechanisms for promoting organizational learning can overcome organizational inertia."[14] In simple terms, change becomes a part of the learning process. Just as in the revolutionary approach, learning facilitates change in the evolutionary approach as well. This is best accomplished in establishing the priorities and facilitating the data, or information, that people need to deal with challenges to growth.

Mindfulness on Trends

Harnish amended the traditional SWOT analysis to SWT, to place emphasis on the role that trends have on the success of a business. By consciously keeping an eye on trends, members can avoid the myopia that nestles into the conventional wisdom of business and industry. He identified seven components of strategy that identify how a firm executes strategy and how it may detect trends that may threaten or embellish a firm's strategic intent. They are revealed in these questions:

- What word(s) do you own in the minds of your targeted customers?
- Who are your customers, what three brand promises are you making them, and how do you know you are keeping them?
- What is your brand promise guarantee?
- What is your One-PHRASE Strategy that likely upsets customers but is key to making a ton of money and blocking your competition?
- What are the three to five activities that differentiate your firm from the competition? i.e., cost, differentiated, and focus (narrow or broad).
- What is your x-factor—a 10 to 100 times underlying advantage over the competition—that completely wipes out any and all rivals?
- What are your economic drivers and BHAG (Big Hairy Audacious Goals)[15] for the company?

When a firm has thoroughly answered these questions, it will have a grounded understanding of its strategy.

TOUGH WORDS IN THE WORKPLACE

Chris brought his people into the dialogue about how to respond to a customer's demand for a witch's brew of a product. It would facilitate a wild grab for revenue but end up a bad business decision resulting in significant loan defaults. Fresh on his mind was not so much saying no, it was accommodating the harmful effects to operations that would follow. This reminded him of messages from his mom when he was just entering business and he chose to take a stroll down memory lane.

CHRIS: *When I got that first job out of college, you took me to J. C. Penney's, I got a suit with two pairs of pants and a reversible vest. One suit; five combinations. What could be better than that from a guy with little money trying to make a good impression on his first job?*

AGNES: *You were dressed for success. I remember our little talk on the way home from the store.*

CHRIS: *Me too… You said, don't talk politics, religion, or money at work.*

AGNES: *Darn right. I remember telling you,* when we're talkin' among friends and family, we're shootin' the breeze, trying to make sense out of life's great mysteries. Politics, religion, and money are the topics that provide a lot of fuel for the fire.

CHRIS: *At work they blow up into a little too much fire. For what it's worth I took your advice... and it has worked out well.*

AGNES: *We can still entertain those barnburners around the dinner table, nothing wrong with a couple of side dishes like that to round out the meal.* They both laughed out loud.

CHRIS: *This week we make the decision on the new product. It's not a discussion. Emotions will heat up... even though we are not talking politics or religion.*

AGNES: *Well, you are talking money!*

CHRIS: *You can say that again. Everyone's understands money and the sales people more than anyone.*

AGNES: *They've got the most to lose.*

CHRIS: *They'll come around, too, once they realize that this is the litmus test of our integrity. If we really mean what we say, we have only one choice.*

AGNES: *Morals in action, that's ethics. It's the way our morals see the light of day.*

CHRIS: *It is a tough talk to have, nonetheless.*

AGNES: *The difference is how you and your people will respond.*

Chris agreed and took a long pause as he finished his cup of coffee. Then he turned to Agnes, kissed her goodbye and returned to work.

When It All Becomes Personal

How many times have you heard somebody in the lunchroom grousing about change? "I just get used to doing something and bam! They make me change." While we get frustrated with what we do, we often keep doing it because changing would be so disruptive. We are creatures of habit. And yet when the environment changes, often we must adapt if we intend to thrive. Chris' message to his troops was that we take our orders from the situation.

There will be times when plans will need to change; but until a new course is determined, people must remain committed to the one in hand. The grousing in the lunchroom is often the voice of the disconnected, the disgruntled. They see a problem; but only from their personal perspective: change will cause me pain.

In an organization, it is external developments that present the need to adapt. In the absence of a free flow of feedback, the big picture can become hazy and cause people to lose their balance and throw the whole department or the whole company into disequilibrium. As we have learned, disequilibrium is not all bad. Remember the disruptive zone of disequilibrium discussed earlier? People facing an adaptive challenge are moved to action because they need to regain balance. But how?

Do I Have the Authority?

In Chapter 5 we learned the nature of authority—the power to influence or command thought, opinion, or behavior. People are taught to respect authority from a very young age. They think of it not as a concept of power, but rather, an individual person or persons. What do you do when *you* are the authority? The reality of adaptive problems is that you must "model the simple act of naming the sensitive issues simmering under the surface, because if you do not, the odds are high that no one else will."[16] This avoidance of controversy gave rise to the phrase, "elephant in the room."

The client's request for a quickie product had developed into an elephant. Chris needed to address this development. Chris, all leaders, need troublemakers—those employees who always seem to be asking the uncomfortable questions—to spark the dialogue that had to take place to force a collective decision on the implications of the product. Yes, Chris could unilaterally decide they would pass on the client request. It is within his authority. Chris hoped to nurture shared responsibility for the organization in each member. Not just for their department, or division, but for the entire organization. People want this privilege. They want to be a part of the solution and even own some of the pain that may cast off after the decision was made. Apex people were about to be given that opportunity.

Living Into the Disequilibrium

Under such conditions, leaders are counseled to live into the disequilibrium. This requires "easing people into an uncomfortable state of uncertainty, disorder, conflict, or chaos at a pace and level that does not overwhelm them yet takes them out of their comfort zones and mobilizes them to engage in addressing an adaptive challenge."[17] It is depicted in Figure 13.2 as living into disequilibrium.

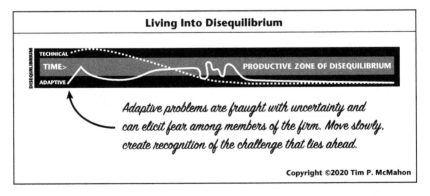

Living Into Disequilibrium

TECHNICAL
TIME>
ADAPTIVE
DISEQUILIBRIUM
PRODUCTIVE ZONE OF DISEQUILIBRIUM

Adaptive problems are fraught with uncertainty and can elicit fear among members of the firm. Move slowly, create recognition of the challenge that lies ahead.

Copyright ©2020 Tim P. McMahon

FIGURE 13.2 Technical problems have defined responses. Adaptive do not. Tread lightly

When change is imminent, the informal communication that operates just below the surface in organizations often takes on a life of its own even to the point of detrimental actions, often in an attempt to stave off management interventions.

Chris recalled an issue several years prior, when he heard rumblings about a manager who was having some disagreements with some of his direct reports. The discourse had devolved into one of personal will, an abuse of authority as was just discussed. Chris said, "I'm not sure I heard it, but it sounded like he said, 'my way or the highway.'" That is language of disgruntlement. It makes people feel like their difference with the opinion is not to be considered, just that the boss said it so the matter is closed. Such occurrences suck the oxygen out of the room.

Such dustups may spur passive-aggressive responses from members. This is resistance of the worst kind, indirect and unspoken, people avoid direct resolution of the issue. Bad things happen, like procrastination, pouting, and even acts of sabotage. This is not the environment in which buy-in occurs. Chris believed such matters called for a solution devised nearly 100 years ago, that to avoid such arbitrary circumstances, it is better for leaders and followers take their direction from the situation at hand.

Take Your Orders From the Situation

In her address to the Executive Conference Group in 1925, pioneering management guru Mary C. Follett framed the issue well in her assessment of scientific management: "Recognizing that orders, nevertheless, have to be given, Follett urged her audience to 'depersonalize the giving of orders, to unite all concerned in a study of the situation, to discover the law of the situation and obey that."[18] Follett believed that "chances of business success were largely diminished when our thinking is constrained within the limits of what has been called an either-or situation."[19] This deference to the collective knowledge of the totality of workers as a source input in decision-making, results in focusing on reliable information and knowledge informs the reality of the situation and that is gravely subject to the preparation needed to resolve the situation.

General David Petraeus served as commander of the 101st Airborne in Mosul, Iraq in 2007.[20] He and Lt. Gen. Raymond Odierno, revamped the American approach in Iraq. Considered outliers, they pursued a course that was quite different from the one they inherited and that produced four years of questionable results. They surrounded themselves with the ability to "think critically, enabling them to arrive at new solutions when their Army training proved insufficient."[21] Troops were moved off of central bases to local posts closer to the front.

Col. Peter Mansoor, would observe, "By the beginning of the surge in early 2007, the military had undergone a renaissance in its ability to connect with the Iraqi people, an adaptation that greatly assisted its ability to conduct counter-insurgency operations."[22] This paradigm shift occurred because leaders dealt with the situation, not preconceived assumptions, personal agendas, misguided biases, or political statements.

This sample of how a leader like Petraeus approaches facts, people, and decision-making is perhaps best summed up in his own words as to how leaders balance the dual role of thinker and doer in the framework of chain of command and the responsibility to challenge the system. He believes leaders must do both: "The bold move is the right move except when it the wrong move ... a leader needs to figure out what's the right move and then execute it boldly."[23] Gibberish, you say?

You know a leader has been battle-tested when they are able to experience brutal reality and without a whimper continue down the path unaffected by conceit or self-pity. Conflict is real. Hardship is inevitable. It is all mind-bending rife with paradox. The beauty of having a strong constitution—a belief system upon which to guide decisions—is that it serves you most in beating back doubt that lives in the brutal reality.

Admiral James Stockdale was the highest-ranking resident of the Hanoi Hilton, a euphemism for the prisoner-of-war camp employed at the height of the Vietnam War. He was tortured, mentally abused, and left in a constant state of uncertainty during his eight years of confinement. Stockdale's focus was to do all in his power to create an environment where his fellow prisoners would eventually leave unbroken.

His story is remarkable in and of itself. His behavior set a standard for emerging from difficult circumstances. Jim Collins wrote of firms that applied Stockdale's brand of thriving in the face of adversity. "On one hand, they stoically accepted the brutal facts of reality. On the other hand, they maintained an unwavering faith in the endgame, and a commitment to prevail as a great company despite the brutal facts." It came to be known as the Stockdale Paradox.

Stockdale summed up his view of life in this statement: "You must never confuse faith that you will prevail in the end—which you can never afford to lose—with the discipline to confront the most brutal facts of your current reality, whatever they might be."[24] When confronted with enormous odds, allowing our self to believe they are insurmountable creates immediate defeat. The leader must find hope for all to believe.

Living Into Disequilibrium at Apex

Chris had circulated among the hallways of Apex and caught the ear of just about anyone who glanced his way, and all did. He had been doing this ever since Mike, Apex VP-sales, delivered the news that the whale client wanted a quickie report—a useless, risk-ridden security blanket that offered no security, but would be sure to invite legal action from clients who approved loans based on its information. Chris knew at that moment Apex would never provide such a report. He had done his homework on the looming housing crisis. He observed the nature of the credit applications coming in and recognized the data on Apex reports indicates applicants were increasingly questionable. Because he was watching he could see the company was headed for an inflection point, and he held the trip trigger. When Apex declined to provide the quickie report, half the business would evaporate.

Every organization has an unwritten, sometimes unrecognized, connection to the status quo. And it's powerful. It guides behavior. It set boundaries. It challenges any attempt to alter business-as-usual in any way. In the pages of this book, it has become clear that Chris has sampled and studied many disciplined approaches to moving human beings to commitment. He has infused the organization with a commitment to learning. He has opened minds and created dialogue. He has used tools of influence and thought leadership. He has done this with the knowledge that all firms will sooner-or-later face a critical decision that will significantly disrupt operations.

He has done this out of his own self-enlightened interest, and out of love for his peeps as affectionately he calls them, the individuals who bring their unique competencies to their individual accountabilities and responsibilities. He is pleased with the progress the firm has made since acquisition. However, the real test would soon be administered.

In all of these actions, Chris has defined leadership as leaders and followers in an influence relationship who intend real changes that reflect their mutual purposes. And now, it's the moment of truth. In a firm that places the customer as the hero, it must now inform the customer that they refuse to deliver a product that will not only fail to help them make progress against their circumstance, it will reverse their progress.

Just Say NO!

The meeting on the quickie product decision was actually uneventful. Every manager and supervisor arrived in agreement that the quickie product would ultimately lead to unintended consequences, and certainly lawsuits when defaults rapidly increased. Taking the high road meant speaking the truth and suffering the loss of half of Apex revenues and certainly many jobs. It was a grave reality. It was necessary.

Chris stood up, welcomed everyone, and laid it out. "A wise man once said, 'if you lose dollars for the firm by bad decisions, I will be very understanding. If you lose reputation for the firm, I will be ruthless'"[25] Those were the words of our homeboy Warren B! We have been asked by a whale-sized client to provide a report accurately dubbed the quickie! Well, as I have talked with each of you ... offering this report would display a flawed character. If Apex becomes known for its 'quickie' we will share a reputation with the seedier side of life that would not make us proud, if you know what I mean (Chris chuckled and all laughed).

He then asked the functional leaders to be accountable for assessing the action from *their* point-of-view. "Be prepared to explain to everyone in this room how this decision will affect your accountabilities, your employees and their competencies. We will meet next week, same time and same place to hear your plans."

Additionally, Chris asked all to review each employee for whom they are responsible, and ask "Would you enthusiastically hire that person today as a valued member of your team? We're going to take action to deal with our new revenue possibilities. Each of us will shoulder the burden of this expected loss of business. Some more than others, but all of us in some way, shape or form. We will do this with the idea that our short-term sacrifice will be met with a renewed commitment to Apex and our purpose over time. I am confident our sacrifices will be rewarded."

Chris had everyone's undivided attention, so he continued to create context around the situation to capture the gravity of the decision. "Apex is not a money tree. It's not a slot machine. It is a business whose aim is to create value by helping our customer's make progress against their situation. We know that challenge better than they do! So, let's get busy writing our next chapter and replace this lost business before we even know it's gone.

The meeting ended with a summary of the discussion and a clear list of deliverables each member would be responsible to accomplish before the next meeting.

Debrief to Complete the Loop

In the wake of the meeting, Chris and members of the senior management team held one-on-ones with each manager and supervisor. In those meetings, they answered questions and clarified any confusion or concerns. They also briefed each one on the details of the agenda. Develop a plan. Communicate to employees. Communicate to customers. Determine the RIF actions. Meet with affected employees. Meet with all in Town Halls to provide details and gather feedback.

The management follow-up meeting was evidence that Chris had the right people on board. They had prepared detailed plans reflecting meetings with leaders in other functional areas and had laid out a plan that would systematically reduce and strengthen the business all in coherent, step-by-step plan addressing the mission and vision of the firm, its values and a re-statement of its purpose and unique selling proposition.

As the leaders progressed through their individual plans a new future emerged. While there would be a price to pay in pruning, if done properly, Apex would grow again and in so doing, win the respect of the industry.

Post-Mortem

In its final form, most of the employees laid off were part-timers. Those full-timers who left were considered below average producers. Chris and the senior managers devised an expense reduction plan that included Chris suspending his full pay until the firm could get back up to full profitability. Members of the senior team each gave up 20% of their salaries to be restored when Apex was healthy again. Finally, the team developed a plan where those employees who would not be enthusiastically hired again were released. The remaining staff—all considered to be valuable and worthy of retention—were asked to take a small reduction in hours (for non-exempt workers) and voluntary unpaid leave time (for exempt workers).

The senior team also investigated leasing its space, developing new market segments and creating compelling sales and marketing to appeal to potential like-minded prospects. This was a source of energy for the team. For example, getting ready for a big industry conference, Mike, the VP-sales and marketing came up with a clever idea depicted in Figure 13.3. They customized a label for containers of breath mints that read: "Got a bad taste, Call Mike at Apex" the tchotchke was a smash hit at the conference and won the attention and admiration of all who saw it as having the last laugh on a serious matter.

The quickie report is the cherry on top of a mortgage sundae heaped with scoops of poor business judgment and drizzled with streams of irrational exuberance. Hardly a dessert treat, within months the wheels came off the mortgage bonanza and sent shockwaves through the industry. Those competitors who offered the quickie product were awarded short-term business but were eventually sued by lenders whose insurance companies refused to pay on the poorly documented default loans.

It so weakened some of Apex competitors that some were acquired for a fraction of their former value. By the following February, Apex business picked up dramatically, including increased business from the whale customer who within a year awarded 100% of their business to Apex for the next decade.

FIGURE 13.3   A clever way to remind clients of your integrity

Buy-in Epilogue

With government bailout money, the industry purged the bad loans and the housing market returned to some semblance of normalcy. Within 10 years (2018), the federal government had recovered all of the $628 billion that was invested, loaned, or granted due to various bailout measures.[26]

TAKEAWAYS

- The desire to change is advanced in the operations of the organization. Recognizing functional (leaders) and process (cross-functioning of leaders) makes adaptive work possible.
- Leaders who suppress dissent may feel strong but are often weakened when blind side threats never see the light of day due to leaders suppressing dissent.
- Culture (the way we do things around here) may be adapted to the mission, but it is through daily operating practices that adaptive work is accomplished.
- In the course of an organization's life, it is likely to face an inflection point, the point that the direction of the firm is altered by a single event. In the life Apex, it lies in the refusal to produce the quickie report.
- Inflection point post-life can be wildly successful or doomed to extinction. The direction is determined by the response of the firm. If it can capitalize on events, it succeeds; if it succumbs or is overpowered it fails.
- Smooth operations depend on two accountabilities: functional (people) and process (people working with people).
- The best functional leaders pass two tests: (a) They don't need to be managed and (b) They regularly wow the team with their insights and output.
- To recruit, engage and retain the best people a firm must ply to people's strengths, dehassle their work, provide line of sight expectations, provide recognition an appreciation, and hire fewer people and pay them more.
- Leaders must know their people beyond their work. By reaching deeply, the relationship has room to develop a relationship that encourages self-renewal through practicing mindfulness, hope, and compassion.
- Change in an organization can come from the grass roots or from the top-of-the house. From the top, it is consider revolution and from the bottom, evolution. Either direction, people are best served in adaptation when learning is actively practiced.

- Being mindful on external change permits members of the firm to see adaptive challenges emerge. Every leader should engage its people in identifying trends that may produce a need to acclimate so as to thrive.
- When people spend a significant part of their day working with one another, often the personal difference overtake the mission and purpose to the firm. This can fog people's minds. The biggest problem is workers lose their focus on what matters, the customer. At its worst, it stirs passive-aggressive responses. A simple remedy is to take your orders from the situation. Create a collective response to the problem, not the personalities.
- Thought leaders throughout history have provided a glimpse into how these things may be resolved. Take your orders from the situation. Nurture and develop integrity in the chain of command. Never forget that life's decisions are not always black and white, and the clear path is not always apparent or easily taken. Yet, when leaders maintain their integrity, fiercely face reality despite the daunting conditions, the rewards are sweet and lasting.

Notes

1 Rhody, R. (1999). *The CEO's playbook: Managing the outside forces that shape success.* Sacramento, CA: Academy Publishing, p. 18. Rhody lists *timidity never won any ballgames and silence never swayed any masses* as one of the five givens concerning the play of the [business] game.

2 Rhody, R. (1999). *The CEO's playback: Managing the outside forces that shape success.* Sacramento, CA: Academy Publishing, (p. 102).

3 Heifetz, R., Grashow, A., & Linsky, M. (2009). *The practice of adaptive leadership: Tools and tactics for changing your organization and the world.* Boston, MA: Harvard Business Press, (p. 303).

4 Harnish, V. (2002). *Mastering the Rockefeller habits: What you must do to increase the value of your growing firm.* Ashburn, VA: Gazelles Inc, (p. 1)

5 Harnish, V. (2014). *Scaling up: How a few companies make, and why the rest don't.* Ashburn, VA: Gazelles Inc., (p. 10)

6 Ibid, (p. 10).

7 Harnish, (p. 11).

8 Ibid, (p. 11).

9 Ibid, (p. 12).

10 Boyatzis, R. & McKee, A. (2005). *Resonant leadership: Renewing yourself and connecting others through mindfulness, hope, and compassion.* Boston, MA: Harvard Business School Press, (pp. 32–33).

11 Carnegie, D. (1981). *How to win friends and influence people.* New York: Simon & Schuster, (p.25).

12 Ibid, p. 26.

13 Jones, G. R. (2001). *Organizational theory: Text and cases.* Upper Saddle River, NJ: Prentice-Hall, (p. 403).

14 Ibid, (p. 403).

15 Jim Collins wrote a seminal business book called *Good to Great*, in which he pioneered observations common with great companies he studied. Two important insights from his work were that companies should have a handle on the key profit drivers for the firm and that it should have a reach goal, what called a Big Hairy Audacious Goal.

16 Heifetz, et al., (p. 167).

17 Ibid, (p. 306).

18 Tonn, J. C. (2003). *Mary P. Follett: Creating democracy, transforming management.* New Haven, CT: Yale University Press, (p. 400).

19 Ibid, (p. 399).

20 Ricks, T. E. (2012). *The generals: American military command from World War II to today.* New York, NY: Penguin. [Kindle Edition].

21 Ibid.

22 Ibid.

23 Tetlock & Gardner, (p. 224).

24 Collins, J. (2001). *Good to great: Why some companies make the leap and others don't.* New York, NY: HarperBusiness, (p. 85).

25 The reference was to Warren Buffett's comments in an address to Salomon employees after he had assumed temporary responsibility for the firm as the result of a scandal-ridden period in 1991. See: Fuerbringer, J. (August 27, 1991). Buffett sets Salomon rules; Stock up on Tisch's buying. *New York Times,* (Sec. D, p. 1). Retrieved December 27, 2020 from https://www.nytimes.com/1991/08/27/business/buffett-sets-salomon-rules-stock-up-on-tisch-s-buying.html

26 Kiel, P., & Nguyen, D. (April 15, 2009). Tracking every dollar and every recipient. *ProPublica.* Retrieved November 9, 202 from projects.propublica.org

PART V
Conclusion

In this final section, the author puts the story into context as in the previous chapter, leadership effectively faced the adaptive challenge and averted a path of certain disaster. While the decision created uncertainty about the eventual livelihoods of the member of the enterprise, it galvanized commitment to setting course on a path to survive.

The author provides the details behind the future of the firm that inspired the fabled Apex Enterprises. It also summarizes the lessons that emerged when leaders and followers who intend real changes that reflect their mutual purposes effectively create an influence relationship to tackle adaptive challenges to allow the firm to thrive.

14

MAKING IT HAPPEN

We have arrived at the destination in our story. Chris is the main character whose eyes you see the real-life lessons come alive in storybook form. While he is make-believe, Chris was inspired by a real leader named Bill Mackintosh. He was an extraordinary businessman, husband, father, friend and, for me, learning partner. I enjoyed a 30-year friendship with Bill until his much too early passing the day after my birthday in 2016. I think of him every week and miss him greatly. He lives on in the pages of this book. While he is the inspiration, there are many elements herein that are attributable to others and for that I am grateful to have had the benefit of their presence in my personal learning about leadership and communication.

This story began with Chris, who had just bought a mortgage services company. He was a natural entrepreneur and recognized the joy in developing a thriving organization occupied by bright people whom he relied upon for their energy, imagination, enthusiasm, and instincts. He had a knack for recognizing raw talent and the knowledge to guide them to full development.

You know that Chris spent many weekday breaks having coffee with his 80-plus-year-old mother who was sharp as a tack and wise as an owl. It was during these shared moments that Chris could relax and reminisce about the mundane matters of the day and occasionally, re-capture a treasured lesson from his youth.

As you see this book revealed a specific scheme of leadership dependent upon leaders and followers actively engaged in an influence relationship. You witnessed Chris modeling this behavior. He saw that the customer was the hero in any business because she financed the operation. He also knew you had to earn the customer's trust and respect and you did that by developing and delivering products—goods and services—that helped them make progress against their circumstance. This was accomplished by understanding and shaping the core competencies of the people at the firm. Chris relentlessly pursued buy-in through their learning, understanding, experimentation, and unfettered comments and observations.

As the reader learns key lessons like taking your orders from the situation, it becomes clear that Chris firmly embraces the three elements of leadership defined in this text that make that possible: (a) vigorously confronting reality, (b) expanding individual and organizational knowledge in purposeful ways, and (c) creating safety for members taking bold, legitimate action. You see these explained as milestones along the journey.

Chris fully embraces a meritocratic form of governance. He recognizes that there are dangers in leaning too far one way or the other into the concept but believes that excess is inherent in every form of administration whether meritocratic, autocratic, or democratic. He holds ethics high and believes by doing so the firm will enjoy an enviable reputation among employees, customers, and even competitors.

His worst fear, as noted on every rendition of the SWOT analysis is losing a major customer. Yes, that is what happens. But it surfaces in a manner that permits Chris and his nascent firm to prepare for the loss and learn a critical lesson about enduring through crisis.

This is accomplished through a deep dive into leadership principles and tools for crafting leadership that causes a firm to thrive. It is through these challenges that thought leaders are introduced to provide new and unique perspectives on how to move people to buy-in to organizational purpose and vision.

Finally, the book explores the most recent thinking on communication strategy and execution, thinking and sensemaking, innovation, innovative leadership, and smooth operations.

It is not your father's textbook. It is not a how-to or inspirational guide. However, there is a bit of both in every chapter.

My goal is to lay out the information in a manner that it is both understandable and enjoyable, yet gives rise to debate. It is not unlike the way I conduct my college courses and management coaching sessions. I have been teaching for more than a decade after a full and exciting life in business running the course from Main Street to Wall Street.

The end is the best part. And it is quite true to form. The real Apex (which will remain anonymous) emerged from the worst financial crisis in decades by holding firm to its ideals, while preparing to thrive, not merely survive.

If you would like to discuss any or all parts of the text, please reach out to me personally at Tim P. McMahon, Creighton University Heider College of Business. My email is tpm@creighton.edu, phone and text is (402) 660–1165. You will find me on LinkedIn @tmacphd.

Hope you enjoyed the read.

BIBLIOGRAPHY

Abbott, H. (Producer). (April 26, 2020). Outbreak Science (Season 52, Episode 30) [TV series episode]. In W. Owens (Executive Producer). *60 minutes.* CBS Television.

Arendt, H. (November 21, 1977). Thinking. *The New Yorker.* pp. 65–140.

Arthur W. Page Society. (2019). The CEO as pacesetter: What it means, why it matters, how to get there. Retrieved November 10, 2020 from https://knowledge.page.org/report/the-cco-as-pacesetter/.

Atlas, J. (May 12, 2012). The amygdala made me do it. *New York Times.* Retrieved December 20, 2020 from https://www.nytimes.com/2012/05/13/opinion/sunday/the-amygdala-made-me-do-it.html.

Baime, A. J. (2017). *The accidental president: Harry S. Truman and the four months that changed the world.* Boston, MA: Mariner Books. (p. 56)

Balding, J. & Beacham, T. (Producers). June 13, 2020. The Playbook (Season 2020, Episode E61320) [TV Series episode].

Barnlund, D. C. (2008). A transactional model of communication. In. C. D. Mortensen (Eds.), *Communication theory* (2nd ed.). New Brunswick, NJ: Transaction.

Bass, B. M. (1990). *Bass and Stogdill's handbook of leadership: Theory, research, and managerial applications.* New York, NY: Free Press.

Bennis, W. (1989/2003). *On becoming a leader.* Cambridge, MA: Perseus Publishing.

Berger, B. (2008). Employee/Organizational Communication. Institute for Public Relations. Retrieved from https://instituteforpr.org/employee-organizational-communications/

Berger, J. (2013). *Contagious: Why Things Catch On.* New York, NY: Simon & Schuster.

Berkun, S. (2009). *The myths of innovation.* Sebastopol, CA: O'Reilly.

Berkun, S. (May 14, 2012). *Why common sense is not common practice.* Retrieved from scottberkun.com/2012/why-common-sense-is-not-common-practice/

Bossidy, L., & Charan, R. (2002). *Confronting reality: Doing matters to get things right.* New York, NY: Crown Business.

Bossidy, L., & Charan, R. (2004). *Execution.* New York, NY: Crown Business.

Bottary, L. (2019). *What anyone can do: How surrounding yourself with the right people will drive change, opportunity, and personal growth.* Abingdon, UK: Bibliomotion, Inc.

Bourne, B. (2020) Top of mind. *Chief Learning Officer, 19*(4).

Boyatzis, R., & Mckee, A. (2005). *Resonant leadership: Renewing yourself and connecting others through mindfulness, hope, and compassion.* Boston, MA: Harvard Business School Press.

Bridges, W. (2004). *Transitions: Making sense of life's changes.* Cambridge, MA: DeCapo Press.

Bryman, A. (1992). *Charisma & leadership in organizations.* London, UK: Sage Publications.

Burns, J. M. (1978). *Leadership.* New York, NY: Perennial.

Bridges, W. with Bridges, S. (2016). *Managing transitions: Making the most of change.* Philadelphia, PA: Perseus Books.

Brown, P. C., Boediger III, R. L., & McDaniel, M. A. (2014). *Make it stick: The science of successful learning.* Cambridge, MA: The Belknap Press of Harvard.

Campbell, J. (1995). *Understanding John Dewey.* Chicago, IL: Open Court Publishing.

Carlzon, J. (1987). *Moments of truth: New strategies for today's customer-driven economy.* New York, NY: Ballinger Publishing Co.

Carnegie, D. (1981). *How to win friends and influence people.* New York: Simon & Schuster.

Carton, A. M., Murphy, C., & Clark, J. R. (2012). A (blurry) vision of the future: How leader rhetoric about ultimate goals influences performance. *Academy of Management Journal, 57,* 1544–1570, Retrieved July 3, 2020 from https://journals.aom.org/action/fedSearchRedirect?doi=10.5465%2Famj.2012.0101

Carton, A. M., & Lucas, B. J. (2018). How can leaders overcome the blurry vision bias? Identifying an antidote to the paradox of vision communication. *Academy of Management Journal, 61*(6)_2110.

Castilla, E. J. (2008). Gender, race, and meritocracy in organizational careers. *American Journal of Sociology, 113,* 1479–1526.

Castilla, E. J., & Benard, S. (December 2010). The paradox of meritocracy in organizations, *Administrative Science Quarterly, 55*(4), 543.

Cathy, S. T. (2002). *Eat mor chikin: Inspire more people.* Decatur, GA: Looking Glass Books.

Chaleff, I. (1995). *The courageous follower: Standing up to and for our leaders.* San Francisco: Berrett-Koehler.

Christensen, C. M. (1997). *The innovator's dilemma: When new technologies cause great firms to fail.* Boston, MA: Harvard Business Review Press.

Christensen, C. M., & Raynor, M. E. (2003). *The innovator's solution.* Boston, MA: Harvard Business School Publishing.

Christensen, C. M., Hall, T., Dillon, K., & Duncan, D. S. (2016). *Competing against luck: The story of innovation and customer choice.* New York, NY: HarperCollins.

Christoffersen, T. (June 1, 2017). Our common core: Deliver WOW through service. *Culture* [company magazine]. Retrieved on November 10, 2020 from https://www.zappos.com/about/stories/core-values-one

Christoffersen, T. (June 5, 2019). 20 years, 20 milestones: How Zappos grew out of just shoes. *Culture* [company magazine]. Retrieved on November 10, 2020, from https://www.zappos.com/about/stories/zappos-20th-birthday.

Coe, F. (Producer), & Penn, A. (Director). (1962) *The miracle worker.* [Motion picture]. USA: Playfilm Productions.

Collins, J. (2001). *Good to great: Why some companies make the leap and others don't.* New York, NY: HarperBusiness.

Conger, J. A., & Kanungo, R. N. (1987). Toward a behavioral theory of charismatic leadership in organizational settings. *Academy of Management Review, 12*(4), 637–647.

Conger, J. A., Spreitzer, G. M., & Lawler III, E. E. (1999). *The leader's change handbook.* [Kindle version]. San Francisco, CA: Jossey- Bass.

Cooper, M. (December 1, 2015). The false promise of meritocracy. *The Atlantic.* Retrieved October 20, 2020 from www.theatlantic.com/business/archive/2015/12/meitocracy/418074.

Covey, S. R. (1990/1991). *Principle-centered leadership.* New York, NY: Fireside.

Covey, S. R. (2013). *The 7 habits of highly effective people: Powerful lessons in personal change.* New York, NY: Rosetta Books.

Doyle, S. (April 7, 2015). Before Lena Dunham, there was Anaïs Nin – now patron saint of social media. *The Guardian.* Retrieved from https://www.theguardian.com/culture/2015/apr/07/anais-nin-author-social-media.

Definition of "Customer Lifetime Value" (n.d.). Retrieved from https://economictimes.indiatimes.com/definition/customer-lifetime-value.

De Mello, A. (1990). *Conversations with the masters.* New York, NY: Crown Publishing.

De Pree, M. (1992). *Leadership jazz: The essential elements of a great leader.* New York, NY: Dell Trade Paperback.

Dietrich, G. (2014). *Spin sucks: Communication and reputation management in the digital age.* Indianapolis, IN: Que Publications. (p. 37).

Drath, W. (2001). *The deep blue sea: Rethinking the source of leadership.* San Francisco, CA: Jossey-Bass.

Drath, W. F., & Palus, C. J. (1994). *Making common sense: Leadership as meaning-making in a community of practice.* Greensboro, NC: Center for Creative Leadership.

Drucker, P. F. (2004). *Managing oneself and what makes and effective leader.* Boston, MA: Harvard Business Review Press.

Duggan W. (2015). *The seventh sense: How flashes of insight change your life.* New York, NY: Columbia Business School.

Dupuy, T. (1984). *A genius for war: The German army and general staff 1807-1945.* London, UK: Hero Books, Ltd.

Dweck, C. (2006, 2016). *Mindset: The new psychology of success.* New York, NY: Random House.

Dwight D. Eisenhower Quotes (n.d.). BrainyQuote.com. Retrieved July 1, 2020 from https://brainyquote.com/quotes/dwight_d_eisenhower_112040.

Drucker. P. (2017). *Managing oneself and what makes an effective executive.* Boston, MA: Harvard Business Review Press.

Edmondson, A. C. (2019). *The fearless organization: Creating psychological safety.* Hoboken, NJ: Wiley & Sons, Inc.

Fader, P. (2012). *Customer centricity: Focus on the right customers for strategic advantage.* Philadelphia, PA: The Wharton Digital Press.

Festinger, L. (1957). *A theory of cognitive dissonance.* Stanford, CA: Stanford University Press.

Fox, J. (June 20, 2014). Instinct dan beat analytical thinking. *Harvard Business Review.* [Reprint HOOVFV].

Friedman, M. (1962). *Capitalism and freedom.* Chicago, IL: University of Chicago Press.

Friedman, M. (September 13, 1970). The social responsibility of business is to increase its profits. *The New York Times Magazine.* p. 17.

Friedman, T. L. (2006). *The world is flat: A brief history of the twenty-first century.* New York, NY: Farrar, Straus, and Giroux.

Friedman, T. L. (2009). *Hot, flat, and crowded* (Release 2.0). New York, NY: Picador/ Farrar/Straus and Giroux.

Fuerbringer, J. (August 27, 1991). Buffett sets Salomon rules; Stock up on Tisch's buying. *New York Times*, D1.

Fuller, B., & Kuromiya, K. (1981). *The critical path*. New York, NY: St, Martin's Press.

Gagnon, C., & Theunissen, R. (September 7, 2017). Organizational health: A fast track to performance improvement. *McKinsey Quarterly*. Retrieved November 22, 2020 from https://www.mckinsey.com/business-functions/organization/our-insights/ organizational-health-a-fast-track-to-performance-improvement#.

Gallup. (n.d.). *Learn how the CliftonStrengths Assessment works*. https://www.gallup.com/ cliftonstrengths/en/253676/how-cliftonstrengths-works.aspx

Garcia, H. G. (2012). *The power of communication: Skills to build trust, inspire loyalty, and lead effectively*. Upper Saddle River, NJ: Pearson Education.

Gardner, H. (1983/2003). *Frames of mind. The theory of multiple intelligences*. New York: Basic Books.

Gass, R. H., & Seiter, J. S. (2019). *Arguing, reasoning, and thinking well*. New York, NY & London, UK: Routledge (Taylor & Francis Group).

Geertz, C. (1975). Common sense as a cultural system. *The Antioch Review, 33*(1), 5–26.

Gergen, K. J. (2007). *An invitation to social construction*. San Francisco: Sage.

Gigerenzer, G. (January 1, 2008). Why heuristics work. *Perspectives on Psychological Science, 1*(3), 20–39.

Gilbert, D. (2006). *Stumbling on happiness*. New York, NY: Alfred A. Knopf.

Gittell, J. H. (2003). *The Southwest Airlines way: Using high power of relationships to achieve high performance*. New York, NY: McGraw-Hill.

Gladwell, M. (2002). *The tipping point: How little things can make a big difference*. New York, NY: Little, Brown and Company.

Gladwell, M. (2007). *Blink: The power of thinking without thinking*. New York, NY: Little, Brown and Company.

Goleman, D. (2006). *Emotional intelligence*. New York: Bantam Books.

Goleman, D., Boyatzis, R., & McKee, A. (2002). *Primal leadership: realizing the power of emotional intelligence*. Boston, MA: Harvard Press.

Goodman, N. (1978). *Ways of worldmaking*. Indianapolis, IN: Hackett.

Goodpaster, K. E. (2007). *Conscience and corporate culture*. Hoboken, NJ: Blackwell Publishing.

Goodreads [Website]. n.d. Buckminster Fuller. Retrieved July 3, 2020 from https:// www.goodreads.com/quotes/467583-if-you-want-to-teach-people-a-new-way-of

Govindarajan, V., & Trimble, C. (2010). *The other side of innovation: Solving the execution challenge*. Boston, MA: Harvard Business Review Press.

Grant, A. (June 11, 2015). The four most important elements of your voice. *Fast Company [Online Magazine]*. Retrieved July 1, 2020 from https://www.fastcompany.com/30471 83/the-4-most-important-elements-of-your-voice

Grenny, J., Patterson, K., Maxfield, D., McMillan, R., & Switzer, A. (2013). *Influencer: The new science of leading change* (2nd ed.). New York, NY: McGraw Hill Education.

Grunig, J.E. (2001). Two-way symmetrical public relations: Past, present, and future. In R. Heath (Ed.), *Handbook of public relations* (pp. 11–30). Thousand Oaks, CA: Sage.

Grunig, J. L. A., Grunig, J. E. & Dozier, D. M. (2002). *Excellent public relations and effective organizations: A study of communication management in three countries*. Mahwah, NJ: Lawrence Erlbaum Associates, Publishers.

Haas, M., & Mortensen, M. (2016, June). The secrets of great teamwork. *Harvard Business Review*. [Reprint R1606E].

Haberman, M. (2020, April 6). Trade adviser warned White House in January of risks of a pandemic. *New York Times*. https://www.nytimes.com/2020/04/06/us/politics/navarro-warning-trump-coronavirus.html

Haidt, J. (2013). *The righteous mind: Why good people are divided by politics and religion*. New York, NY: Vintage Books.

Hamel, G., & Välikangas, L. (2003). The quest for resilience. *Harvard Business Review*. [Reprint R0309C]. Retrieved November 15, 2020 from https://hbsp.harvard.edu.

Harris, J. D., Wicks, A. C., & Parmar, B. L. (July 31, 2015). Ethical business decisions: The framework. *UVA ideas to action*. Retrieved November 15, 2020 from ideas.darden.virginia.edu/ethical-business-decisions-the-framework.

Harnish, V. (2002). *Mastering the Rockefeller habits: What you must do to increase the value of your growing firm*. Ashburn, VA: Gazelles Inc.

Harnish, V. (2014). *Scaling up: How a few companies make, and why the rest don't*. Ashburn, VA: Gazelles Inc.

Heifetz, R. A. (1994). *Leadership without easy answers*. Cambridge, MA: Belknap.

Heifetz, R., Grashow, A., & Linsky, M. (2009). *The practice of adaptive leadership: Tools and tactics for changing your organization and the world*. Boston, MA: Harvard Business Press.

Hess, E. D. (2014). *Learn or die: Using science to build a leading-edge learning organization*. New York, NY: Columbia University Press.

Howe, J. (2009). *Crowdsourcing: Why the power of the crowd is driving the future of business*. New York, NY: Three Rivers Press.

Hurst, D. K. (2012). *The new ecology of leadership: Business mastery in a chaotic world*. New York, NY: Columbia Business School Publishing.

Hussain, S. T., Lei, S., Akram, T., Haider, M. J., Hussain, S.H. & Ali, M. (June 22, 2016). Kurt Lewin's change model: A critical review of the role of leadership and employee involvement in organizational change. *Journal of Innovation & Knowledge*. Retrieved November 23, 2020, from https://reader.elsevier.com/reader/sd/pii/S2444569X16300087?token=5ED1B6F3DCF3D1E0A42122B380C58A8F6D5C1003B4AB5524E64B3C1A251440F5640478514328CC924277B00AB843BC78.

Idiomic.com. (n.d.). (I've) got your back. In *Idiomic.com*. Retrieved June 24, 2020 from http://idiomic.com/got-your-back/

Immergluck, D. (2011). *Foreclosed: High-risk lending, deregulation, and the undermining of America's mortgage market*. Ithaca, NY & London, UK: Cornell University Press.

Jackson, P. & Delehanty, H. (1995). *Sacred hoops: Spiritual lessons of a hardwood warrior*. New York, NY: Hyperion.

Jones, G. R. (2001). *Organizational theory: Text and cases*. Upper Saddle River, NJ: Prentice-Hall.

Jovanovic, N. (June 29, 2014). *Gene Kranz – Tough and competent (NASA Speech)*. [Video]. YouTube. https://www.youtube.com/watch?v=9zjAteaK9lM&feature=emb_logo.

Jung, C. G. (1971). *Psychological Types*. Princeton, NJ: Princeton University Press.

Kahan, S. (2010). *Getting change right: How leaders transform organizations from the inside out*. San Francisco, CA: Jossey-Bass.

Kahneman, D. (2011). *Thinking, fast and slow*. New York, NY: Farrar, Straus and Giroux.

Kaushik, A. (2010). *Web analytics 2.0: The art of online accountability & science of customer centricity*. Indianapolis, IN: Wiley Publishing, Inc.

Keller, S., & Price, C. (2011). *Beyond performance: How great organizations build ultimate competitive advantage.* Hoboken, NJ: John Wiley & Sons, Inc.

Kiel, P., & Nguyen, D. (April 15, 2009). Tracking every dollar and every recipient. *ProPublica.* Retrieved November, 2020 from projects.propublica.org

Kim, W. C. & Mauborgne, R. (2005). *Blue ocean strategy: How to create uncontested market space and make the competition irrelevant.* Boston, MA: Harvard Business School Publishing.

Klein, G. (1998/2018) *Sources of power: How people make decisions.* Cambridge, MA: MIT Press. [Kindle edition].

Knaus, B. (November 19, 2013,). It's not what you say—It's how you say it. *Psychology Today.* https://www.psychologytoday.com/us/blog/science-and-sensibility/201311/it-s-not-what-you-say-it-s-how-you-say-it.

Kotter, J. P. (1990). *A force for change: How leadership differs from management.* New York, NY: Free Press.

Kotter, J. P. (2012). *Leading change.* Boston, MA: Harvard Business Review Press.

Kotler, P., Kartajay, H., & Setiawan, I. (2017). *Marketing 4.0: Moving from traditional to digital.* Hoboken, NJ: Wiley.

Kouzes, J. M., & Posner, B. Z. (2002). *The leadership challenge* (3rd ed.). San Francisco: Jossey-Bass.

Kouzes, J. M. & Posner, B. Z. (2017). *The leadership challenge* (6th ed.). Hoboken, NJ: Wiley & Sons, Inc.

Kranz, G. (2000). *Failure is not an option.* New York, NY: Berkley Publishing Group.

Kristof, N. (November 30, 2009). Nicholas Kristof's advice for saving the world. *Outside Online.* Retrieved December 20, 2020 from https://www.outsideonline.com/1909636/nicholas-kristofs-advice-saving-world

Lauer-Williams, K. (October 11, 2004) Channeling Mark Twain: Hal Holbrook performs one-man show In Easton. *The Morning Call.* Retrieved November 26, 2020 from www.mcall.com/entertainment/art-theater/mc-hal-holbrook-easton-state-theatre-2 0141011=stpry.html.

Lawler, E. E. (1982). Increasing worker involvement to enhance organizational effectiveness. In P. S. Goodman (Ed.), *Changes in organizations.* San Francisco: Jossey-Bass.

Lerner, J. S., & Tetlock, P. E. (1999). Accounting for the effects of accountability. *Psychological Bulletin, 125,* 255–275.

Lewin, K. (1947). Group decision and social change. In T. N. Newcomb & E. L. Hartley (Eds.), *Readings in social psychology* (pp. 340–344). New York: Holt, Rinehart and Winston.

Lewin, K. (1951). *Field theory in social science* (D. Cartwright, Trans.). New York: Harper & Brothers.

Lowney, C. (2003). *Heroic leadership: Best practices from a 450-year-old company that changed the world.* Chicago, IL: Loyola Press.

Maister, D. (2008). *Strategy and the fat smoker.* Boston, MA: Spangle Press.

Maslow, A. (1943). A theory of human motivation. *Psychological Review, 50,* 370–396.

Matthews, M. D. (May 3, 2016). The three C's of trust. *Psychology Today,* https://www.psychologytoday.com/us/blog/head-strong/201605/the-3-c-s-trust.

Maxwell, J. C. (February 12, 2019). Are you a "Go First" leader? John C. Maxwell blog. www.johnmaxwell.com/blog/are-you-a-go-first-leader/

McChesney, C., Covey, S., & Huling, J. (2012). *The four disciplines of execution: achieving your wildly important goals.* New York, NY: Free Press.

McGrath, R. G., & MacMillan. I. C. (July-August 1995). Discovery-driven planning. *Harvard Business Review*. Reprint 95406. Retrieved July 4, 2020 from https:// hbsp.harvard.edu.

McGregor, D. (1960). *The human side of enterprise*. New York, NY: McGraw-Hill.

McMahon, T. P. (2020). *Integrated communication*. In Doorley, J. & Garcia, H. F. (2020). *Reputation Management* (4th Ed.). New York, NY: Routledge.

McMahon, T. P. (2009). *Social construction of charismatic leadership: a case study*. (Unpublished doctoral dissertation). Spokane, WA: Gonzaga University.

Melo S., Guedes J., & Mendes S. (2019) Theory of cumulative disadvantage/advantage. In: Gu D., Dupre M. (Eds.), *Encyclopedia of Gerontology and Population Aging*. Cham: Springer. https://doi.org/10.1007/978-3-319-69892-2_751-1.

Merriam-Webster, Inc. (2020). *[App version]*

Milgram, S. (May 1967). The small world problem. *Psychology Today*, *1*(1), pp. 61–67.

Miller, D. (2017). *Building a story brand*. New York, NY: HarperCollins Leadership.

Mintzberg, H. (1994). *The rise and fall of strategic planning*. New York, NY: The Free Press.

Mintzberg, H. (2004). *Managers Not MBAs: A hard look at the soft practice of managing and marketing development*. San Francisco, CA: Berrett-Koehler.

Mintzberg, H. (2009). *Managing*. Sab Francisco, CA: Berrett-Koehler.

Morrell, M., & Capparell, S. (2001). *Shackleton's way: Leadership lessons from the great Antarctic explorer*. New York, NY: Penguin Books.

Northouse, P. G. (2007). *Leadership: Theory and practice*. (4th ed.). Thousand Oaks, CA: Sage.

Northouse, P. G. (2019). *Leadership: Theory and practice*. (8th ed.). Thousand Oaks, CA: Sage.

Oliver, M. (December 30, 2020). Vaccine rollout slower than expected as Americans wait for doses. *CBS News*. Retrieved on December 30, 2020 from https:// www.cbsnews.com/news/covid-vaccine-rollout-slower-than-expected/

Olson, R. (2015). *Houston, we have a narrative: Why science needs a story*. Chicago, IL, and London, UK: University of Chicago Press.

Orlowski, J. (Producer). 2020, September, The Social Dilemma. [TV documentary, drama]. Netflix Television.

Owens, W. (Executive Producer). (1968-present). *60 minutes* [TV news series]. CBS Television.

Patterson, K., Grenny, J, McMillan, R., & Switzler, A. (2012). *Crucial conversations*. New York, NY: McGraw-Hill.

Peters, T., & Waterman, R. H. (1982/2004) *In search of excellence*: Lessons from America's best-run companies. New York, NY: HarperCollins.

Phillips, D. T. (1992). *Lincoln on leadership: Executive strategies for tough times*. Illinois, USA: DTP/Companion Books.

Phillips, M. (December 9, 2020). Azar says vaccinations could begin next week, 20M people inoculated by end of year. *Fox Business*. Retrieved December 15, 2020 from https://www.foxbusiness.com/politics/azar-says-vaccinations-could-begin-next-week-20m-by-end-of-year.

Pink, D. H. (2009). *Drive: The surprising truth about what motivates us*. New York, NY: Riverhead Books.

Pisano, G. P. (June 2015). You need an innovation strategy. *Harvard Business Review*. Retrieved December 1, 2020 from hbr.org/2015/06/you-need-an-innovation-strategy.

Porter, M. (1985). *Competitive advantage: Creating and sustaining superior performance*. New York, NY: The Free Press.

Quote Investigator. [Website]. *Tell 'em what you're going to tell 'em; tell 'em; Next, tell 'em what you told them.* Retrieved from https://quoteinvestigator.com/2017/08/15/tell-em/#return-note-16654-1

Rafferty, A. E., & Griffin, M. A. (2004). Dimensions of transformational leadership: Conceptual and empirical extensions. *The Leadership Quarterly*, *15*(3), 329–354. Retrieved July 3, 2020 from https://doi.org/10.1016/j.leaqua.2004.02.009

Rhody, R. (1999). *The CEO's playback: Managing the outside forces that shape success.* Sacramento, CA: Academy Publishing.

Ricks, T. E. (2012). *The generals: American military command from World War II to today.* New York, NY: Penguin.

Robinson, K. (2014). *Finding your element: How to discover your talents and passions and transform your life.* New York, NY: Penguin Books.

Rokeach, M. (1973). *The nature of human values.* New York, NY: The Free Press.

Rokeach, M. (1979). *Understanding human values: Individual and societal.* New York, NY: The Free Press.

Romm, J. (2018). *How to go viral and reach millions: Top persuasion secrets from social media superstars, Jesus, Shakespeare, Oprah, and even Donald Trump.* Eugene, OR: Luminare Press.

Rost, J. C. (1993). *Leadership for the 21st century.* Westport, CT: Praeger.

Ryan, R. M., & Deci, E. L. (January 2000). Self-determination theory and the facilitation of intrinsic motivation, social development and well-being. *American Psychologist*, *55*(1), 68–78. selfdeterminationtheory.org/SDT/documents/2000_RyanDeci_SDT.pdf.

Ryan, R. M., & Deci, E. L. (2017). *Self-determination theory: Basic psychological needs in motivation, development, and wellness.* New York, NY: The Guilford Press.

Saffo, P. (July–August 2007). Six rules for effective forecasting. *Harvard Business Review.* Retrieved July 18, 2020 from https://hbsp.harvard.edu/download?url=%2Fcatalog %2Fsample%2FR0707K-PDF-ENG%2Fcontent&metadata=eyJlcnJvck1lc3NhZ2 UiOiJZb3UgbXVzdCBiZSByZWdpc3RlcmVkIGFzIGEgUHJlbW11 bSBFZHVjYXRvcibvbiB0aGlzIHdlYiBzaXRlIHRvIHNlZSBFZHVjYXRvciBD-b3BpZXMgYW5kIEZyZWUgVHJpYWxzLiBOb3QQgcmVnaXN0ZXJlZD8gQXB wbHkgb 93LiBBYY2Nlc3MgZXhwaXJlZ8gUmVhZHRRob3JpemVmUgbm93LiJ9

Salganik, M. J., & Watts, D. J. (2011). Social influence: The puzzling nature of success in cultural markets. In P. Hedstrom & P. Bearman (Eds.). *The Oxford handbook of analytical sociology*, Topics in cognitive science, *1*, 439–468.

Schaffer, J. (2000). *The leadership solution.* New York, NY: McGraw-Hill.

Schaffer, J. (n.d.). *Straight talk about employee engagement.* [White Paper]. Retrieved from https://jimshaffergroup.com/.

Schein, E. H. (2017). *Organizational culture and leadership* (5th ed.). Hoboken, NJ: Wiley & Sons, Inc.

Schultz, D., & Schultz, H. (2004). *IMC: the next generation.* New York, NY: McGraw Hill.

Schloemer, E., Li, W., Ernst, K., & Keest, K. (2006). *Losing ground: Foreclosures in subprime market and their cost to homeowners.* Durham, NC: Center for Responsible Lending.

Schwartz, J. M. & Begley, S. (2002). *The mind and the brain: Neuroplasticity and the power of mental force.* New York, NY: Harper Collins.

Schwartzman, E. (2013). Social Media Bootcamp. Slide Retrieved November 26, 2020 from www.linkedin.com/profile/view?id=3016595&locale=en_US&trk-tyah

Senge, P. M. (2006). *The fifth discipline: The art and practice of the learning organization* (Rev. ed.). New York, NY: Currency Doubleday.

Silk, A. J. (2006). *What is marketing?* Boston, MA: Harvard Business Review Press.

Silver, N. (2012/2020). *The signal and the noise.* New York, NY: Penguin Books.

Simon, H. A. (1987). Making management decisions: The role of intuition and emotion. *Academy of Management Executive, 1*(1), 57–64.

Sinek, S. (2014/2017). *Leaders eat last: Why some teams pull together and others don't.* New York, NY: Penguin Books.

Solnit, R. (2009). *A paradise built in hell.* New York, NY: Penguin Books.

Shirky, C. (2010). *Cognitive surplus: Creativity and generosity in a connected age.* New York, NY: Penguin Press.

Skarzynski, P., & Gibson, R. (2008). *Innovation to the core: A blueprint for transforming the way your company innovates.* Boston, MA: Harvard Business Press.

Stanier, M. B. (2016). *The coaching habit: Say less, ask more & change the way you lead forever.* Toronto, ON: Box of Crayons.

Stiglitz, J. E., & Greenwald, B. C. (2015). *Creating a learning society: A new approach to growth, development, and social progress.* [Reader's Edition]. New York, NY: Columbia University Press.

Strunk, Jr., W. & White, E. B. (2000). *The elements of style.* (4th ed.). New York, NY: Longman.

Taylor, C. C. (1947). Sociology and common sense. *American Sociological review 12*(1), 1–9.

TED (March 2015). *Bill Gates: The next outbreak, we're not ready.* [Video file] Retrieved from https://www.youtube.com/watch?v=6Af6b_wyiwI.

Tetlock, P. E., & Gardner. D. ((2015). *Superforecasting: The art and science of prediction.* New York, NY: Crown Publishers.

The Institute for Public Relations (1997, 2003). *Guidelines for measuring the effectiveness of PR programs and activities.* [White Paper]. Retrieved from https://www.instituteforpr.org/wp-content/uploads/2002_MeasuringPrograms.pdf

T. I. (2010). Got your back [Song]. On *No Mercy* [Digital Download]. Grand Hustle.

Tichy, N. M., & Sherman, S. (2001). *Control your destiny or someone else will.* New York: HarperBusiness.

Tonn, J. C. (2003). *Mary P. Follett: Creating democracy, transforming management.* New Haven, CT: Yale University Press.

Weick, K. E. (1995). *Sensemaking in organizations.* Thousand Oaks, CA: Sage.

Urban Dictionary. (2014). Got your back. In *Urban Dictionary.* Retrieved June 24, 2020 from https://www.urbandictionary.com/define.php?term=Got%20your%20back.

Wakabayashi, D., Alba, D., & Tracy, M. (April 17, 2020). Bill Gates, at odds with Trump on virus, becomes right-wing target. *New York Times.* https://www.nytimes.com/202 0/04/17/technology/bill-gates-virus-conspiracy-theories.html

Watkins, M. D. (2007). Organizational immunology (Part 1: Culture and change). *Harvard Business Review.* Retrieved June 25, 2020 from https://hbr.org/2007/06/organizational-immunology-part-1

Watts, D. J. (2011). *Everything is obvious once you know the answer.* New York, NY: Crown Books.

Weber, M. (1963). *The sociology of religion.* Beacon, NY: Beacon Press. (Originally published in 1922).

Weinberger, D. R., Weintraub Austin, E. & Pinkleton, B. E. (2015). *Strategic public relations management* (3rd ed.). New York, NY: Routledge – Taylor & Francis Group.

Welch, J., & Welch, S. (2005). *Winning.* New York, NY: HarperBusiness.

Willingham, R. (2003). *Integrity selling for the 21st century: How to sell the way people want to buy.* New York, NY: Currency Doubleday.

Wilson, E. O. (1984). *Biophilia.* Cambridge, MA: Harvard University Press.

Yong, E. (2020). America is trapped in a pandemic spiral. *The Atlantic.* Retrieved September 12, 2020 from https://www.theatlantic.com/health/archive/2020/09/pandemic-intuition-nightmare-spiral-winter/616204/.

Zacharias, N. A., Nijssen, E. J., & Stock, R. M. (2016). Effective configurations of value creation and capture capabilities: Extending Treacy & Wiersema's value disciplines. *Journal of Business Research, 69*(10), 4121–4131. www.sciencedirect.com/science/article/pii/S0148296316300595

Zaleznik, A. (2004). Managers and leaders: Are they different? *Harvard Business Review, 82*(1), 74–82

Zimmerman, P. (1984). *The new thinking man's guide to pro football.* New York, NY: Simon & Schuster.

Zinsser, W. (2006). *On writing well.* New York, NY: HarperCollins.

Zenger. J. H., & Folkman, J. (2009). *The extraordinary leader.* New York, NY: McGraw-Hill.

INDEX

Printed in the United States
by Baker & Taylor Publisher Services